Intestinal Calcium Absorption and Its Regulation

Author

Alexander D. Kenny
Professor and Chairman
Department of Pharmacology and Therapeutics
Texas Tech University Health Sciences Center
Lubbock, Texas

CRC Press, Inc.
Boca Raton, Florida

Library of Congress Cataloging in Publication Data

Kenny, Alexander D
Intestinal calcium absorption and it's regulation.

Bibliography: p.
Includes index.
1. Calcium--Metabolism. 2. Intestinal absorption.
I. Title. [DNLM: 1. Intestinal absorption. 2. Calcium --Metabolism. 3. Vitamin D--Metabolism. QV 276 K36i]
QP535.C2K46 599.01'33 80-27881
ISBN 0-8493-5701-2

This book represents information obtained from authentic and highly regarded sources. Reprinted material is quoted with permission, and sources are indicated. A wide variety of references are listed. Every reasonable effort has been made to give reliable data and information, but the author and the publisher cannot assume responsibility for the validity of all materials or for the consequences of their use.

Direct all inquiries to CRC Press, Inc., 2000 N.W. 24th Street, Boca Raton, Florida 33431.

International Standard Book Number 0-8493-5701-2

Library of Congress Card Number 80-27881
Printed in the United States

PREFACE

This review will encompass the gastrointestinal absorption of calcium and its regulation. The importance of calcium in biological systems is unquestionable. Its role in maintaining the integrity of cell membranes and normal function in muscle, nerve, and secretory organs is well known. It is not surprising that the calcium level in plasma and extracellular fluid is sustained within very narrow limits by homeostatic mechanisms. These mechanisms, at least in mammals, involve three endocrine messengers: parathyroid hormone, calcitonin, and 1,25-dihydroxyvitamin D_3. Three organs — kidneys, gut, and bone — are the targets of these hormones.

The decade since 1970 has seen tremendous advances in our understanding of the physiological role of vitamin D. These developments have focused on the hormonal function of vitamin D_3 with the recognition of the role of the renal-vitamin D endocrine system.

In the review to follow emphasis will be placed on: (1) the recent developments in the metabolism, transport, and endocrine function of vitamin D; (2) the concepts and techniques concerning calcium transport by the gastrointestinal tract; and (3) the physiological and pharmacological aspects of gastrointestinal absorption of calcium.

AUTHOR

Dr. Alexander D. Kenny obtained his Bachelor of Science degree in Chemistry at the Imperial College of Science and Technology, University of London, in 1945. He obtained his Ph.D. degree in Biochemistry at the Institutum Divi Thomae, Athenaeum of Ohio, in 1950. After receiving postdoctoral training in endocrinology with Dr. Paul L. Munson at the Harvard School of Dental Medicine, he has held academic appointments in Pharmacology at Harvard Medical School, West Virginia University, University of Missouri (Pharmacology and Biochemistry), and The University of Texas Medical Branch in Galveston. In 1976, Dr. Kenny was appointed Professor and Chairman of the Department of Pharmacology and Therapeutics and Director of the Tarbox Parkinson's Disease Institute at the Texas Tech University Health Sciences Center in Lubbock. Dr. Kenny has also held appointments in the Medical Unit, University College Hospital in London, at the Massachusetts General Hospital, and at the Sidney Farber Cancer Institute in Boston during the 1950s. It was during his association with the late Professor Charles E. Dent, M.D., F.R.S. at University College Hospital in London in 1950–51 that Dr. Kenny first became interested in the endocrine aspects of calcium metabolism.

ACKNOWLEDGMENTS

The author is indebted to Ingrid M. Green, whose assistance in assembling the references and performing a myriad of other tasks in connection with the generation of this monograph was invaluable. Additional thanks are due to Virginia M. Davis and her office staff. Among the latter, Betty R. Brashears deserves special mention for her dedication and patience in typing the monograph.

TABLE OF CONTENTS

PART II CALCIUM ABSORPTION

Chapter 5
Calcium Transport

Chapter 10

Endocrine Aspects and Calcium Absorption

Chapter 11

Pharmacological Aspects of Calcium Absorption

Part I
Vitamin D Metabolism

INTRODUCTION

Rapid developments in our understanding of vitamin D metabolism took place in the three-year span 1968 to 1971. It was during this period that important contributions from the work of Kodicek, DeLuca, Norman, Haussler, and their respective associates led to our recognition of the renal-vitamin D endocrine system.[1] The early reports indiated that vitamin D_3 was converted to a more polar metabolite which was identified as 25-hydroxyvitamin D_3[2] and that the liver was the site of this conversion.[3] A second metabolite, subsequently known as 1,25-dihydroxyvitamin D_3, was detected in avian intestinal nuclear chromatin and was proposed as the active form of vitamin D_3.[4] This metabolite was subsequently shown to be formed exclusively in the kidney[5] and identified as 1,25-dihydroxyvitamin D_3.[6,7] It is now accepted that vitamin D_3 and its liver metabolite, 25-hydroxyvitamin D_3, are physiologically inactive precursors or prohormones of 1,25-dihydroxyvitamin D_3, the active form of the vitamin. The latter is now designated a hormone secreted by its endocrine organ, the kidney. The overall scheme describing our present knowledge concerning vitamin D metabolism is presented in Figure 1. Plasma concentrations of vitamin D and its major metabolites are presented in Table 1, Chapter 2. The major circulating form of vitamin D is 25-hydroxyvitamin D (30 ng/mℓ); vitamin D itself is much lower (1 ng/mℓ). The plasma concentration of the hormonal form, 1,25-hydroxyvitamin D, is considerably less (0.03 ng/mℓ).

In the more detailed discussion to follow, attention will be focused on four major areas of vitamin D metabolism relevant to calcium absorption by the gastrointestinal tract: (1) hepatic metabolism; (2) renal metabolism; (3) vitamin D transport; and (4) regulation of the renal-vitamin D endocrine system. Certain important areas of vitamin D research, considered less relevant to the topic of calcium absorption, will not be reviewed. These include the actions of vitamin D on bone and kidney function and the possible roles of metabolites other than 1,25-dihydroxyvitamin D_3.

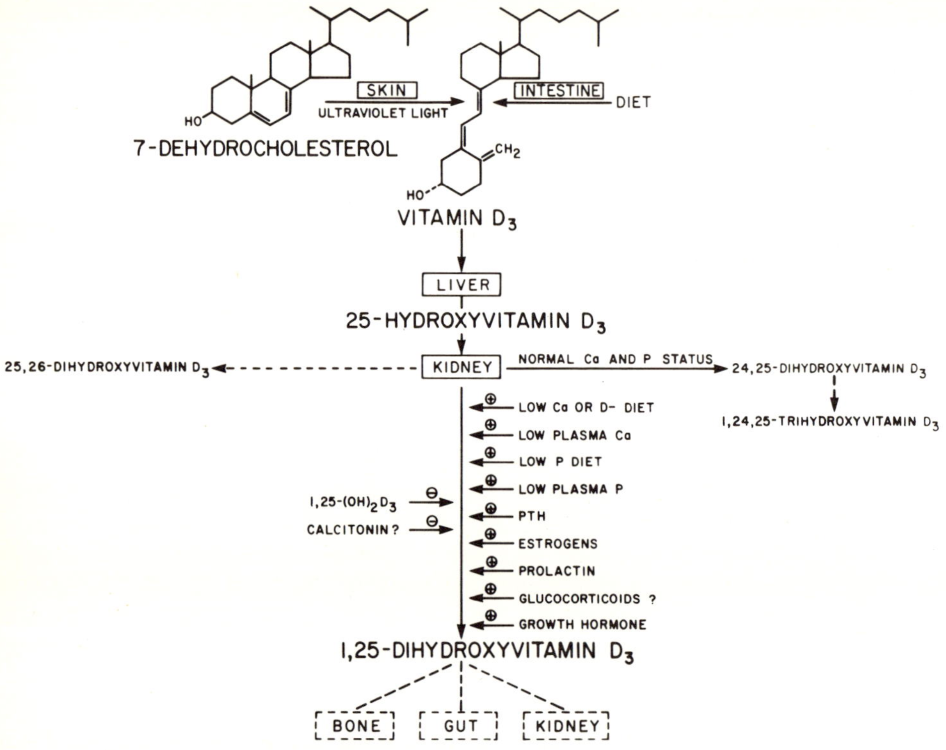

FIGURE 1. Overall scheme of the major metabolic pathways of vitamin D metabolism indicating possible physiological, nutritional, and pharmacological regulatory factors. Vitamin D_3 is synthesized photochemically in the skin from its precursor, 7-dehydrocholesterol. It is transported in the blood bound to vitamin D binding protein and is converted by the liver to 25-hydroxyvitamin D_3 by a hydroxylation reaction which is subject to minimal regulation. The liver metabolite, 25-hydroxyvitamin D_3, circulates at around 30 ng/mℓ, most of which is firmly bound to vitamin D binding protein. The kidney converts 25-hydroxyvitamin D_3 either to 1,25-dihydroxyvitamin D_3, the active hormonal form of vitamin D_3, or to less active forms such as 24,25-dihydroxyvitamin D_3. Tight regulatory control is exercised over the renal 25-hydroxyvitamin D_3-1-hydroxylase enzyme. Of the regulatory factors listed, parathyroid hormone is considered to play a major physiological role. Ingested vitamin D_3 and vitamin D_2 undergo similar pharmacokinetic behavior. Not indicated are the water-soluble, side-chain oxidation products of 1,25-dihydroxyvitamin D_3 and 24,25-dihydroxyvitamin D_3, namely calcitroic acid and cholacalcioic acid, respectively (Table 1, Chapter 10).

Chapter 1

HEPATIC METABOLISM OF VITAMIN D

I. NORMAL METABOLISM

Although Kodicek was the first to study the metabolic fate of radioactively labeled vitamin D, he was unable to report the production of any biologically active metabolites. The availability of labeled vitamin D_3 of high specific activity enabled Lund and DeLuca[8] to demonstrate the existence in rats of a metabolite which was active with respect to curing rickets in rats. This metabolite was subsequently isolated in pure form from pig[2] and human[9] plasma and identified as 25-hydroxyvitamin D_3. The liver was determined to be the major production site of this metabolite.[3,10,11] There have been reports of extrahepatic sites in the rat but these sites are claimed to be of minor significance.[3,10,12] These extrahepatic sites, particularly in the intestine and kidney, appear to be more significant in the chicken.[13–15]

A large proportion of administered vitamin D rapidly accumulates in the liver of rats.[16–19] Within the liver, a vitamin D_3-25-hydroxylase enzyme responsible for converting vitamin D to 25-hydroxyvitamin D is located in the smooth endoplasmic reticulum (microsomal) fraction both in rats[20,21] and in chickens.[15] The microsomal enzyme of rat liver is supported by NADPH, molecular oxygen, and a cytoplasmic protein, and is classified as a mono-oxygenase or mixed-function oxidase.[22] Controversy exists over whether or not the microsomal enzyme is cytochrome P-450 dependent and inducible by phenobarbital. Devlin et al.[23] maintain it is, whereas Madhok et al.[22] claim it is not. Another vitamin D_3-25-hydroxylase has been reported to be present in the mitochondria of rat livers.[21] This enzyme also requires NADPH and molecular oxygen and is classified as a mixed-function oxygenase. It is inhibited by carbon monoxide, requires cytochrome P-450, and is subject to induction by phenobarbital.[21] The relative contributions of these two enzymes to the 25-hydroxylation of vitamin D is unclear.

It is well known that vitamin D_2 (ergocalciferol) is approximately ten times less active in the chicken than vitamin D_3 (cholecalciferol).[24,25] No definitive explanation for this discrimination has been proposed. Jones et al.[26] examined the hepatic conversion of vitamin D_2 to 25-hydroxyvitamin D_2 using liver homogenates prepared from immature rachitic chickens, and compared it with the conversion of vitamin D_3 to its 25-hydroxylated metabolite. No difference in the hydroxylation reactions were observed and they concluded that the basis for the discrimination must be elsewhere.

II. REGULATION OF HEPATIC 25-HYDROXYLASE

Although regulation of hepatic 25-hydroxylase activity has been proposed to be present in both rats[27] and chickens,[14] the weight of the evidence indicates that the enzyme is not tightly controlled, at least under *chronic* conditions. Bhattacharyya and DeLuca[14,27] found that administration of *acute* doses of vitamin D_3 decreased hepatic 25-hydroxylase activity; circulating levels of the product of the enzyme, 25-hydroxyvitamin D_3, were not implicated as exerting the regulatory influence. This claim that 25-hydroxylase activity is regulated by *acute* administration of vitamin D is supported by acute studies using the perfused rat liver preparation.[28,29] There is agreement that the mechanism of this acute regulation is not through product

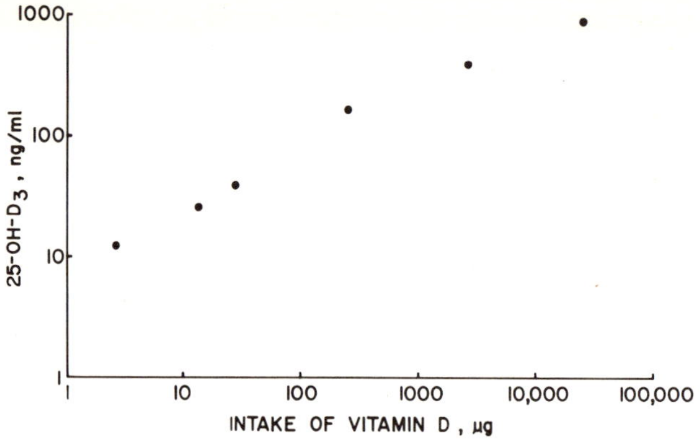

FIGURE 1. Serum 25-hydroxyvitamin D_3 levels in vitamin D-deficient rats supplemented with increasing doses of vitamin D_3. The data are presented in a logarithmic mode on both axes. There is a linear relationship between the intake of vitamin D_3 and the serum level of 25-hydroxyvitamin D_3. (From Clarke, M. B., and Potts, J. T., Jr., *Calcif. Tissue Res.*, 22S, 29, 1977. With permission.)

inhibition of the 25-hydroxylase enzyme,[13,16,23,27,29] as had been proposed originally by Horsting and DeLuca.[30] Other studies conclude that little regulation of hepatic 25-hydroxylase activity is exerted *chronically* either in rats[31] or in man.[32,33] The data obtained by Clark and Potts[31] in rats are presented in Figure 1. In this study young rats were first made vitamin D-deficient and then placed on diets containing different amounts of vitamin D ranging from 0.032 µg to 2.5 mg once or three times weekly. Plasma 25-hydroxyvitamin D levels were determined at weekly intervals and showed no evidence of reaching a plateau.

The explanation for this apparent confusion — whether or not hepatic 25-hydroxylase activity is regulated under physiological conditions — may reside in an examination of the kinetics of the enzyme. In an important study, Fukushima et al.[28] perfused rat livers removed from vitamin D-deficient rats and found 25-hydroxylation occurred in two modes: (1) a fast, high-affinity (K_m, 5.6 n*M*), low-capacity reaction; and (2) a slow, low-affinity (K_m, 1000 n*M*), high-capacity reaction. It is proposed that the high-affinity mode is responsible for 25-hydroxylation of *physiological* levels of vitamin D_3 (<2.5 n*M*), and that the low-affinity mode comes into play with supraphysiological or toxic levels of the prohormone (<2.5 n*M*). Devlin et al.,[23] using microsomal preparations obtained from vitamin D-deficient and vitamin D-replete rats, found that the K_m of the 25-hydroxylases differed under two nutritional states (D-deficient, K_m = 180 n*M*; D-replete, K_m = 440 n*M*). Although Devlin et al.[23] claim that their data are at variance with those of Suda and his colleagues,[28] the lowest substrate concentration used was 20 n*M*, considerably above the K_m (5.6 n*M*) of the high-affinity mode of the 25-hydroxylation reaction reported in the Japanese study. It is understandable, in the light of these kinetic considerations, that regulation is observed in certain studies depending upon the conditions. Acute injection of vitamin D into vitamin D-deficient animals might rapidly saturate the fast high-affinity/low-capacity mode and move into the slow low-affinity/high-capacity mode. This would have the appearance of decreasing the 25-hydroxylase activity. Most of the chronic studies, in which regulation appears to be absent, may be involved only with the slow low-affinity/high-capacity mode.

Whereas vitamin D_3, the natural substrate for hepatic 25-hydroxylase, is regulated to some degree, the pharmacologically important synthetic derivatives, 1α-hydroxyvitamin D_3[28] and dihydrotachysterol$_2$,[27] appear to be subject to little or no regulation. Both agents, inactive per se, require only 25-hydroxylation by the liver to render them biologically active.

There has been a preliminary report that estrogens may regulate hepatic 25-hydroxylase activity in Japanese quail.[34] Egg-laying birds had greater hepatic 25-hydroxylase activity than did immature birds or mature males; injection of estrogen enhanced the activity in the latter birds.

III. HEPATIC 25-HYDROXYLASE IN LIVER DISEASE

Bone pathology is frequently associated with liver disease, whether the latter is in patients with primary biliary cirrhosis[35] or with alcoholic cirrhosis.[36] Naturally, attention was turned to the question whether or not hepatic 25-hydroxylation was seriously impaired in these conditions.

In patients with primary biliary cirrhosis, circulating levels of 25-hydroxyvitamin D were found to be low (5 ng/mℓ) when compared with patients with normal liver function (9–44 ng/mℓ).[37,38] In those patients treated with monthly intramuscular injections of 100,000 units of ergocalciferol, serum 25-hydroxyvitamin D levels were normal (24 ng/mℓ), indicating that there was no absolute block in the 25-hydroxylation mechanism. Whether the source of the 25-hydroxyvitamin D was hepatic or extrahepatic is not clear. Alcoholic cirrhosis is also associated with low plasma levels of 25-hydroxyvitamin D.[39–42] Again, the impairment in 25-hydroxylation is not absolute; chronic treatment with vitamin D will raise the plasma levels of 25-hydroxyvitamin D to normal or above normal.[39,41,42] The impairment appears to be more extensive when studied following *acute* administration of vitamin D: no significant rise in serum 25-hydroxyvitamin D concentration was seen 24 hr after intravenous administration of 120 μg (4800 units) of cholecalciferol.[40]

Children with hepatitis and congenital biliary atresia have likewise been observed to have low plasma 25-hydroxyvitamin D levels (5.7 and 2.2 ng/mℓ, respectively) when compared with those found in normal children (19.5 ng/mℓ.[33] A marked difference in response to oral administration of 2000 units per day of ergocalciferol for 2 weeks was observed between the hepatitis and the congenital biliary atresia groups. The former responded by an elevation of their plasma 25-hydroxyvitamin D levels (from 8.0 to 22.1 ng/mℓ), whereas no significant response was seen in the children with congenital biliary atresia.

IV. HEPATIC 25-HYDROXYLASE IN ANTICONVULSANT THERAPY

In 1970, reports began to appear that individuals on long-term anticonvulsant therapy such as phenobarbital and phenytoin (Dilantin®) often developed bone disease resembling that seen in vitamin D deficiency.[43–45] Early data indicated that plasma levels of 25-hydroxyvitamin D were low in these patients,[44,46] and the effects of anticonvulsants were attributed to accelerated degradation of vitamin D and 25-hydroxyvitamin D to more polar inactive metabolites by the liver.[44] It was tacitly assumed that the lower levels of 25-hydroxyvitamin D would naturally lead to depressed levels of the physiologically active form of vitamin D, 1,25-hydroxyvitamin D. However, the more recent report that in patients on chronic anticonvulsant therapy plasma 1,25-hydroxyvitamin D levels were not depressed, but were either normal or elevated,[47] did not confirm this assumption. These studies were supported by the finding that chronic administration of phenobarbital and phenytoin to chickens resulted in low levels of plasma 25-hydroxyvitamin D and enhanced renal 25-hydroxyvitamin D_3-1-hydroxylase activity.[48]

What is the mechanism by which anticonvulsant therapy lowers the plasma levels of 25-hydroxyvitamin D? It is known that hepatic 25-hydroxylase activity has been reported to be present in both the microsomal[20,21] and the mitochrondrial[21] fractions of rat liver. Phenobarbital treatment does not enhance the *microsomal* 25-hydroxylation[49] but does enhance the *mitochondrial* 25-hydroxylation of vitamin D_3. Recently, Baran et al.[50] have been reinvestigating the effects of anticonvulsants on 25-hydroxylation of vitamin D using the isolated perfused rat preparation. This system permits the study of the effects of anticonvulsants on the total microsomal and mitochondrial 25-hydroxylation. Treatment of the rats with phenobarbital for 5 days enhanced the production of 25-hydroxyvitamin D_3 from vitamin D_3. They made the additional interesting observation that when livers removed from vitamin D-deficient rats, which had not been treated with phenobarbital, were perfused with blood taken from phenobarbital-treated rats, 25-hydroxylation was enhanced when compared with similar preparations perfused with blood removed from untreated rats. Addition of phenobarbital or its major metabolite, p-hydroxyphenobarbital, to the perfusate had no effect on 25-hydroxyvitamin D_3 production. This finding suggests that stimulation of 25-hydroxyvitamin D_3 production by chronic phenobarbital treatment for 5 days is due either to a metabolite of phenobarbital other than p-hydroxyphenobarbital, or to a humoral factor induced by phenobarbital, its major metabolite, or both.

Chapter 2

RENAL METABOLISM OF VITAMIN D

Around the time that the biologically important metabolite 1,25-dihydroxyvitamin D_3 was discovered, identified, and shown to be of renal origin,[4–7,51] another metabolite was identified in pig plasma. This metabolite, originally designated 21,25-dihydroxyvitamin D_3,[52] was subsequently identified as 24,25-dihydroxyvitamin D_3.[53] This second metabolite is also produced in the kidney,[54] but there is evidence that some 24,25-dihydroxyvitamin D_3, unlike 1,25-dihydroxyvitamin D_3, may arise from extrarenal sources at least in rats[55] and in man[56]. The enzymes responsible for production of these major renal metabolites, 25 hydroxyvitamin D_3-1-hydroxylase and 25-hydroxyvitamin D_3-24-hydroxylase, are located in the mitochondria. There appears to be a reciprocal relationship between these two metabolites; when one is being synthesized and released, production of the other is suppressed.[57] Of the two metabolites, 1,25-dihydroxyvitamin D_3 is the more active biologically and has been designated the hormonal form of vitamin D_3. Whether or not 24,25-dihydroxyvitamin D_3 has any physiological function remains unclear.

Two other metabolites produced by the kidney have been identified. These are 25,26-dihydroxyvitamin D_3[58] and 1,24,25-trihydroxyvitamin D_3[59]. The renal origin of 1,24,25-trihydroxyvitamin D_3 has been demonstrated in rats,[60] in chickens,[61,62] and in Japanese quail.[63] The kidney production of 25,26-dihydroxyvitamin D_3 has been observed in chickens[64] and in Japanese quail[65]. The physiological role of both these metabolites is unknown; perhaps 24- and 26-hydroxylations are initial steps in terminating the potential and actual physiological activity of circulating 25-hydroxyvitamin D_3 and 1,25-dihydroxyvitamin D_3, respectively.

In the discussion to follow the renal production of the two major metabolites, 1,25-dihydroxyvitamin D_3 and 24,25-dihydroxyvitamin D_3, only will be reviewed.

I. RENAL PRODUCTION OF 1,25-DIHYDROXYVITAMIN D_3

A. Species Distribution

The existence of 1,25-dihydroxyvitamin D_3 was first indicated in the chicken,[4,66] its renal origin was first demonstrated in the rat.[5] Since that time these two species, particularly the chicken, have served as the main experimental models for studying the renal-vitamin D endocrine system. Nevertheless, the renal metabolite, 1,25-dihydroxyvitamin D_3, and/or its associated renal enzyme, 25-hydroxyvitamin D_3-1-hydroxylase, have been found to be widely distributed throughout the vertebrate classes. Few systematic studies of species distribution have been reported. Norman and his associates have conducted the most thorough study covering fishes, amphibia, reptiles, birds, and mammals.[67,68] Reports from Kenny's laboratory have included representative species from fish, amphibia, birds, and mammals.[69–72]

Mammals — Either the metabolite, 1,25-dihydroxyvitamin D_3, or the renal 1-hydroxylase enzyme, has been shown to be present in a variety of mammalian species including the rat,[57] pig,[73] dog, man,[67] monkey,[68,74] rabbit, mouse, guinea pig, cow, sheep, and bison.[68] Attempts to demonstrate in vitro either 1-hydroxylase or 24-hydroxylase activity in mammalian kidney homogenate preparations has not met with universal success, particularly in the more common experimental species such as the rat. Although Norman's laboratory has claimed some success in this regard,[67,68] DeLuca and his associates have failed to demonstrate either of the enzyme activities in the rat.[75] The latter group attribute this failure to the presence of an inhibitor of the 1-hydroxylase enzyme.[75,76] The inhibitor has been isolated from rat serum; it contains iron, has a molecular weight of 52,000, and binds the substrate, 25-hydroxyvitamin D_3. The presence of this inhibitor has seriously hampered studies of vitamin D_3 metabolism and regulation in the rat by eliminating the in vitro renal homogenate approach. This problem has been circumvented by using in vivo administration of the labeled 25-hydroxyvitamin D_3 substrate and subsequent extraction and identification of the metabolite from plasma or various tissues. Such an approach has been used in studies of regulation of 1-hydroxylase activity in the rat.[71,77] As radioreceptor and other sensitive assays for 1,25-dihydroxyvitamin D become more readily available, it will be possible to study regulation and metabolism by measuring plasma levels of the hormone. Such an assay is that developed by Haussler and his associates.[78]

Birds — The immature chicken has been used extensively for studies of vitamin D metabolism from the earliest beginnings of the discovery of 1,25-dihydroxyvitamin D_3 and its associated renal 1-hydroxylase.[4,66] Kenny and his associates pioneered the use of the Japanese quail as a model for examining vitamin D metabolism and its regulation.[63,69,71,72,79–85] Other laboratories have confirmed its usefulness as a model.[86,87] Additional avian species studied have included the duck, pigeon,[68] and turkey.[68,88]

Reptiles — In their survey of vertebrate species Henry and Norman[68] examined kidney homogenates removed from green iguana, box turtle, caiman, and garter snake, for renal 1-hydroxylase activity. The box turtle contained the most activity of these species.

Amphibia — Amphibian renal 1-hydroxylase activity has been examined by two laboratories, those of Norman,[68] and of Kenny.[69] In the latter, bullfrogs were studied; in the former green and thick-tongued frogs were used. In neither study was 1-hydroxylase activity found to be at high levels.

Fish — The presence of renal 1-hydroxylase activity in fish was first reported by Henry and Norman[68] who examined goldfish, rainbow trout, carp, rockfish, sea bass, sculpin, bonito, and kelp bass. Of these only carp showed considerable activity; 1-hydroxylase activity was indetectable in rainbow trout. Killifish and lungfish were studied by Kenny et al.;[70] little 1-hydroxylase activity was reported. The blood levels of 1,25-dihydroxyvitamin D have been measured in male and spawning female trout using a radioreceptor assay and found to be 131 and 59 pg/mℓ, respectively.[89] Holick et al.,[90] on the other hand, failed to find any evidence of conversion of vitamin D_3 to 25-hydroxyvitamin D in marine fish.

B. Subcellular Location and Properties of the Renal 1-Hydroxylase

The first major study of the subcellular location and requirements of the renal 25-hydroxyvitamin D_3-1-hydroxylase enzyme was that of Gray et al.,[91] who identified its presence in the mitochondria. This subcellular location in chicken renal homogenates has been confirmed in other laboratories.[67,68,92,93] The mitochondrial enzyme has been reported to have a pH optimum of 7.4[91], apparent K_m values of $2.2 \times 10^{-6} M$[91], 1 to $2 \times 10^{-7} M$[68], and $3.2 \times 10^{-7} M$[92], and a requirement for molecular oxygen,[91,94] NADPH,[91,95] cytochrome P-450,[68,91,95] and ferredoxin.[96] These properties permit the enzyme to be designated as a mixed-function oxidase. The renal 1-hydroxylase in the Japanese quail has an appreciably lower K_m of $2 \times 10^{-8} M$[72], an observation which has been confirmed by Turner.[712]

The enzyme activity appears to be inhibited by its product, 1,25-dihydroxyvitamin D_3.[97–101] The mechanism of this inhibition is not clear; although the inhibitory effect is mediated directly on kidney cells it does not appear to be one of simple competitive product inhibition of the enzyme.[102]

C. In Vitro Kidney Preparations

Most of the in vitro studies of renal vitamin D metabolism have been performed using either homogenates or, to a lesser extent, mitochondria. More sophisticated in vitro preparations have been used less frequently. These include isolated chicken renal tubules, kidney cell cultures of chicken, Japanese quail, and monkey origin, and the isolated perfused rat kidney.

Isolated Avian Renal Tubule Preparations — Rasmussen's laboratory[92,103–106] pioneered the use of isolated renal tubule preparations for studies of the renal-vitamin D endocrine system. The isolated tubules were prepared from kidneys removed from immature vitamin D-deficient chickens. Similar preparations have been used by others.[97,98,100,107]

Primary Kidney Cell Cultures — Isolated tubule preparations have limited viability and therefore limited application in studies of regulatory mechanisms normally requiring several hours in vivo for their effectiveness. For this reason a few investigators have resorted to the use of primary kidney cell cultures. Juan and DeLuca[74] first described the use of primary cultures of rhesus monkey kidney cells but failed to observe any 25-hydroxyvitamin D_3-1-hydroxylase activity. Henry,[99] on the other hand, found that primary cultures of kidney cells prepared from immature vitamin D-deficient chickens did retain 1-hydroxylase activity, an observation which has been confirmed by MacIntyre and his associate.[101] Primary cultures of Japanese quail kidney cells have also been used successfully.[108]

Isolated Rat Kidney Perfusion — A preliminary report of the use of the isolated perfused rat kidney has appeared.[109] Synthesis of 1,25-dihydroxyvitamin D_3 was observed under certain favorable conditions but was not sustained. Evaluation of the usefulness of this technique must await more extensive reports.

D. Renal Production of 1,25-Dihydroxyergocalciferol

As mentioned above (Chapter 1,I), the chicken discriminates between ergocalciferol (vitamin D_2) and cholecalciferol (vitamin D_3) with respect to biological potency. Jones et al.,[26] who examined the response of the chicken hepatic vitamin D-25-hydroxylase system to the two substrates and found no difference, also examined the renal 25-hydroxyvitamin D-1-hydroxylase response to its respective substrates, 25-hydroxyergocalciferol and 25-hydroxycholecalciferol. Again they found no difference in response and concluded that the basis for the discrimination is not associated with either the known hepatic or renal pathways of vitamin D metabolism.

II. RENAL PRODUCTION OF 24,25-DIHYDROXYVITAMIN D

The vitamin D_3 metabolite, 24,25-dihydroxyvitamin D_3, was first isolated from pig plasma.[52] Erroneously designated 21,25-dihydroxyvitamin D_3, it was subsequently identified as 24,25-dihydroxyvitamin D_3.[53] The kidney appears to be the major source of this metabolite,[54] but a minor amount of 24,25-dihydroxyvitamin D_3 may originate from extrarenal sources at least in rats[55] and man.[56] Since the biological function of 24,25-dihydroxyvitamin D_3 is less clearly defined than that of 1,25-dihydroxyvitamin D_3, certainly with respect to the main theme of this review, gut calcium absorption, discussion of its production will be purposefully limited. In any case, the literature on this metabolite is less abundant than that on the 1-hydroxylated renal metabolite.

Knutson and DeLuca[110] were the first to study the subcellular location and properties of the renal 25-hydroxyvitamin D_3-24-hydroxylase enzyme. In the chicken, it is a mitochondrial enzyme requiring NADPH[110] and molecular oxygen.[111] In this respect it is a mixed-function oxidase and resembles the 1-hydroxylase enzyme, but unlike the latter it is not inhibited by carbon monoxide. The apparent K_m of the 24-hydroxylase in the chicken is $1 \times 10^{-6}M$[110], close to that of the chicken 1-hydroxylase (see Chapter 2,I.B above), but above the K_m of $1 \times 10^{-8}M$ for the 24-hydroxylase in Japanese quail.[72]

III. RENAL VITAMIN D METABOLISM IN KIDNEY DISEASE

The association of rickets and osteomalacia with chronic renal failure has a long history,[112] but it is only in the past decade, since the breakthrough in our understanding of vitamin D metabolism, that the problem has received more intensive attention both in man and in experimental models.

A. Clinical Uremia

Avioli and his associates[113–115] were the first to study vitamin D metabolism in patients with chronic renal failure. They concluded that the apparent resistance to vitamin D observed in uremic patients was due to defects in the normal metabolism and excretion of vitamin D. These studies were, of course, initiated before the existence of 1,25-dihydroxyvitamin D_3 and its renal origin were known. Subsequent studies have indicated that, whereas hepatic 25-hydroxylation appears to function adequately in uremic patients,[116–119] defects in renal 1-hydroxylation have been reported.[115,120] The study of Holick et al.,[119] although performed in a single uremic patient, is particularly noteworthy for its novel design. The patient was injected intravenously with tritiated 1α-hydroxyvitamin D_3, the synthetic derivative which requires only 25-hydroxylation for its activation. The presence of tritiated 1,25-dihydroxyvitamin D_3 in plasma extracts was demonstrated, indicating the existence of 25-hydroxylation function.

The development of radioreceptor and other sensitive assays for determining plasma levels of 1,25-dihydroxyvitamin D has allowed the application of this methodological advance to an examination of plasmas obtained from normal subjects and uremic patients. Patients with chronic renal failure have been found to have consistently low circulating levels of 1,25-dihydroxyvitamin D (5 pg/mℓ, compared with normals of 30 to 40 pg/mℓ.[1,121] (See also Table 1). This defect in renal 1-hydroxylation is generally accepted as playing a main role in the development of vitamin D resistance in chronic renal failure.[112] Nevertheless, until more information is available, it cannot be assumed to be the only defect.

B. Experimental Uremia

Attempts have been made to study animal models of clinical uremia with respect to vitamin D metabolism with the hope that such studies will throw further light on the nature of the defect leading to vitamin D resistance. Both chickens[123] and rats[124,125] have been used. In rats made acutely uremic either by bilateral nephrectomy or by urethral ligation, Wong et al.[125] found that, whereas 25-hydroxyvitamin D_3 was unable to stimulate gut calcium transport in uremic rats, 1,25-dihydroxyvitamin D_3 did stimulate calcium absorption at very small doses. They suggested that the defect was probably in the renal 1-hydroxylation mechanism, a conclusion which was confirmed with more direct evidence by Van Stone et al.[124] The latter

Table 1
PLASMA CONCENTRATIONS OF VITAMIN D METABOLITES IN SEVERAL SPECIES

Species	Physiological or pathological status	Plasma metabolite concentration: 1,25-$(OH)_2D$ (pg/mℓ)	25-(OH)D (ng/mℓ) [Mean ± SD or (range)][b]	24,25-$(OH)_2D$ (ng/mℓ)	Methods[a] 1,25/25/24,24	Ref.
Man	Normal		35.2 ± 3.6[c]		-/RS/-	136
	Hypoparathyroidism + D		1250 (500—3200)			
	Anticonvulsant therapy		19.4 ± 3.3			
	Normal males and females	36 ± 12	24 ± 8		RRA/RS/-	193
	Primary hyperparathyroidism	83 ± 23[d]	16 ± 8			
	Stone-formers	62 ± 31[d]	18 ± 8			
	Normal males					
	P+[e]	44 ± 13				
	P−[e]	78 ± 15				
	Normal females					
	P+[e]	29 ± 8				
	P−[e]	40 ± 13				
	Normal females	52.8 ± 14.8	38.9 ± 18.7		RRA/RS/-	214
	Early pregnancy	87.1 ± 52.8	41.7 ± 7.9			
	Lactating	103.0 ± 56.6				
	Normal					
	January—February		20.5 ± 9.7		-/RK/-	702
	March—April		19.8 ± 9.8			
	May—June		28.1 ± 12.7			
	July—August		32.1 ± 12.8			
	September—October		25.5 ± 9.9			
	November—December		19.3 ± 8.2			
	Normal + D[f]					
	January—February		27.0 ± 14.1		-/RK/-	702
	March—April		35.0 ± 16.6			
	May—June		28.7 ± 9.5			
	July—August		33.9 ± 12.6			
	September—October		31.7 ± 7.8			
	November—December		34.5 ± 14.4			

Table 1 (Continued)
PLASMA CONCENTRATIONS OF VITAMIN D METABOLITES IN SEVERAL SPECIES

		Plasma metabolite concentration				
Species	Physiological or pathological status	$1,25-(OH)_2D$ (pg/mℓ)	25-(OH)D (ng/mℓ) [Mean ± SD or (range)][b]	$24,25-(OH)_2D$ (ng/mℓ)	Methods[a] 1,25/25/24,24	Ref.
	Normal					
	18—60 Years		28.2 ± 12.1		-/RK/-	702
	61—93 Years		19.9 ± 9.2[d]			
	Normal + D[f]					
	18—60 Years		36.3 ± 14.3			
	61—93 Years		28.2 ± 11.0[d]			
	Normal postmenopausal	20—52	8—30		RRA/RS/-	703
	Postmenopausal osteoporosis	22—27	21—38			
	Normal					
	5—10 Years	64 ± 9			RRA/-/-	704
	> 18 Years	33 ± 6				
	Pregnant (38 weeks)	73 ± 19				
	Hypoparathyroidism	28 ± 9				
	Primary hyperparathyroidism	54 ± 21				
	Pseudohypoparathyroidism	29 ± 14				
	Nutritional osteomalacia	14 ± 5				
	Anticonvulsant therapy	47 ± 36				
	Hypophosphatemic rickets	33 ± 14				
	Juvenile osteoporosis					
	10—15 Years	34 ± 4				
	Postmenopausal osteoporosis	34 ± 12				
	Sarcoidosis	36 ± 13				
	Idiopathic hypercalciuria	50 ± 16				
	Hypervitaminosis D	36 ± 15				
	Normal males	24(20—28)			RRAQ/-/-	700
	Normal females	38(20—56)				
	Children (winter)		11.0 ± 4.8[c]		-/RS/-	705
	Adults (winter)		11.9 ± 5.7[c]			

Normal		19.2 ± 1.6[c]		-/RS/-	706
Anticonvulsant therapy		8.6 ± 0.8[c]			
Anticonvulsant therapy + D[f]		62.6 ± 9.3[c]			
Primary hyperparathyroidism					
Before PTX[g]	53 ± 13			RRA/-/-	644
After PTX[g]	37 ± 9[d]				
Normal	30.5(18.4—50.7)			RRA/-/-	215
Chronic renal failure	ND[h]				
Pregnancy (33—34 weeks)	87.7 ± 11.2[d]				
Acromegaly	48.4 ± 4.6[d]				
Primary hyperparathyroidism	55.0 ± 5.5[d]				
Prolactinoma	40.4 ± 3.2[d]				
Normal					
20—49 Years		36.9 ± 4.0[c]		-/RS/-	133
50—70 Years		23.1 ± 3.1[c,d]			
Gastrectomized					
20—49 Years		18.6 ± 2.9[c]			
50—70 Years		18.5 ± 2.5			
Uremia		22.9 ± 5.0			
Cirrhosis		11.5 ± 2.0[d]			
Osteoporosis		14.7 ± 1.6[d]			
Normal		22.3 ± 9.2		-/HS/-	137
Hyperlipidemia		17.6 ± 10.3			
Liver disease		2.6 ± 1.9			
Chronic renal failure		23.4 ± 6.9			
Paget's disease		20.9 ± 4.0			
Hypoparathyroidism + D[f]					
Normocalcemic		100[i]			
Hypercalcemic		286(236—336)			
Primary hyperparathyroidism		15.5[i]			
Normal					
20—40 Years		39.5 ± 9.3		-/RS/-	134
40—60 Years		30.0 ± 7.8			
60—80 Years		23.4 ± 16.2			
Alcoholic cirrhosis		13.0 ± 8.9[d]			
Normal		8.8—35.7	1.68 ± 0.82	-/RK/RK	128
+ D[f]		52—186	2.39—4.41[d]		
− D[j]			ND[h]		

Table 1 (Continued)
PLASMA CONCENTRATIONS OF VITAMIN D METABOLITES IN SEVERAL SPECIES

Species	Physiological or pathological status	Plasma metabolite concentration: $1,25-(OH)_2D$ (pg/mℓ)	25-(OH)D (ng/mℓ) [Mean ± SD or (range)][b]	$24,25-(OH)_2D$ (ng/mℓ)	Methods[a] 1,25/25/24,24	Ref.
	Normal		24.3 ± 1.5[c]	3.7 ± 0.2[c]	-/RSP/RS	56
	Anephric		23.2 ± 4.0[c]	3.0 ± 0.7[c]		
	Normal	39 ± 8			RRA/-/-	146
	Chronic renal failure					
	Untreated	13 ± 5[d]				
	Hemodialyzed	ND[h]				
	Anephric	ND[h]				
	Females					
	20—29 Years		29.4 ± 16.5	0.86 ± 1.00	-/RS/RS	131
	30—39 Years		26.0 ± 14.1	0.84 ± 0.84		
	40—49 Years		20.7 ± 8.6	0.80 ± 0.61		
	50—59 Years		37.0 ± 19.9	0.14 ± 0.06		
	60—69 Years		43.0 ± 26.2	0.20 ± 0.08		
	70—79 Years		21.6 ± 14.4	0.34 ± 0.33		
	Normal	29 ± 2[c]			RRA/-/-	149
	Chronic renal failure	ND[h]				
	Anephric	ND[h]				
	Normal	33 ± 6	25—40		RRA/RRA/-	144
		ND(D_2)[k]	ND(D_2)[k]			
		33(D_3)[l]	32(D_3)[l]			
	Hypervitaminosis D_2	52	592			
		52(D_2)[k]	592(D_2)[k]			
		ND(D_3)[l]	ND(D_3)[l]			
	Normal	64 ± 12			RRA/-/-	78
	Chronic renal failure	26 ± 5[d]				
	Hypoparathyroidism	47 ± 18[d]				
	Primary hyperparathyroidism	114—123				
	Normal	33.5 ± 1.8[c]			RRA/-/-	121

	Chronic renal failure	5.1 ± 1.2[c,d]			
	Hypoparathyroidism	18.3 ± 2.8[c,d]			
	Primary hyperparathyroidism	61.4 ± 7.1[c,d]			
	Hyperthyroidism				
	Hypercalcemic	42.1 ± 8.4[c,d]			
	Normal				
	Summer		29.1 ± 7.8	-/RK/-	32
	Winter		20.3 ± 6.1[d]		
	Normal (6—17 years)	37.1 ± 11.9		RRA/-/-	707
	X-Linked hypophosphatemia[f]	15.6 ± 7.8[d]			
	Vitamin D-dependent rickets[f]	9.5 ± 2.9[d]			
	Autosomal hypophosphatemia	30.2 ± 6.3			
	Normal				
	Hospitalized	39 ± 23	15.5 ± 10.4	RRA/-/-	47
	Ambulatory	29 ± 5	22.9 ± 3.0		
	Anticonvulsant therapy				
	Phenytoin	56 ± 37	9.3 ± 5.2		
	Phenobarbital	60 ± 18[d]	7.9 ± 2.7[d]		
	Combined therapy	37 ± 31	7.4 ± 6.3[d]		
	Normal (winter)		16 ± 3.9(31% D_2)	-/UV/-	139
	Normal	55 ± 10		MF/-/-	708
Rat	Normal males	30(16—44)		RRAQ/-/-	700
	Normal males + LCD[m]	60[d](29—97)			
	Normal		22(18—26)	-/RS/-	136
	Vitamin D deficient		3(ND[h]—6)		
	Vitamin D treated				
	Normocalcemic		380(100—1800)		
	Hypercalcemic		3500(2000—6000)		
	Normal	100 ± 8[c]		RRA/-/-	148
	Pregnant (21 days)	180 ± 8[c,d]			
	Lactating				
	1—2 Days	112 ± 11[c]			
	7—8 Days	164 ± 8[c,d]			
	13—16 Days	156 ± 5[c]			
	Postlactation				
	2 Days	34 ± 3[c,d]			
	7 Days	100 ± 11[c]			
	Nonlactating (sham-op)	39 ± 9[c]			

Table 1 (Continued)
PLASMA CONCENTRATIONS OF VITAMIN D METABOLITES IN SEVERAL SPECIES

Species	Physiological or pathological status	Plasma metabolite concentration: 1,25-$(OH)_2$D (pg/mℓ)	25-(OH)D (ng/mℓ) [Mean ± SD or (range)][b]	24,25-$(OH)_2$D (ng/mℓ)	Methods[a] 1,25/25/24,24	Ref.
	Lactating					
	Sham-op	220 ± 8[c]				
	PTX[g]	95 ± 9[c]				
	Control (sham-op)	66.7 ± 13.0[c]			RRA/-/-	250
	Hypophysectomized	30.0 ± 5.0[c,d]				
	Hypophysectomized + GH					
	100 μg/day	76.7 ± 7.9[c,d]				
	500 μg/day	61.7 ± 7.1[c]				
	Hypophysectomized + PRL					
	100 μg/day	33.8 ± 8.8[c]				
	Normal	199 ± 1.4			RRA/-/-	222
	LCD[m]					
	3 Weeks	1118 ± 173[d]				
	6 Weeks	446 ± 140				
	Normal	183 ± 4				
	LPD[n] (6 weeks)	612 ± 117[d]				
	Normal	60—900			RRA/-/-	704
	Normal	210 ± 24	13.1 ± 2.3		RRA/RRA/-	196
	Hypervitaminosis D	136 ± 18[d]	466 ± 54[d]			
	Normal adult females	64 ± 12			RRA/-/-	213
	Weanling	173 ± 14[d]				
	Lactating	187 ± 29[d]				
	Normal		11.5		-/RS/-	126
	Vitamin D deficient		ND[h]			
	Normal	173			RRA/-/-	145
	LCD[m]	900[d]				
	TPTX[g]	62				
	TPTX[g] + LCD[m]	123				

	LPD[n]	820[d]				
	TPTX[g] + LPD[n]	913[d]				
Chicken	Laying hens (6 hr post-ovulation)				RRA/-/-	701
	32 Weeks	116 ± 21				
	80 Weeks	244 ± 53				
	Normal	20—150			RRA/-/-	704
	Normal	60 ± 13	29.3 ± 7.3		RRA/RRA/-	196
	Vitamin D deficient	ND[h]	ND[h]			
	Hypervitaminosis D	42 ± 7	103.7 ± 13.3[d]			
	Hens					
	Nonlaying	20 ± 8			RRA/-/-	213
	Laying	174 ± 35[d]				
	Young	42 ± 4[d]				
	Normal (immature)	98 ± 24			RRA/-	147
	Testosterone	96 ± 17				
	Diethylstilbestrol (DES)	254 ± 26[d]				
	Testosterone + DES	298 ± 19[d]				
	Post-ovulation					
	2 Hr	90			RRA/-/-	210
	4 Hr	250				
	6 Hr	160				
	8 Hr	210				
	10 Hr	250				
	12 Hr	75				
	14 Hr	90				
	16 Hr	120				
	18 Hr	75				
	Immature females	30—50	14.5—20.5	0.76—1.74	RRA/RS/RS	209
	Laying hens (without egg)	140 ± 20	14.0 ± 2.0[c]	0.63 ± 0.18[c]		
	Post-ovulation					
	1 Hr	130	17	1		
	4 Hr	105	12	1		
	6 Hr	110	10	1		
	15 Hr	300	16	1		
	21 Hr	110	18	1		

Table 1 (Continued)
PLASMA CONCENTRATIONS OF VITAMIN D METABOLITES IN SEVERAL SPECIES

		Plasma metabolite concentration				
Species	Physiological or pathological status	1,25-$(OH)_2D$ (pg/mℓ)	25-(OH)D (ng/mℓ) [Mean ± SD or (range)][b]	24,25-$(OH)_2D$ (ng/mℓ)	Methods[a] 1,25/25/24,24	Ref.
Japanese quail	Normal, immature	18.4 ± 3.3			RRAQ/-/-	700
	LCD[n], 10 days	67.8 ± 26.9[d]				
	Adult females (7—20 hr post-ovulation)				RRA/-/-	701
	8 Weeks	126 ± 7				
	20 Weeks	102 ± 19				
	120 Weeks	34 ± 6[d]				
	Normal males					
	4 Weeks		11.8 ± 1.6	2.6 ± 0.9	-/RS/RS	713
	6 Weeks		15.9 ± 3.8	2.2 ± 0.8		
	Normal females					
	4 Weeks		10.8 ± 3.2	2.1 ± 0.9		
	6 Weeks		15.6 ± 3.8	2.1 ± 0.5		
Dog	Normal	40			RRA/-/-	704
Bovine	Cow	60			RRA/-/-	704
	Pregnant				RRA/-/-	709
	1 day preparturient	40				
	2 days postparturient	140				
Sheep	Normal adult ewe		65.6 ± 3.5[c]		-/RS/-	710
	Pregnant		39.7 ± 3.2[c,d]			
	Fetus		26.3 ± 2.4[c]			
	Newborn					
	30 Min		31.0 ± 4.8[c]			
	4 Days		14.8 ± 1.4[c]			
	Lambs		23.2 ± 3.1[c]			
	Lactating ewe		46.4 ± 4.8[c]			

Pig	Unspecified	120			RRA/-/-	704
Trout	Unspecified	70			RRA/-/-	704
	Adult males	130.7 ± 20.7	4.2 ± 0.2	ND[h]	RRA/RS/RS	711
	Females					
	Nonspawning	130.7 ± 20.7	2.9 ± 0.3[d]	ND[h]		
	Spawning	58.8 ± 7.6[d]	2.8 ± 0.2	ND[h]		

[a] The methods, indicated by the abbreviations below, are given for 1,25-$(OH)_2D$/25-(OH)D/24,25-$(OH)_2D$, respectively. For example, RRA/RS/RS would indicate that the 1,25-$(OH)_2D$ was determined by radioreceptor assay and the other two metabolites by the rat serum vitamin D binding protein assay; RRA: radioreceptor assay, *chicken* gut cytosolic receptor; RRAQ: radioreceptor assay, *Japanese quail* gut cytosolic receptor; RS: *rat serum* vitamin D binding protein assay; RK: *rat kidney* vitamin D binding protein assay; HS: *human serum* vitamin D binding protein assay; MF: HPLC: determination by mass fragmentography; UV: HPLC: determination by UV absorptiometry.

[b] Mean ± SD; range enclosed in parentheses.

[c] SE (instead of SD).

[d] Significantly different from normal or appropriate control ($p < 0.05$).

[e] P− and P+ mean dietary phosphate depletion and repletion, respectively.

[f] Supplemented with vitamin D.

[g] PTX: parathyroidectomized (rats); removal of adenoma (humans); TPTX: thyroparathyroidectomized.

[h] ND: not detectable.

[i] Single value.

[j] Vitamin D deficient.

[k] D_2 metabolite.

[l] D_3 metabolite.

[m] LCD: low calcium diet.

[n] LPD: low phosphorus diet.

group measured the plasma content of tritiated 1,25-hydroxyvitamin D_3 following intravenous injection of labeled 25-hydroxyvitamin D_3 and found the production of the dihydroxymetabolite significantly depressed in uremic rats when compared with normal animals. Similar conclusions were drawn by Hartenbower et al.[123] using chickens rendered uremic by partial ureteral ligation.

Chapter 3

VITAMIN D TRANSPORT

I. PLASMA LEVELS OF VITAMIN D AND ITS METABOLITES

Several types of assays have been developed for the determination of the major circulating metabolites of vitamin D: 25-hydroxyvitamin D, 1,25-dihydroxyvitamin D, and 24,25-dihydroxyvitamin D. With few exceptions the assays have not been designed to distinguish between the metabolites of vitamin D_2 (ergocalciferol) and vitamin D_3 (cholecalciferol). The types of assays include:

1. Competitive protein binding assays, using binding proteins obtained from rat, human, and chicken plasma, or rat kidney, for the determination of 25-hydroxyvitamin D and 24,25-dihydroxyvitamin D
2. High-pressure liquid chromatography using ultraviolet absorption for detection of those metabolites circulating at sufficiently high concentrations
3. Radioreceptor assays, using chicken or Japanese quail intestinal cytosolic receptor, for the determination of 1,25-dihydroxyvitamin D
4. Radioimmunoassays for the determination of 1,25-dihydroxyvitamin D

A. Assay Methods

All the assays developed to date require preparative separation of the metabolite in question by extraction from plasma followed by one or more chromatographic separations.

1. Competitive Binding Protein Assays

Competitive binding protein assays were the first to be developed for determining the plasma levels of vitamin D. Binding proteins are prepared from either rat serum[126] or rat kidney tissue.[127] All animals are rendered vitamin D-deficient prior to removal of the serum or kidney tissue. These assays were designed originally for the determination of 25-hydroxyvitamin D; they have subsequently been applied to the determination of plasma levels of 24,25-dihydroxyvitamin D.[56,128–132] The assay method using binding proteins prepared from rat serum[126] has proved to be the most popular method for determining 25-hydroxyvitamin D levels in the plasma.[56,129,132–135] In a subsequent report, Belsey et al.[136] claim that the rat serum competitive binding protein assay can be used without prior preparative chromatography. Human serum[137] and chicken serum[138] binding proteins have also been used. The applications of these methods are summarized in Table 1, Chapter 2. Plasma levels of 25-hydroxyvitamin D have been determined in human, rat, ovine, Japanese quail, and trout plasma.

2. High-Pressure Liquid Chromatography

High-pressure liquid chromatography is invariably a preparative step in the purification of the metabolites prior to their determination by either competitive protein binding, radioreceptor, or radioimmunological assays. Nevertheless, the method itself has been proposed as the end, rather than the means, for the assay of those forms of vitamin D, such as vitamin D itself, 25-hydroxyvitamin D, and 24,25-dihydroxyvitamin D, which circulate in sufficiently high quantities (>0.5 ng/mℓ) to permit detection by ultraviolet absorption.[139–142] This method has been used for the determination of plasma vitamin D, 25-hydroxyvitamin D, and 24,25-dihydroxyvitamin D levels mainly in man[139,141,142] (see also Table 1, Chapter 2). A preliminary report describes its application to the analysis of Japanese quail plasma.[140]

3. Radioreceptor Assays

The methods described above are not sufficiently sensitive to detect normal plasma levels of the hormonal form of vitamin D, namely 1,25-dihydroxyvitamin D, which circulates at pg/mℓ rather than at ng/mℓ concentrations. In 1974, Haussler and his associates first described a radioreceptor method using a cytosolic receptor-nuclear chromatin complex prepared from the small intestine of vitamin D-deficient immature chickens.[78,143–146] Initially, the assay had a sensitivity of 80 pg of 1,25-dihydroxyvitamin D and a requirement for approximately 20 mℓ of plasma. The latter restricted the application of the assay to those larger species, such as man, from which such quantities can be obtained for individual samples. When applied to rats it was necessary to pool the plasmas from seven to ten rats.[145] Further modifications, particularly the use of higher specific activity tritiated 1,25-hydroxyvitamin D_3, have increased the sensitivity first to 10 pg by using 11.2-Ci/mmol material,[147] and then to 1 pg by employing 94-Ci/mmol hormone.[148]

Eisman et al.[149] reported a radioreceptor assay for 1,25-dihydroxyvitamin D based on the method of Haussler and his associates, with one major modification: the chromatin binding step was eliminated and cytosolic receptor-bound 1,25-dihydroxyvitamin D was separated from the free form by precipitation with polyethylene glycol. Sensitivity is about 10 pg and allows normal human levels to be determined on 5 mℓ of plasma. Other modifications for separating bound from free 1,25-dihydroxyvitamin D have included the use of dextran-charcoal[121] and hydroxyapatite.[150]

Kenny and his associates[151] have developed a radioreceptor assay using vitamin D-replete Japanese quail intestinal cytosolic receptor; the advantage of not placing the birds on vitamin D-deficient diets for several weeks is obvious. The assay is based on the cytosol receptor-chromatin complex of Haussler and his associates.[78] The receptor preparation exhibits 90 to 95% high-affinity, low-capacity (specific) binding and a sensitivity of 5 pg or less per tube.

Dissociation constants for the binding of 1,25-dihydroxyvitamin D_3 to the intestinal cytosolic receptor preparations have been reported as 7.1 p*M*[152], 200 p*M*[153], 200 to 500 p*M*[154], 1.7 n*M*[155], and 2200 p*M*[156] in the chicken, and 730 p*M* in the Japanese quail.[151]

4. Radioimmunoassays

In 1979, preliminary reports began to appear describing radioimmunoassay methods for determining 1,25-dihydroxyvitamin D.[157–159] The sensitivity of these assays is around 5 to 10 pg/tube, which is no more sensitive than the better radioreceptor assays (5 pg/tube or less). Full evaluation of the radioimmunoassay approach must await further developments and applications.

II. VITAMIN D BINDING PROTEINS IN PLASMA

It was recognized prior to the discovery of the monohydroxylated and dihydroxylated metabolites of vitamin D, that the latter migrated with the plasma α-globulin fraction at least in man[160,161] and in the rat.[162] Subsequently, these findings have been confirmed in man[163–165] and in rats,[166,168] and have been extended to the pig and Old World monkeys,[168] and to the baboon.[169] New World monkeys do not appear to have the same binding pattern.[168] Whereas in most mammalian species vitamin

D is associated with a binding protein which migrates on electrophoresis with the α-globulin fraction, the vitamin D binding protein is associated with the β-globulin fraction in chickens[168] and with albumin in New World monkeys.[170]

Purification of the vitamin D binding protein (DBP) has revealed that mammalian species appear to possess a single high-affinity binding protein[163,166,171,172] with a molecular weight of 52,000 to 59,000 (Svedberg constant 3.49S to 4.1S) and an isoelectric point of between 4.1 and 5.2. It is suggested that DBP is the common transport protein for all three physiologically important vitamin D secosteroids, namely vitamin D, 25-hydroxyvitamin D, and 1,25-dihydroxyvitamin D, and that it is the sole transport protein for 25-hydroxyvitamin D and 1,25-dihydroxyvitamin D.[166] Its concentration in human plasma has been reported.[173] Vitamin D, on the other hand, is not exclusively bound to DBP. The vitamin D binding protein circulates in mammalian plasma at high molar ratios relative to its secosteroid ligands[137,166,174] and, therefore, circulates mostly as the apoprotein not containing any bound secosteroids. Affinity for 25-hydroxyvitamin D_3 is high; the dissociation constant has been reported to be $2.0 \times 10^{-10}M$[166] and $6.4 \times 10^{-8}M$[174,175] in man and $3.3 \times 10^{-9}M$ in rats.[176] The human plasma DBP has been identified with the group-specific component (Gc) proteins.[137,164,175,177]

Chicken plasma, unlike mammalian plasmas, contains two vitamin D binding proteins which migrate with the β-globulin fraction. One of these proteins, with a molecular weight of 60,000, binds vitamin D_3 while the other (molecular weight 54,000) binds 25-hydroxyvitamin D_3 preferentially.[168]

The relative binding of vitamin D_2 and D_3 metabolites to plasma proteins has been studied in two species, the chicken and the New World monkey, which exhibit discrimination with respect to biological response between the two major classes of vitamin D. Whereas chickens exhibit differences in binding properties,[178] New World monkeys do not.[179] The latter finding indicates that the basis for the biological discrimination in the latter species must reside in other differences.

The comparative aspects of plasma vitamin D binding proteins have been studied by Hay and Watson.[180–182] All the major vertebrate classes have been investigated, including 22 species of fish, 12 species of amphibians, 5 species of reptiles, 19 species of birds,[180,182] and 72 species of mammals.[181,182] The general conclusions were that 25-hydroxyvitamin D_3 was bound: to lipoproteins in amphibian and cartilaginous fish; to an α-globulin protein in bony fish, reptiles, 3 species of birds, and 65 mammalian species; to a β-globulin protein in 12 species of birds; and to albumin in 4 species of birds and in the remaining 7 species of mammals.

Chapter 4

REGULATION OF RENAL VITAMIN D-ENDOCRINE SYSTEM

Several factors or agents have been implicated in the regulation of the renal vitamin D-endocrine system. Nutritional factors such as dietary calcium, phosphorus, and vitamin D were among the first to be reported. These observations led to studies of ionic regulation mainly by calcium and inorganic phosphate. The regulatory influence of hormonal agents has received sustained attention during the past decade; such studies have revealed that a wide spectrum of hormones influences the vitamin D-endocrine system. Finally, a few additional agents of pharmacological and toxicological interest have been investigated for their effects on this endocrine system.

Two points should be made before launching into a more detailed discussion of these regulatory influences. First, the discussion will be concerned almost exclusively with the regulation of 1,25-dihydroxyvitamin D_3 production by the kidney, or to the activity of its renal enzyme, 25-hydroxyvitamin D_3-1-hydroxylase. The regulation of the 24-hydroxylase enzyme will not receive detailed attention and will be mentioned only where appropriate. Secondly, the terms "regulation" or "regulatory influence" are not being used in any special sense. By itself, regulation does not imply *physiological* regulation. The term "regulation" is being used essentially synonymously with perturbation, i.e., a shift, either upwards or downwards, in the level of 25-hydroxyvitamin D_3-1-hydroxylase activity. Some of these influences may eventually prove to be of physiological importance. The vast majority of the effects reported may, when the research dust has fallen, prove to be of pharmacological, therapeutic, or toxicological interest only.

I. NUTRITIONAL REGULATION

Three major nutritional factors have been reported to influence the renal production of 1,25-dihydroxyvitamin D_3: (1) dietary calcium; (2) dietary phosphorus; and (3) vitamin D.

A. Dietary Calcium

The first observation that low calcium diet stimulated the production of 1,25-dihydroxyvitamin D_3 was made in the rat by Boyle et al.,[57] a finding which has been subsequently confirmed in rats,[183,184] in chickens,[54,185–187] in Japanese quail,[80,81,188] and in pigs.[73]

B. Dietary Phosphorus

Tanaka and DeLuca[183] were the first to report that rats, when placed on a low phosphorus diet, exhibited enhanced synthesis of 1,25-dihydroxyvitamin D_3. This stimulatory response, unlike that to calcium deprivation, does not require the presence of the parathyroid glands. Thyroparathyroidectomy does not abolish the response to phosphorus deprivation as it does the response to low calcium diet. This is an important observation and indicates that the plasma or tissue phosphate level may play a direct regulatory role with respect to renal 1-hydroxylase activation. These authors suggest that the renal tubular cell inorganic phosphate levels underlie the control of 1,25-dihydroxyvitamin D_3 synthesis.[183] This initial observation of the effect of phosphorus deprivation on enhanced synthesis of 1,25-dihydroxyvitamin D_3 has been confirmed in rats,[184,189,190] in chickens,[191,192] and in pigs.[73,189] In the human, females responded to phosphorus deprivation by a rise in plasma 1,25-dihydroxyvitamin D levels but males failed to exhibit any such response.[193] The basis for this difference may be associated with the fact that whereas the females became hypophyosphatemic, the males did not. The findings in the chicken are more controversial. Whereas some investigators have failed to find a stimulatory effect of phosphorus deprivation on 1,25-dihydroxyvitamin D_3 production in chickens,[187,192] others have reported a positive response.[191,194,195] Part of the disagreement may be attributable to the level of dietary phosphorus; low levels are required to see the stimulatory response. In any case, the response to phosphorus deprivation is not as dramatic as that to calcium deprivation.

C. Dietary Vitamin D

When the dietary calcium and phosphorus levels are adequate, vitamin D deficiency results in marked stimulation of renal 1-hydroxylase activity in rats[57] and in chickens.[92,185,187,196,197] Plasma 1,25-dihydroxyvitamin D levels will obviously depend upon the availability of the substrate, 25-hydroxyvitamin D. In severely vitamin D-depleted chickens, in which the plasma 25-hydroxyvitamin D levels were undectable, the plasma levels of 1,25-dihydroxyvitamin D were also undetectable.[196] Increasing vitamin D intake to toxic levels in rats actually suppressed the plasma levels of 1,25-dihydroxyvitamin D (from 210 to 136 pg/mℓ) in spite of a 36-fold rise in plasma 25-hydroxyvitamin D levels from 13,100 to 466,000 pg/mℓ.

II. IONIC REGULATION

It is obvious that the nutritional regulatory influences discussed above must mediate their effects on renal 1-hydroxylase activity indirectly, i.e., through a messenger or series of messengers. Plasma calcium and inorganic phosphate levels have been implicated as playing either direct or indirect roles. Indirectly, these ions could be working through their influence on the secretion of other messengers such as parathyroid hormone, a known regulator of 1-hydroxylase activity (see Section IV.A). Equally attractive is the concept that the ions may affect the renal enzyme directly. Various investigators have turned their attention to this possibility.

A. Calcium

The possible relationship between the plasma calcium and the renal production of 1,25-dihydroxyvitamin D_3 was first suggested by Boyle et al.[57] in their rat studies. This relationship is depicted in Figure 1. Below 9.0 mg/dℓ 1,25-dihydroxyvitamin D_3 synthesis is stimulated; above 9.5 mg/dℓ it is suppressed. MacIntyre and his associates proposed that intracellular calcium, particularly in the appropriate renal cells, may exert a controlling influence on 1-hydroxylase activity.[185,198]

These in vivo experiments led to attempts to demonstrate regulatory effects of calcium ion when manipulated in the incubation medium of in vitro preparations of chicken kidney mitochondria.[93,107,199–201] The results have been conflicting. Several reports claim a biphasic effect of ionic calcium concentration in the incubation medium; lower concentrations stimulate while higher concentrations inhibit 1-hydroxylase activity.[105,107,199,201] Others report mostly stimulation over the range of calcium concentrations studied.[93] Henry and Norman,[200] in a more limited study, claimed that addition of calcium at $2 \times 10^{-5}M$ inhibited 1,25-dihydroxyvitamin D_3 synthesis by renal mitochondria.

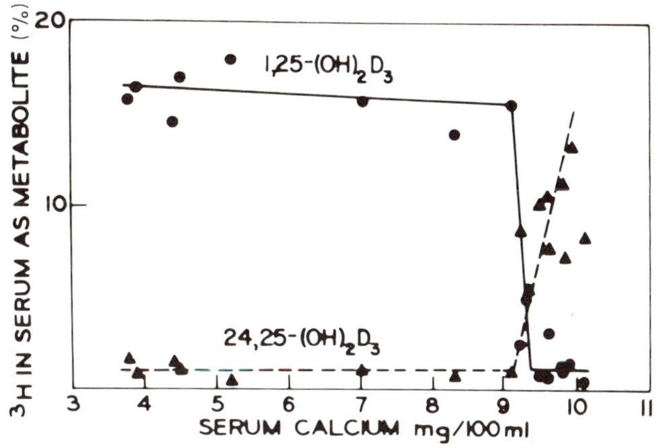

FIGURE 1. The relationship between serum calcium concentration and the conversion of ^{3}H-25-hydroxyvitamin D_3 to either 1,25-dihydroxyvitamin D_3 or 24,25-dihydroxyvitamin D_3. Rats were fed a variety of semipurified diets for a period of 2 weeks. At that time all animals were injected with ^{3}H-25-hydroxyvitamin D_3, and 12 hr later the plasma was removed, extracted, and chromatographed on Sephadex LH-20 to reveal ^{3}H-1,25-dihydroxyvitamin D_3 or 24,25-dihydroxyvitamin D_3. The amount of these metabolites is plotted *vs.* serum calcium concentration. The normal value of the latter in these animals is 9.5 mg/dℓ. The data were taken from Boyle, et al.[57] (From DeLuca, H. F., *Vitamin D. Metabolism and Function*, Springer-Verlag, New York, 1979, 26. With permission.)

B. Inorganic Phosphate

Tanaka and DeLuca[183] suggested that 1,25-dihydroxyvitamin D_3 synthesis by the rat kidney may be subject to some control by the plasma or kidney intracellular levels of inorganic phosphate. Low levels of inorganic phosphate in the plasma and/or kidney cortex stimulated, and high levels suppressed, 1-hydroxylase activity. Henry et al.[187] failed to find support for this relationship in chickens.

In vitro studies of ionic control of renal 1-hydroxylase activity by inorganic phosphate, like those with calcium, have resulted in conflicting findings.[93,105,200,201]

III. REGULATION IN REPRODUCTION AND LACTATION

A. Avian Reproduction

Kenny was the first to demonstrate that reproductive activity in the female Japanese quail and chicken led to enhanced synthesis of 1,25-dihydroxyvitamin D_3 relative to the biologically less active dihydroxylated metabolite, 24,25-dihydroxyvitamin D_3.[63,72,202–204] The studies in the Japanese quail indicated that the renal 1-hydroxylase activity stays steadily elevated when the bird is undergoing consecutive ovulations. Clutch pauses were associated with a decline in 1-hydroxylase activity. Especially important was the observation that 1-hydroxylase activity was already enhanced during the first 6 hr following ovulation, during the period when the ovum is traveling down the upper part of the oviduct (infundibulum, magnus, and isthmus) and *prior* to its lodging in the uterus (shell gland) where calcification of the eggshell is initiated and completed. Figures 2 and 3, taken from Kenny's report,[72] illustrate these findings. Kenny concluded that at least in the situation of consecutive ovu-

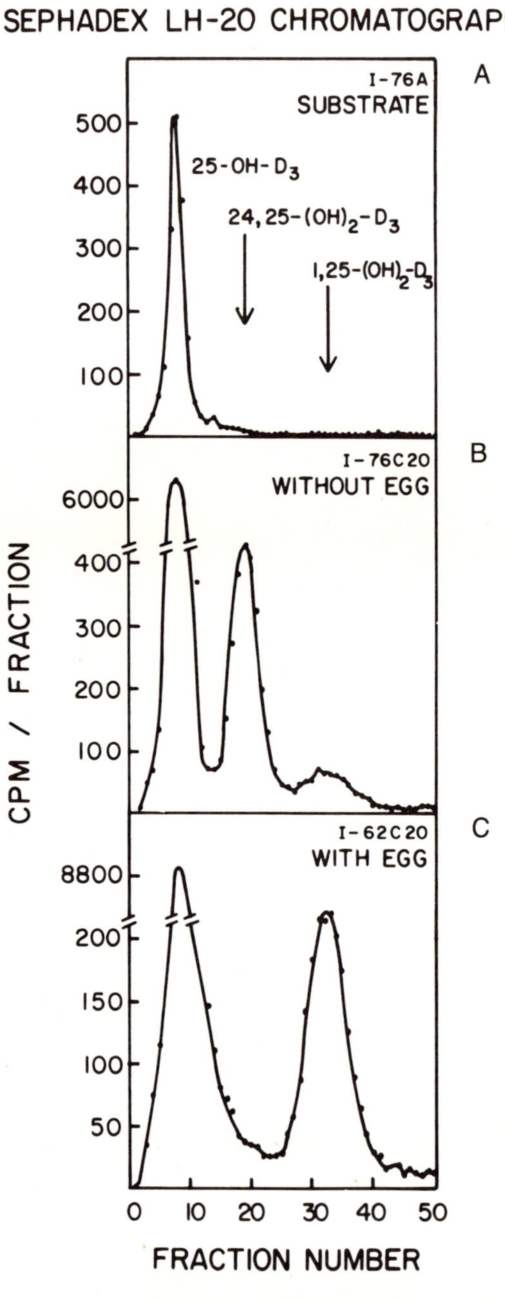

FIGURE 2. Typical chromatographic profiles using a 0.7 × 18 cm column of Sephadex LH-20, chloroform-Skellysolve B (65:35) solvent system, and 125-drop (0.92 mℓ) fractions. (A) 25-[26,27-^{3}H]hydroxyvitamin-D_3 substrate alone; (B) extract prepared following a 20-min incubation of $8 \times 10^{-9} M$ 25-[26,27-^{3}H]hydroxyvitamin D_3 with a kidney homogenate prepared from a reproductively active female Japanese quail *without* an egg in oviduct; 24,25-dihydroxyvitamin D_3 is the predominant metabolite; (C) similar to middle profile except that the kidney homogenate was prepared from a bird *with* a calcified egg in oviduct; 1,25-dihydroxyvitamin D_3 is the predominant metabolite. (From Kenny, A.D., *Am. J. Physiol.*, 230, 1612, 1976. With permission.)

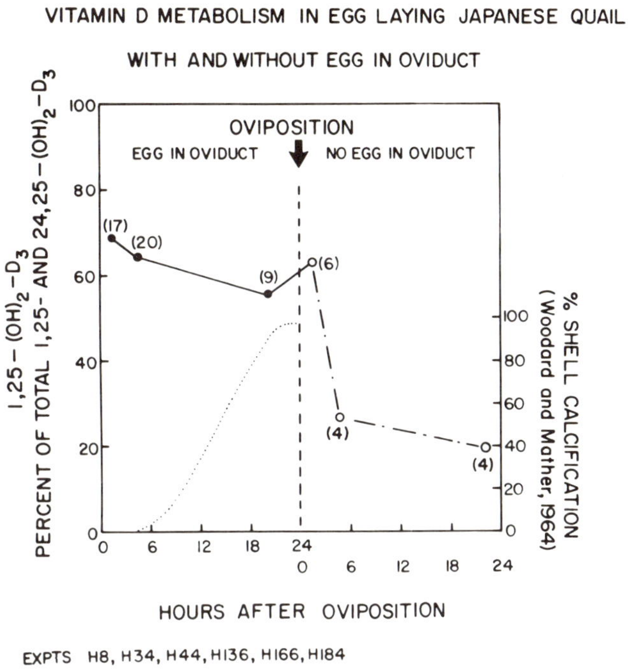

FIGURE 3. In vitro renal production of 1,25-dihydroxyvitamin D_3, expressed as a percent of total 1,25- and 24,25-dihydroxyvitamin D_3 biosynthesis, at different periods (1–3, 3–6, and 18–24 hr) after oviposition in Japanese quail *with* (●——●) and *without* (○—·—○) an egg in oviduct. Ovulation, when it occurs, is within 30 min after oviposition. The production of 1,25-dihydroxyvitamin D_3 is already enhanced (69 and 64%) at 1 to 3 and 3 to 6 hr after oviposition/ovulation (left side of figure) at a time *before* calcification of eggshell has begun, and remains enhanced throughout the 24-hr ovulatory cycle. If oviposition is not followed immediately by ovulation (right side of figure) then 1,25-dihydroxyvitamin D_3 production, although still enhanced 1 to 3 hr after oviposition, falls rapidly and significantly ($P < 0.05$) to 27 and 20% at 3 to 6 and 18 to 24 hr after oviposition, respectively. Data taken from Woodard and Mather (1964) and indicating eggshell calcification rate are plotted on left side of figure (.........). Number in parentheses represents number of birds contributing to mean value. (From Kenny, A.D., *Am. J. Physiol.*, 230, 1613, 1976. With permission.)

lations, calcification of the eggshell was not the signal for increasing the renal 1-hydroxylase activity. In a later report,[205] birds were studied in which ovulation had not been immediately preceded by oviposition, i.e., the bird had not ovulated during the previous 24 hr but had taken an egg-laying pause. In this study the birds still exhibited enhanced 1-hydroxylase activity during the first 5 hr following ovulation prior to the onset of eggshell calcification, again indicating that the latter is not necessary to activate 1,25-dihydroxyvitamin D_3 synthesis. The basic observation, that ovulation leads to enhanced 1-hydroxylase activity, was early confirmed by Kenny and his associates in the chicken[204] and later by reports from other laboratories in both Japanese quail[86,206–208] and in chickens.[206,207,209,210] In addition, measurements of plasma 1,25-dihydroxyvitamin D levels support the renal enzyme studies.[209,211] Determination of plasma 1,25-dihydroxyvitamin D levels throughout the ovulatory cycle has led to slightly conflicting data. Whereas DeLuca and his associates[210] report that the plasma 1,25-dihydroxyvitamin D levels are higher during the period 4 to 10 hr after ovulation, Abe et al.[209] find that the levels are highest 15 hr after ovulation. Certain differences between the two studies, the omission of important details concerning photoperiod, and a possible misunderstanding of avian reproductive physiology in one of the reports, do not permit an immediate resolution of this apparent discrepancy. In one study, white leghorns were used,[210] while in the other report shavers, a strain known for its higher rate of egg production and shorter ovulatory cycle, were used,[209] The lack of photoperiod details in the study of Castillo et al.[210] is an important omission. Nevertheless, if one reduces the high lag time of 3 hr erroneously assumed by Castillo et al. to represent the lag time between oviposition and ovulation to the generally accepted value of around 30 min,[212] and if one assumes that the peak for plasma 1,25-dihydroxyvitamin D, attributed to 15 hr post-ovulation, might in fact be earlier if points between 6 and 15 hr had been determined, then the peaks in the two studies may essentially coincide.

B. Pregnancy

Plasma 1,25-dihydroxyvitamin D levels are elevated in the pregnant rat[148] and human female,[213–215] as is indicated in Table 1, Chapter 2.

In the human female, Pike et al.[213] found plasma levels of 73 pg/mℓ at 38 weeks of pregnancy, compared with 39 pg/mℓ in normal females. In a more detailed study Kumar et al.[214] found that plasma 1,25-dihydroxyvitamin D levels were elevated early in pregnancy, being 87 pg/mℓ as compared with age-matched control levels of 53 pg/mℓ, and continued to rise throughout pregnancy, reaching values around 140 pg/mℓ close to term (38 weeks). Plasma 25-hydroxyvitamin D levels, on the other hand, remain normal (41,700 pg/mℓ) during the first two trimesters.

The report of Pike et al.[148] of elevated plasma 1,25-dihydroxyvitamin D levels in the pregnant rat (control rats around 100 pg/mℓ; 21-day pregnant rats around 180 pg/mℓ) is supported by the work of Lester et al.,[216] who found that 1,25-dihydroxyvitamin D_3 was the predominant dihydroxylated metabolite of vitamin D_3 circulating in the pregnant rat. On the other hand, 24,25-dihydroxyvitamin D_3 was the predominant metabolite in fetal tissues.

C. Lactation

Lactation is also associated with elevated levels of plasma 1,25-dihydroxyvitamin D in rats[148,213,217] and in the human female.[214] Lactating women had levels of 103 pg/mℓ compared with control levels of 53 pg/mℓ. In the lactating rat the plasma 1,25-dihydroxyvitamin D levels fell to control levels (around 100 pg/mℓ) at 1 to 2 days post partum and then rose to levels of around 160 pg/mℓ at 7 to 8 and 14 to 15 days post partum, respectively. There was a sharp decline 2 days after weaning to levels (around 40 pg/mℓ) below those found in control rats; 1 week after weaning the levels had returned to normal.

IV. HORMONAL REGULATION

Several hormones have been implicated as exhibiting a regulatory influence on 1,25-dihydroxyvitamin D_3 production. These include parathyroid hormone, calcitonin, vitamin D, sex hormones (particularly estradiol), prolactin, growth hormone, and glucocorticoids. All, with the exception of calcitonin and vitamin D, cause stimulation of 1,25-dihydroxyvitamin D_3 synthesis and release. How many of these agents are involved in *physiological* regulation is not known with certainty; parathyroid hormone comes close to being recognized as important in this regard.

A. Parathyroid Hormone

In the early 1970s, three laboratories, using different approaches, independently demonstrated that parathyroid hormone has a regulatory influence on the renal 25-hydroxyvitamin D_3-1-hydroxylase enzyme. Garabedian et al.[77] were the first to report the relationship in rats. These investigators found that thyroparathyroidectomy reduced the production of 1,25-dihydroxyvitamin D_3 in calcium-deprived rats and that injection of parathyroid extract was able to restore the production to normal. Similar results were reported by Fraser and Kodicek[197] in the chicken; subacute injections of parathyroid extract into intact chickens led to enhanced renal 1-hydroxylase activity when the activity was measured 3 hr after the last injection. Parathyroidectomy resulted in a decline of enzyme activity 15 hr after the endocrinectomy. Using isolated renal tubules of the chicken, Rasmussen et al.[106] demonstrated that bovine parathyroid hormone, when added in vitro at low concentrations (0.5 n*M*), stimulated 1-hydroxylase activity. All three groups emphasized the physiological significance of the relationship between parathyroid hormone and the renal vitamin D-endocrine system.

There is agreement that parathyroid hormone, at least pharmacologically, regulates renal production of 1,25-dihydroxyvitamin D_3 by enhancing its synthesis. The original observations of Garabedian et al.[77] in the rat have been amply confirmed.[218–224] In addition, Baksi and Kenny[65,85] have observed this response in the Japanese quail and Nagode and Steinmeyer[225] report a stimulatory effect of parathyroid hormone in thyroparathyroidectomized dogs. Nevertheless, Tanaka et al.,[226] using conditions not designed specifically for revealing such an effect, failed to observe a stimulatory effect of parathyroid hormone on renal 1-hydroxylase activity in the chicken.

The rapidity with which parathyroid hormone enhances 1,25-dihydroxyvitamin D_3 synthesis is worthy of note. Most investigators have used subacute dosage schedules involving several daily doses for periods varying from 2 to 11 days. In other cases prolonged intravenous infusions were administered. Fraser and Kodicek[197] did study one group of chickens 3 hr after they had received a single injection of the hormone, but failed to observe any response in renal 1-hydroxylase activity. Hill and Mawer[223] observed a response 20 hr after a single injection into thyroparathyroidectomized rats. The only systematic study of this aspect of the regulatory influence of parathyroid hormone remains that of Baksi and Kenny[85] who studied the response at three time intervals (4, 12, and 24 hr) to three doses (30, 90, and 270 USP units/kg) of parathyroid extract in Japanese quail (Figure 4). Enhanced synthesis of 1,25-dihydroxyvitamin D_3 was exhibited by all three doses but was seen only at the 12-hr interval. No response was seen at 4 hr, and production rates had returned to control levels by 24 hr. In contrast, marked hypercalcemic and hyphosphatemic responses were observed at 4 hr. The rapid onset and short duration of the hypercalcemic response to parathyroid hormone in Japanese quail have been reported before by Kenny and Dacke.[227,228]

The effects of parathyroidectomy on the renal vitamin D-endocrine system have also been studied. In the rat, investigators have confirmed the original observation of Garabedian et al.[77] by reporting that decreased production of 1,25-dihydroxyvitamin D_3 follows parathyroidectomy.[218–220] Similarly, in the chicken, the original observation of Fraser and Kodicek[197] has been confirmed in more than one laboratory.[187,229] Larkins et al.[230] have demonstrated in rats that 1,25-dihydroxyvitamin

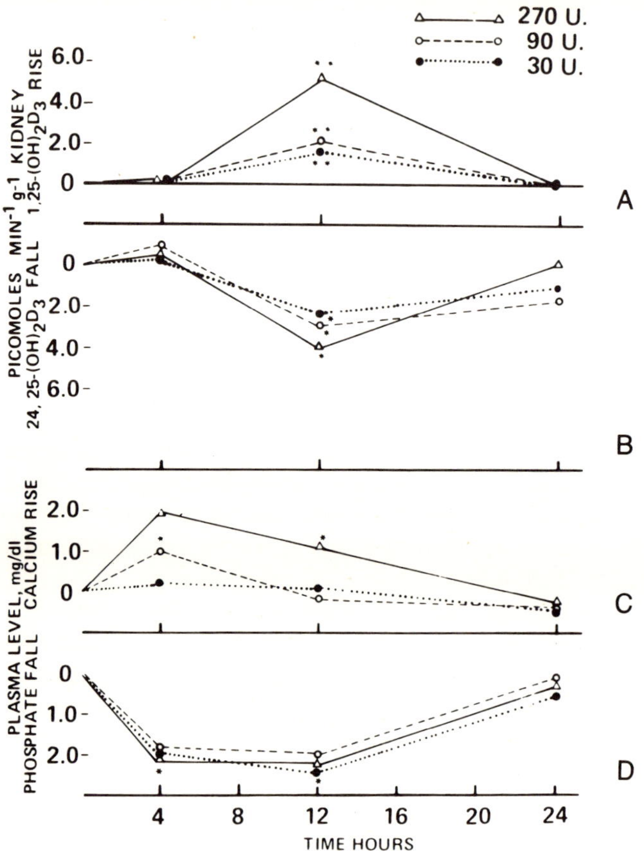

FIGURE 4. Effect of parathyroid hormone (PTH) injection on in vitro renal metabolism of tritiated 25-(OH)D_3, plasma calcium and plasma inorganic phosphate levels in immature (4-week) female Japanese quail. PTH was injected at 30 (●), 90 (○), or 270 (△) USP units/kg intramuscularly. The kidneys were removed 4, 12 or 24 hr later, homogenized, and incubated with $1.0 \times 1.0^{-7}M$ 25-hydroxyvitamin D_3 for 20 min. The rise in 1,25-dihydroxyvitamin D_3 production is expressed in picomoles min^{-1} g^{-1} kidney (A and B). The plasma calcium and inorganic phosphate data are presented in C and D. All responses are relative to controls receiving vehicle alone. Asterisks indicate significant responses (* = $p < 0.05$; ** = $p < 0.01$). (From Baksi, S. N. and Kenny, A. D., *Pharmacology*, S. Karger AG, Basel 18, 171, 1979. With permission.)

D_3 production could be stimulated by dietary manipulation in the absence of the parathyroid glands and concluded that the production of 1,25-dihydroxyvitamin D_3 did not have an absolute dependence on parathyroid hormone. This conclusion is supported by the indirect evidence of Pento et al.,[231] who found that parathyroid hormone was not required for enhanced gut calcium absorption following *long-term* (3-week) calcium deprivation in rats. Short-term deprivation, however, did exhibit a dependence.

Whether or not parathyroid hormone has a direct in vitro effect on the renal 1-hydroxylase enzyme is unclear. Although the early positive report of Rasmussen et al.[106] has been recently confirmed using primary cultures of chicken kidney cells,[97,167] other laboratories have failed to find a direct stimulatory effect of parathyroid hormone on 1-hydroxylase activity, whether primary cultures of kidney cells[99,232] or isolated renal tubules[104] were used. Larkins et al.[97] found a stimulatory effect of parathyroid hormone only when calcium was absent from the incubation medium; in the presence of calcium no effect on 1,25-dihydroxyvitamin D_3 synthesis was observed.

B. Calcitonin

The regulatory effects of calcitonin on the vitamin D-endocrine system are highly controversial. Galante et al.[198] were the first to demonstrate that salmon calcitonin, when injected repeatedly every 6 hr for 3 days into rats, led to enhanced production of 1,25-dihydroxyvitamin D_3. Independently, Rasmussen et al.[106] reported that calcitonin, when added in vitro to isolated renal tubules of the chicken, inhibited parathyroid hormone-stimulated synthesis of 1,25-dihydroxyvitamin D_3. Subsequently, Larkins et al.[97] claimed that salmon calcitonin added in vitro enhanced 1-hydroxylase activity in a similar renal tubular preparation.

In an attempt to resolve the question, Lorenc et al.[224] repeatedly injected salmon calcitonin every 8 hr for 2 days into either intact or thyroparathyroidectomized rats and determined 1,25-dihydroxyvitamin D_3 production rates. Confirming Galante et al.,[198] Lorenc et al. found that 1,25-dihydroxyvitamin D_3 synthesis was enhanced in *intact* rats. However, they made the additional observation that this response was abolished in the absence of the parathyroid glands and concluded that the response to calcitonin was probably secondary to parathyroid hormone release. It is reasonable to conclude that until additional evidence is presented calcitonin does not have important direct regulatory effects on the vitamin D-endocrine system.

C. 1,25-Dihydroxyvitamin D_3

In 1974, Henry et al.[187] reported that chronic administration of 1,25-dihydroxyvitamin D_3 to vitamin D-deficient immature chickens suppressed renal 1-hydroxylase activity. Subsequently, Tanaka et al.[226] demonstrated that this inhibitory response could be observed within 12 hr following intravenous injection of 325 pmol of 1,25-dihydroxyvitamin D_3 into vitamin D-deficient immature chickens. This response appears to be directly on the kidney; several laboratories have reported a similar response when 1,25-dihydroxyvitamin D_3 was added in vitro to either kidney tubular[97,98,100] or cell[101] preparations of the chicken.

D. Sex Hormones

1. *Estrogens*

In 1974, a series of reports began emanating from Kenny's laboratory indicating that avian reproductive activity in the female is accompanied by enhanced synthesis of 1,25-dihydroxyvitamin D_3 in both Japanese quail and chickens.[72,202–204] Details of these observations have been described in Section III.A. These findings led Kenny to suggest that a certain qualitative and quantitative combination of gonadal hormones might stimulate renal 1-hydroxylase activity.[72] Experiments had been initiated in 1973 to determine whether or not the ovarian steroid hormones, estradiol and progesterone, either singly or in combination, would regulate the renal production of 1,25-dihydroxyvitamin D_3 in the Japanese quail. These studies led to a series of reports, beginning in 1976, which documented the fact that estradiol administration to Japanese quail, using acute (1 to 24 hr following a single dose), subacute (daily doses for 3 days), and chronic (repeated doses for 4 weeks) dosage schedules, led to marked stimulation of 1,25-dihydroxyvitamin D_3 production.[79,81,82,233] Ovariectomy and treatment with the antiestrogen, tamoxifen, both influence renal 1-hydroxylase activity in Japanese quail.[80,81] Independently, DeLuca and his associates observed that estradiol injection in Japanese quail and chickens stimulated 1,25-dihydroxyvitamin D_3 production, and made the additional claim that estradiol can influence renal 1-hydroxylase activity only in the presence of circulating androgen.[86,87,234] The stimulatory effect of estradiol on renal 1-hydroxylase activity in the chicken has been confirmed by Pike et al.[147] who, incidentally, used the nonsteroidal estrogen, diethylstilbestrol. Sommerville et al.,[235] on the other hand, failed to observe the response.

The claim that androgen is an absolute requirement for the estradiol-induced stimulation of renal 1-hydroxylase activity is not supported by the finding of Kenny and Baksi[236] that the antiandrogen cyproterone, failed to block the response in immature (4-week old) female Japanese quail. In addition, the 1-hydroxylase response to estradiol in immature (4-week old) female Japanese quail was little influenced by androgen priming of the birds by pretreatment with testosterone propionate.[82] These findings do not completely eliminate any role for androgen. Cyproterone, a known antiandrogen in mammalian species, has not been demonstrated to exhibit such a characteristic in avian species. Also, immature female quail are not necessarily devoid of androgen. Nevertheless, injection of estradiol daily for 3 days does not induce medullary bone formation (a phenomenon which requires both estrogen and androgen) in these birds as it does in immature males.[79] The absolute need for androgen for the stimulation of renal 1-hydroxylase activity by estradiol must remain unsettled until further evidence is forthcoming.

The vitamin D response to estradiol was first demonstrated in avian species using the in vitro kidney homogenate technique following in vivo administration of the estrogen. More recently, radioreceptor assay methods have become available for measuring plasma levels of 1,25-dihydroxyvitamin D_3 (see Section I.A). Application of these methods to an investigation of the estradiol response has confirmed the earlier findings. Administration of either estradiol[234] or diethylstilbestrol[147] resulted in a two- to tenfold rise in plasma levels of 1,25-dihydroxyvitamin D within 12 to 24 hr following a single dose.

There is no doubt that, in avian species, pharmacological doses of estradiol lead to enhanced production of 1,25-dihydroxyvitamin D. An important question is whether this effect of estrogen may be seen with physiological doses of estradiol. Kenny has attempted to answer this question.[237] First, plasma estradiol levels of Japanese quail of both sexes were determined at 3, 4, 5, 6, 7, 8, and 12 weeks of age in order to gain insight into what levels can be expected to occur physiologically. Secondly, plasma estradiol levels were measured at intervals ranging from 2 min to 4 hr after intramuscular (i.m.) injection of estradiol benzoate. When 0.01 mg/kg of estradiol benzoate was injected, the peak plasma levels of estradiol ($\ngtr$400 pg/mℓ at 15 min) were never more than the highest levels found to occur naturally. This dose of estradiol (0.01 mg/kg, i.m.) is capable of activating the renal 1-hydroxylase enzyme at 24 hr after injection.[82] Thus, it is possible for estradiol to influence the renal vitamin D-endocrine system at doses which are in the physiological range. It does not follow, necessarily, that estradiol is of importance in regulating the endocrine system physiologically.

Does the estradiol response result from a direct effect on the renal 1-hydroxylase enzyme or is the estrogen acting secondarily through the mediation of a nonrenal pathway? Attempts to demonstrate a direct in vitro stimulatory effect of estradiol on the 1-hydroxylase activity in primary kidney cell cultures[101,167,232,238] have met with failure, indicating that the estradiol response is probably indirectly mediated.

Kenny and his associates were the first to demonstrate that the response to estrogen is not restricted to avian species. They reported that estradiol enhances 1,25-dihydroxyvitamin D_3 production in rats[71,239] and in bullfrogs.[69,70] Gallagher et al.[240] have shown that treatment of postmenopausal osteoporotic females with estrogen raises their low plasma 1,25-dihydroxyvitamin D levels (22.6 pg/mℓ) to levels (36.3 pg/mℓ) observed in age- and sex-matched normal individuals.

Estrogens have been reported to have an additional effect in avian species. Nicholson et al.[34,241] have shown that hepatic conversion of vitamin D_3 to 25-hydroxyvitamin D_3 is enhanced in adult male and immature Japanese quail treated with estrogen. This observation awaits confirmation.

2. *Progesterone*

Baksi and Kenny[79] first reported that subacute doses of progesterone (5 mg/kg i.m. daily for 3 days) significantly enhanced renal 1-hydroxylase activity in immature male and female Japanese quail maintained on a normal diet. Subsequently, they demonstrated that chronic doses of progesterone (5 mg/kg, i.m. three times a week for 4 weeks) also led to enhanced renal 1-hydroxylase activity in ovariectomized quail maintained on a normal diet.[81] The birds were ovariectomized at 4 weeks of age at which time the 4-week injection period was started. The stimulatory effect of progesterone was not as marked as that seen with estradiol, but no attempt was made to determine the relative potencies of the two gonadal hormones by varying their doses. When the ovariectomized birds were maintained on a low calcium diet, progesterone, like estradiol, effected a paradoxical suppression of 1-hydroxylase activity. Castillo et al.[86] have also reported a slight response to progesterone in mature Japanese quail.

The renal 1-hydroxylase enzyme of the chicken does not respond to progesterone, whether the enzyme activity itself[147,234] or the plasma 1,25-dihydroxyvitamin D levels[147] are measured. Nevertheless, progesterone acts synergistically with estradiol alone or with a combination of estradiol and testosterone.[234]

3. *Androgens*

It has been reported that the renal 1-hydroxylase response to estrogen has an absolute requirement for androgen. Tanaka et al.[87] found that the renal 1-hydroxylase enzyme of immature male Japanese quail, unlike that of mature males, did not respond well to estradiol stimulation. Injection of estradiol plus testosterone led to a good response. Subsequently, Castillo et al.,[86] using castrated male chickens, found that the estradiol response had an absolute requirement for testosterone. The estradiol response could be elicited only when the castrates were pretreated with testosterone. The discrepancy between these findings and those of Kenny and Baksi[236,242] has been discussed (Section IV.D.1).

E. Prolactin

Spanos et al. found that immature vitamin D-deficient chickens responded to subacute injections of ovine prolactin by an increase in renal 1-hydroxylase activity[243] and in plasma 1,25-dihydroxyvitamin D levels.[211] The prolactin was administered once or twice daily for 5 to 7 days at doses of 100 μg/day or less. An acute response, 1 hr after a single injection, was also reported.[243] Kenny and his associates have confirmed the subacute response in the Japanese quail[69,70] but have failed to confirm acute (1- to 4-hr) response in this species.[714] A subacute dose of ovine prolactin failed to elicit any 1-hydroxylase response in the bullfrog; the usual hypercalcemic response was observed, indicating that the hormone was at least active in this species.[69] MacIntyre and his associates[244] have demonstrated that prolactin also stimulates 1-hydroxylase activity when added in vitro to chicken kidney cell cultures, and that bromocriptine, an inhibitor of prolactin release, lowers plasma 1,25-dihydroxyvitamin D levels in rats. Others have failed to demonstrate effects of prolactin on avian kidney cells in vitro[232] or on in vivo production of 1,25-dihydroxyvitamin D_3 in hypophysectomized rats.[245] A patient with a prolactinoma exhibited elevated levels of plasma 1,25-dihydroxyvitamin D.[215] The fact that lactation in rats and humans is associated with increased levels of plasma 1,25-dihydroxyvitamin D (see Section III.C) also supports the concept of a physiological role for prolactin with respect to regulation of the renal vitamin D-endocrine system.

One concept which needs exploring is the role that prolactin might play in the phenomenon of adaptation to calcium deprivation. We suggest that long-term adaptation might lead to increased secretion of prolactin, which in turn leads to increased production of 1,25-dihydroxyvitamin D_3 and enhanced absorption of calcium by the intestine. Kenny and his associates[231,246] have suggested that, although parathyroid hormone is important for short-term adaptation, it is not required for longer periods. Prolactin, in general, is not known for being a rapidly acting hormone; the acute (1-hr) response reported by Spanos et al.[243] remains to be confirmed. The hypothesis poses several questions which are amenable to experimental solution. Does calcium deprivation, especially that of several weeks duration, lead to elevated prolactin levels in the plasma? Would bromocriptine administration prevent the adaptive response (increased intestinal absorption of calcium) to a low calcium diet? Particularly intriguing is the possibility that prolactin may influence the vitamin D-endocrine system in lower vertebrates, especially in fish which lack the regulating hormone, parathyroid hormone. Prolactin is well recognized as a hypercalcemic hormone in lower vertebrates[247] but the mechanism of this response is unclear.

F. Growth Hormones

Spencer and Tobiassen[245,248] were the first to report that growth hormone has a regulatory influence on the renal vitamin D-endocrine system. They found that hypophysectomy in rats leads to a fall in 1,25-dihydroxyvitamin D_3 production and that treatment with growth hormone restored the production rate towards normal. Subsequently, MacIntyre and his associates confirmed this finding; they found that hypophysectomy diminished, and growth hormone treatment increased plasma 1,25-dihydroxyvitamin D levels.[249,250]

The response of the renal vitamin D-endocrine system to growth hormone in man is more controversial. Although there are reports that injection of growth hormone has no effect on plasma 1,25-dihydroxyvitamin D levels[251] and that plasma 1,25-dihydroxyvitamin D levels are not elevated in acromegaly,[252] another laboratory has observed that the latter condition is associated with elevated levels of plasma 1,25-dihydroxyvitamin D and that bromocriptine administration lowers the levels.[253]

G. Glucocorticoids

Early reports of the influence of glucocorticoids on vitamin D metabolism were concerned with the effect on 25-hydroxyvitamin D_3 production in rats.[254,255] In these studies, cortisone was found to enhance 25-hydroxyvitamin D_3 production, a conclusion which was subsequently supported by clinical observations.[256]

The first studies concerned with effects of glucocorticoids on the rate of 1,25-dihydroxyvitamin D_3 production were also made in the rat,[257,258] but with conflicting findings. In one study, prednisolone administration to rats increased plasma 1,25-dihydroxyvitamin D levels[258], an observation not supported by the negative findings of Favus et al.,[257] nor the experience in man where chronic prednisone treatment of children led to a decline in plasma 1,25-dihydroxyvitamin D levels.[259]

In the chicken, cortisol was found to increase 1,25-dihydroxyvitamin D_3 production both in vivo and in vitro. The response was rapid, being manifested within 4 hr of injection.

V. OTHER REGULATORY AGENTS

A. Lead

The first experimental study of the effect of lead ingestion on the rate of 1,25-dihydroxyvitamin D_3 production is that of Baksi and Kenny[83] in immature female Japanese quail, who found that incorporation of lead acetate in the drinking water (0.32 mg Pb/mℓ) resulted in enhanced renal synthesis of 1,25-dihydroxyvitamin D_3. The relationship of this finding to that of Sorrel and Rosen,[260] who observed that lead-burdened children have low plasma 1,25-dihydroxyvitamin D levels, is unclear.

B. Diphosphonates

Hill et al.[261] presented indirect evidence which suggested that high doses of the diphosphonate, ethane-1-hydroxy-1,1-diphosphonate (EHDP), inhibit 1,25-dihydroxyvitamin D_3 production in rats, a conclusion which was rapidly confirmed by Baxter et al.[262] in immature chickens. These observations are consistent with the known rachitogenic properties of larger doses of EHDP. Low doses of EHDP, on the other hand, appear to stimulate renal 1-hydroxylase activity, at least in rats.[263]

C. Strontium

Strontium feeding leads to suppression of renal 1-hydroxylase activity in immature chickens[264,265] and accounts for decreased rates of calcium absorption by the intestine in strontium-treated animals.

Part II
Calcium Absorption

INTRODUCTION

Calcium is necessary for the integrity of cell membranes and is essential for maintaining normal function in muscle, nerve, and secretory organs. For this reason, the calcium level in the extracellular compartment is kept within very narrow limits by endocrine systems concerned with calcium homostasis. These regulatory systems involve three messengers (parathyroid hormone, 1,25-dihydroxyvitamin D_3, and calcitonin) and three target organs (gut, bone, and kidney). During the 1970–1979 decade, our understanding of the endocrine role of vitamin D and its relationship to calcium absorption from the intestine has taken such an explosive form that much of the present review has been devoted to that topic. Relative to this massive thrust in vitamin D research, developments in our perception of the mechanism of gut calcium transport have been very modest.

The review of calcium absorption will consider the concepts concerning calcium transport followed by a discussion of how it is influenced by growth and senescence, reproductive states and the stress of calcium deprivation, and nutritional and endocrine factors. Finally, the pharmacological aspects of calcium transport will be surveyed.

Chapter 5

CALCIUM TRANSPORT

I. TECHNIQUES FOR STUDYING GUT CALCIUM TRANSPORT

Most of the techniques which have been used in other areas of gut transport research [266–268] have been applied to an examination of calcium absorption. In vivo methods include the balance technique, perfusion of isolated loops, and ligated loops. The most widely used in vitro preparation is the everted gut sac of Wilson and Wiseman.[269] Other in vitro approaches have utilized intestinal slices, isolated villi, and organ culture of the duodenum. The techniques available for clinical studies in man are more limited;[270] the balance method remains the most widely used in spite of its tedium expense.

A brief description of these techniques and their application to studies of calcium absorption follows.

A. In Vivo Techniques in Animals

1. Balance Method

The classical approach for studying calcium absorption is the balance method. In its simplest form, the total fecal output subtracted from the total dietary intake to give the quantity of calcium absorbed. The latter may be expressed as a percentage of the intake. Fecal collection errors may be minimized by gathering specimens over several days and using an unabsorbed marker in the diet to mark the beginning and the end of the collection period. Chromium sesquioxide and ^{91}Y are examples of markers. This simple balance technique has been used by Henry and Kon[271] and Benson et al.[272] in the rat, by Hurwitz and Griminger[273] in the laying hen, and by Gershoff et al.[274] in the dog.

Ignored in this simple approach is the contribution of the endogenous component of fecal calcium. Albright and his associates recognized the existence of this component in their pioneer studies in man, where they found fecal losses of 300 mg/day on a calcium intake of only 100 mg/day.[275] Since the mid-1950s this problem was tackled with the aid of intravenously administered ^{45}Ca. Endogenous fecal loss of calcium was thus demonstrated and measured in cattle,[276,277] rats,[278–281] and man.[282]

Does this mean that studies which ignore the endogenous component necessarily lead to false conclusions? Data taken from Hansard and Plumlee[279] and Sammon et al.[281] have been assembled in Table 1 to indicate the differences in the values for percent calcium absorbed both by the simpler and the more accurate approaches. It is obvious that the classical approach (apparent absorption) gave lower values than those corrected for endogenous loss (true absorption). However, conclusions concerning the relative effects of dietary calcium level on the percent absorbed would be similar based on either set of data.

The endogenous fecal calcium component is not a constant value but varies with the dietary level of calcium. The higher the dietary intake, the greater is the endogenous less (Table 1[281,283,284]). Is the determination of endogenous fecal calcium a *sine qua non* of acceptable work in studies of calcium absorption using the balance method? More needs to be known about the physiology of the endogenous loss before a definitive answer can be given. It is still uncertain to what extent the endogenous calcium, secreted into the intestine, is subject to partial reabsorption.[285]

The balance method has one major advantage: it is the most physiological. Its

Table 1
CALCIUM BALANCE DATA IN RATS ON VARIOUS CALCIUM INTAKES

Dietary Ca (%)	Ca intake v_i (mg/day)	Ca absorbed v_a (mg/day)	Endogenous fecal loss v_f (mg/day)	Ca absorption: Apparent[a] (%)	Ca absorption: True[b] (%)	Ref.
0.01	0.8	0.78	0.78	—	98	279
0.3	24.0	20.6	8.4	65	86	
0.5	45.0	28.4	24.3	46	63	
1.0	102.0	47.9	64.3	37	47	
0.05	7.3	6.6	0.3	86	90	281
0.5	72.8	44.5	5.1	54	61	
1.4	205.0	75.9	11.1	32	37	

[a] $(v_i - v_F)100/v_i$.
[b] $(v_i - v_F + v_f)100/v_i$ or $v_a \times 100/v_F$ = total fecal Ca.

drawbacks, in addition to the problem of endogenous fecal loss, lie in its tedium, its fecal collection errors, and its inability to pinpoint mechanism or site of absorption.

2. *Isolated Loop: Perfusion of Chronic Preparation*

The chronically prepared isolated loop (Thiry-Vella fistula) has been used mainly in larger animals such as the dog[286–292] and the sheep.[293–295]

Solutions of varying but known composition are perfused through the loop at a volume rate which is estimated to be physiological. Care and van't Klooster[293] used 180 mℓ/hr in 2- to 3-year old sheep, for example. The perfusate may be concentrated by fluid absorption or be diluted by intestinal secretions; either event will introduce an error in interpretation. This artifact may be minimized by the addition to the perfusate of a material such as polyethylene glycol[293] which is not absorbed and can be measured readily by the turbidometric method of Hydén.[296]

Disuse atrophy of the Thiry-Vella loop can occur as a result of its being isolated from the normally functioning gastrointestinal tract. This problem can be largely circumvented by the use of the re-entrant cannulae which permit the flow of food through the loops except when isolated during an experiment.[294]

The chronically isolated loop preparation, although less physiological than the balance technique, is certainly more reliable quantitatively. Certain kinetic aspects can be studied, such as unidirectional flow and saturation kinetics. It can render information on sites of absorption and on the direct influence of pharmacological agents at these sites. It cannot readily distinguish between the active and passive components of calcium absorption and hence the mechanisms underlying its absorption.

3. *Isolated Loop: Perfusion of Acute Preparation*

Perfusion of the isolated loop in an acute preparation has had more limited application in studies of intestinal calcium absorption. Its use has been restricted mostly to smaller animals such as the rat[297–300] and the chicken.[301] An isolated segment of the small intestine is cannulated at both ends under anesthesia and is perfused at a constant rate with[298,299,301] or without[300] recirculation of the fluid. The advantages of the acute perfusion technique are similar to those of the chronic preparation. In addition, the problem of disuse atrophy does not arise.

4. Isolated Loop: Injection into Ligated Segment

This is the most widely used in vivo technique in smaller animals, especially in rats,[231,302–307] in chickens,[305,308–320] and in the hamster.[321] The animal is anesthetized and a segment of the intestine is exposed and ligated at both ends following the injection of a ^{45}Ca solution. In studies involving the proximal duodenum the bile duct is also ligated. The laparotomy is closed and the animal allowed to recover from anesthesia. After an interval (usually 1 hr), the animal is bled and the segment of gut removed. The radiocalcium contents of the plasma, gut loop tissue, and loop contents and washings are determined and used to calculate indexes of calcium absorption. The technique is simple and relatively physiological. It can be used for studies of unidirectional fluxes. The active and passive components of calcium absorption can be determined indirectly by the use of flux ratios at varying luminal calcium concentrations.[319] It can also be used to identify sites of absorption. A somewhat similar technique has been used in dogs.[322]

B. In Vitro Techniques in Animals

1. Everted Gut Sac

The everted gut sac preparation was first described by Wilson and Wiseman[269] in studies of glucose and methionine absorption by rat and hamster intestine. A short segment (2 to 3 cm) of the intestine is removed, everted, and ligated at both ends following the insertion of a small volume (0.5 mℓ) of a buffer solution containing ^{45}Ca with or without glucose. The everted sac is placed in a 25-mℓ Erlenmeyer flask containing a larger volume (3 mℓ) of the labeled buffer solution. After incubation at 37°C for 1 to 3 hr with shaking, the final ^{45}Ca concentration ratio [inside/outside (I/O) or serosal/mucosal (S/M)] is determined.

The development of the everted gut sac preparation gave a great impetus to research in intestinal absorption in general. It allowed active transport to be examined directly and to be demonstrated more conclusively. The influence of environment, metabolic inhibitors, and pharmacological agents can be studied in isolation from neural and humoral factors (Table 2).

Since its first applications to calcium absorption in 1959,[323,324] our understanding of several aspects of mineral absorption has greatly increased. First applied to both rats and rabbits,[323] the technique has subsequently been applied almost exclusively to rats.[324–339,341–349] Passive transport may be studied by incubating at lower temperatures (5 or 22°C), or under other conditions, such as anaerobiosis and addition of metabolic inhibitors, which suppress active transport. The everted gut sac preparation has been used in studies of calcium absorption in chickens.[301,315,317] A disadvantage of the technique is that it cannot address such questions as to where the *bulk* of the calcium is absorbed in the gastrointestinal tract.

The everted gut sac as described above is the most popular in vitro preparation. Modified preparations have been developed for special purposes. Morehead and Kessner[350] used an open-ended gut sac of the rat similar to that described by Parsons and Paterson.[351] Schachter[352] and Wasserman and Taylor[353] adapted the preparation described by Crane and Wilson[354] for calcium absorption studies. This technique, in which a segment of the everted gut is ligated at one end, and at the other end tied to a cannula suspended in a test tube, permits serial sampling and the measurement of bioelectric phenomena.

Table 2
EVERTED GUT SAC OF THE RABBIT: EFFECT OF METABOLIC INHIBITORS ON ACTIVE TRANSPORT OF CALCIUM

Inhibitor	Concentration (m*M*)	Serosal/mucosal ratio	
		Control	Inhibitor
Nitrogen (anaerobiosis)	—	3.7	0.8
5°C	—	4.8	1.0
Sodium fluoride	2.0	5.2	1.0
Sodium cyanide	0.5	4.6	1.1
Sodium azide	3.0	6.0	1.1
Sodium iodoacetate	0.3	5.0	1.6
Mercuric chloride	1.0	4.6	1.1
Sodium malonate	20.0	5.0	2.5
2,4-Dinitrophenol	0.05	7.2	1.2
Magnesium chloride	1.0	4.6	2.0
Strontium chloride	1.0	4.3	5.5
Barium chloride	1.0	4.5	4.6

From Schacter, D. and Rosen, S. M., *Am. J. Physiol.*, 196, 357, 1959. With permission.

2. *Other In Vitro Techniques*

These include the use of (1) rat intestinal slices;[355-358] (2) rat isolated intestinal villi for tissue uptake studies;[359] (3) a modification of the Ussing and Zerahn[360] technique for measuring transmural unidirectional fluxes and electrical potentials;[356,361,362] and (4) more recently, embryonic chicken duodenum in organ culture.[363-370]

C. Clinical Techniques in Man

1. *Balance Method*

The balance method has been unquestionably the most widely used approach for studies of calcium absorption in man. The early history and the experimental details associated with balance studies in man have been adequately reviewed by Malm.[371] The method can yield data subject to quantitative errors unless the endogenous component of fecal calcium is taken into considerations, as has been discussed (see Section I.A.1). Blau et al.[372] and Bronner and Harris[282] were the first to present direct evidence for the existence of this phenomenon in man. Its physiological significance has been discussed by Bronner.[373]

2. *Other In Vivo Techniques*

During the past 2 decades, simpler methods for approaching the problem of studying calcium absorption in man have been developed. There are several reports of using a single oral dose of radiocalcium followed by monitoring the plasma level of the radioisotope.[374-381] Birge et al.[382] developed a method involving the administration of a single oral dose of ^{47}Ca followed by monitoring the plasma ^{47}Ca level over the next 8 hr. An intravenous dose of ^{47}Ca was administered one to two weeks later and similarly monitored. They subjected their data so obtained to kinetic analysis based on a model of calcium kinetics which enabled them to make physiological interpretation of the data in both the normal and diseased state. Szymendera et al.[383]

modified the method of Birge et al.[382] by administering ^{47}Ca orally, followed 2 hr later by an intravenous dose of a different radioisotope of calcium, ^{45}Ca.

Wensel et al.[384] have used a different approach in the human. The small intestine was directly intubated and perfused using a triple-lumen polyvinyl tube. The perfusate (10 mℓ/min) emerged from the proximal lumen and was continuously sampled through the second and third lumens located 10 and 60 cm, respectively and distally, below the point of infusion. Polyethylene glycol was used to measure water movement (see Section I.A.2.)

II. MECHANISMS OF GUT CALCIUM ABSORPTION

Various mechanisms have been proposed as contributing to the absorption of calcium from the intestine. Some of the mechanisms, such as active transport, are well substantiated. Others, such as the existence and contribution of a Ca-activated adenosinetriphosphatase (CaATPase), are more controversial. It is not intended to take a stand at this point on the importance of a particular mechanism; this will depend on the circumstances (species, intestinal site, age, physiological and pharmacological factors) and will be discussed later where appropriate. It is hoped that a brief description of the individual mechanisms will serve as an introduction to the terminology, to the techniques used in the study of a certain mechanism, and to the evidence for the existence of that mechanism.

In considering the transport of calcium from the intestinal lumen to plasma, it should be remembered that the barrier through which calcium has to cross is not a simple, unicellular, anatomical membrane, but consists of several layers of tissues. In vivo, blood vessels are found close to the basement membrane so that the ion being transported must pass at least through the epithelial cells, basement membrane, lamina propria, and the vascular endothelium. Certain in vitro preparations, such as the everted gut sac, exaggerate this barrier by requiring the ion to be translocated through additional layers of tissue (muscularis mucosa, submucosa, circular and longitudinal muscle, and the serosa).

There may be situations where the barrier, at least from a kinetic or functional viewpoint, might take the form of a simple unicellular layer, the other layers not being rate limiting. It is usually assumed that the epithelial cells of the mucosal membrane are rate limiting and therefore form the barrier of most interest in calcium transport studies. It is in this tissue layer that agents, active in controlling calcium transport, such as 1,25-dihydroxyvitamin D_3, are thought to act. Although this concept is reasonable in the light of current knowledge, there is little direct evidence in its support. We know that the epithelial cell is polarized anatomically (microvillar surface *vs.* basal surface without microvilli), and therefore assume that certain functions such as active transport are polarized but there is little direct evidence for the exact location of these functions within the cell.[353]

A. Active Transport

1. Active Transport: Theoretical Aspects

Active transport in simplest terms is defined as movement against an electrochemical gradient, a process which requires work or energy input. This gradient consists of two components, electrical and chemical. The electrical part is the potential difference across the barrier or membrane and could either enhance or oppose cation transport depending upon which side of the barrier is electrically negative. The chemical component is the chemical concentration, or more correctly the *activity*, gradient existing across the barrier. These two components are related to each other according to the Nernst equation:

$$E = \frac{RT}{nF} \ln \frac{a_1}{a_2}$$

where E = potential difference; R = gas constant; T = absolute temperature; n = valence of ion; F = Faraday; a_1 and a_2 are the *activities** (concentrations) of the ion on either side of the barrier. The in vivo potential difference between the intestinal lumen and the blood is normally positive with respect to the lumen and is between 5 and 40 mV depending upon the site and species.[295,385] This means that with no active transport one would anticipate the ratio of the *activities* (blood/lumen) of a cation to be less than 1.0 under steady state conditions. A qualitatively and quantitatively similar potential difference exists in vitro. Table 3 summarizes some in vitro and in vivo bioelectric data taken from the calcium transport literature.[295,300,319,332,339,353,356,361,362] All these reports indicate that the serosa is positive with respect to the mucosa, a situation which opposes cation transport. Martin and DeLuca[356] calculate from their observed potential difference (1.3 mV) that a flux ratio (mucosal to serosal/serosal to mucosal) of not more than 0.9 would be expected in the absence of active transport; Walling and Rothman[362] suggested a value of 0.68. These values are consistent with the observation that, under conditions which inhibit active transport (anaerobiosis or metabolic inhibitors), the serosal/mucosal ratios often drop to values of 0.7 to 0.9[323,346] (Table 2).

As a first approximation the electrical component is usually ignored and the total calcium concentration is normally equated with the *activity*. Under these circumstances an equilibrium concentration ratio (serosal/mucosal) of 1.0 is assumed to represent no active transport; values significantly greater than 1.0 indicate an energy-dependent transport system or, more colloquially, a calcium pump.

A more precise approach to the problem of demonstrating active transport is to use flux ratio analysis,[386,387] an approach which has had considerable application in studies of calcium transport by the gut.[297,299,339,353,361,362] One advantage of this approach is that it is applicable to both the in vitro and in vivo situation. This method involves a comparison between the *observed* flux ratios (lumen to plasma/plasma to lumen) and the *theoretical* flux ratios calculated from the known chemical and electrical gradients (ignoring solvent drag) as described by Koefoed-Johnson and Ussing.[386] If the observed ratio equals the theoretical flux ratio, then only passive transport is involved. If the observed ratio is significantly larger than the theoretical, then active transport is partly or wholly involved.

2. *Active Transport: Experimental Aspects*

In 1959, the existence of a calcium pump in the intestine was first demonstrated in vitro by Schachter and Rosen[323] in both the rat and the rabbit. The evidence was clear-cut (Table 2). First the concentration ratio (serosal/mucosal) was always greater than 1.0 (3.7 to 7.2) in the absence of metabolic inhibitors. In the presence of the latter, the ratio was reduced towards 1.0 or below. This initial demonstration of active Ca transport has been amply confirmed in rats using: (1) the everted gut sac technique;[231,324,328–334,337–339,341–347] (2) an open everted gut sac preparation;[350] and (3) the Ussing and Zerahn method.[362] Active transport of calcium has been shown

* The thermodynamic term, *activity*, is synonymous with the *ionic* Ca concentration, but may be equal to, or less than, the total Ca concentration.

Table 3
TRANSMURAL POTENTIAL DIFFERENCES IN SMALL INTESTINES OF VARIOUS SPECIES *IN VIVO* AND *IN VITRO*

Species	Site	Technique	Potential difference[a] (mean or range)	Ref.
Rat	Duodenum	*In vitro*[b]	+3.0—+4.5	361
	Duodenum	*In vitro*[b]	+1.3	356
	Duodenum	*In vitro*[b]	+5.2	362
	Duodenum	*In vitro* ligated loop	+8.1	300
	Duodenum	*In vitro* everted sac	+4.9	339
	Jejunum	*In vitro* everted sac	+9.5	339
	Ileum	*In vitro* everted sac	+4.4	339
	Colon	*In vitro* everted sac	+7.2	332
Rabbit	Duodenum	*In vitro* membrane	+3.0	353
Chicken	Duodenum	*In vivo* ligated loop	+6.1	319
Sheep	Duodenum	*In vivo* Thiry-Vella loop	+14.0	295
	Upper jejunum	*In vivo* Thiry-Vella loop	+13.0	295
	Lower jejunum	*In vivo* Thiry-Vella loop	+7.5	295
	Ileum	*In vivo* Thiry-Vella loop	+7.6	295

[a] + sign indicates that the serosa is positive with respect to mucosa.
[b] Short-circuit apparatus of Ussing, H. H. and Zerahn, K.[360]

by Schachter and his colleagues to be present also in the intestine of the rabbit, guinea pig and mouse,[352] as well as the hamster.[343,352]

The in vivo evidence for active transport in the rat has been well summarized by Wasserman and Taylor.[353] The positive evidence is largely that reported by Wasserman et al.[318] and by Krawitt and Schedl.[299] These groups used an acute in vivo perfusion technique, measured unidirectional fluxes in all segments of the small intestine, and determined the observed flux ratios. Wasserman et al.,[300] from a knowledge of the luminal and plasma calcium *activities* and the potential difference, calculated the theoretical flux ratios and compared them with the observed values. Over a luminal calcium concentration range of 0.3 to 1.97 m*M* the *observed* flux ratio values were approximately tenfold the *theoretical* ratios, which was interpreted as evidence for active transport. Krawitt and Schedl[299] made no bioelectric measurements but found that, even when the perfusion fluid calcium concentration (0.4 or 0.85 m*M*) was kept below the plasma ionic calcium level (1 m*M* or above), there was still a net flux of calcium from the lumen to the plasma. In view of the fact that the plasma is always electrically positive with respect to the lumen (Table 3) and that the concentration ratio (lumen/plasma) was kept below 1.0, Krawitt and Schedl can claim that this net flux was observed in the face of an opposing electrochemical gradient, or, in other words, that active transport was involved.

The negative evidence in the rat is represented by the work of Helbock et al.[361] and of Dumont et al.[297] The work of the former group is impressive. They used several approaches including the Ussing short-circuit apparatus. Although they demonstrated active Na transport in a 400-g male rat duodenum, they were unable to find any evidence for active transport of calcium in the same preparation. The negative findings of Dumont et al.[297] in 300- to 400-g male rats also cannot be ignored, although the intestinal segment (mainly ileal) used is not considered the best for demonstrating active transport of calcium.[334] Both these studies[297,361] used heavy rats. The age of the rats cannot be estimated with any degree of accuracy from weight data alone—they could have been any age after 6 months—but it is possible that very old rats were used and that the active transport mechanism had degenerated. Schachter et al.[341] found that active transport, as determined with the in vitro gut sac technique, decreased with age, but they still observed significant active transport in 400- to 500-g male rats over 12 months of age. Walling and Rothman[362] reported similar findings. However, more recently Schachter et al.[343] used a calcium-specific electrode in conjunction with the everted duodenal sac preparation and found no evidence of active transport in rats over 500 g. In view of the overwhelming in vitro evidence and of the existence of positive in vivo evidence, and in spite of the two reports to the contrary, the author feels that the existence of an active process for the transport of calcium in the rat's upper small intestine can be accepted as an established fact.

The existence of active transport for calcium in chicken intestine is less certain. Hurwitz et al.[315] were unable to demonstrate it in vitro in any part of the small intestine under normal circumstances; only in a low sodium medium did the ileum indicate an energy-dependent system. Norman and his associates on the other hand have reported finding it in the ileum.[388] Wasserman and Kallfelz[319] used an in vivo acute perfusion technique and found, at luminal calcium concentrations of 5.2 m*M* and less, flux ratios (lumen to plasma/plasma to lumen) which were always greater than the theoretical flux ratios calculated with the equation of Ussing.[387] These data were interpreted as indicating an active process. The presence of an active transport mechanism for calcium in the sheep is still controversial.[293–295] The data of Wensel et al.[384] would suggest the presence of an active transport system in the human proximal small intestine.

3. *Active Transport: Saturation Kinetics*

Wasserman and Taylor[353] and Walling and Rothman[362] have pleaded a case for the existence of an active transport system which becomes saturated at intestinal luminal concentrations of around 3 to 5 m*M* calcium. Wasserman's case is based largely on his earlier work[319] using an in vivo preparation (injection into an isolated loop) in the chicken. There appears to be no question that, as the intraluminal concentration of calcium is increased, the efflux (lumen to plasma) changes rather abruptly from a faster to a slower flux around 5 m*M* (Figure 1). This was interpreted as indicating that one process had become saturated and that this process was active transport. The latter conclusion is based on the fact that at the lower luminal calcium concentrations (1.3 to 5.2 m*M*) the observed flux ratios (lumen to plasma/plasma to lumen) were always greater than the theoretical flux ratios which would pertain in the absence of an active process. The authors note that the point where one process becomes saturated (around 5 m*M*) is also the point at which the electrochemical gradient becomes theoretically zero. In other words, at luminal calcium concentrations greatly above 5 m*M*, transport would occur passively by a downhill process. However, no saturation of the downhill process was observed even with intraluminal calcium concentrations as high as 135 m*M*. Walling and Rothman[362] have confirmed these findings in the rat duodenum; active transport became saturated at 3 m*M* whereas passive transport did not become saturated with calcium concentrations up to 12.4 m*M*. In humans, Wensel et al.[384] found no evidence of saturation in the proximal small intestine but the highest luminal calcium concentration used was only around 4 m*M*.

B. Passive Transport

The transport of an ion across a membrane is considered completely passive if its movements can be explained entirely and quantitatively in terms of physical

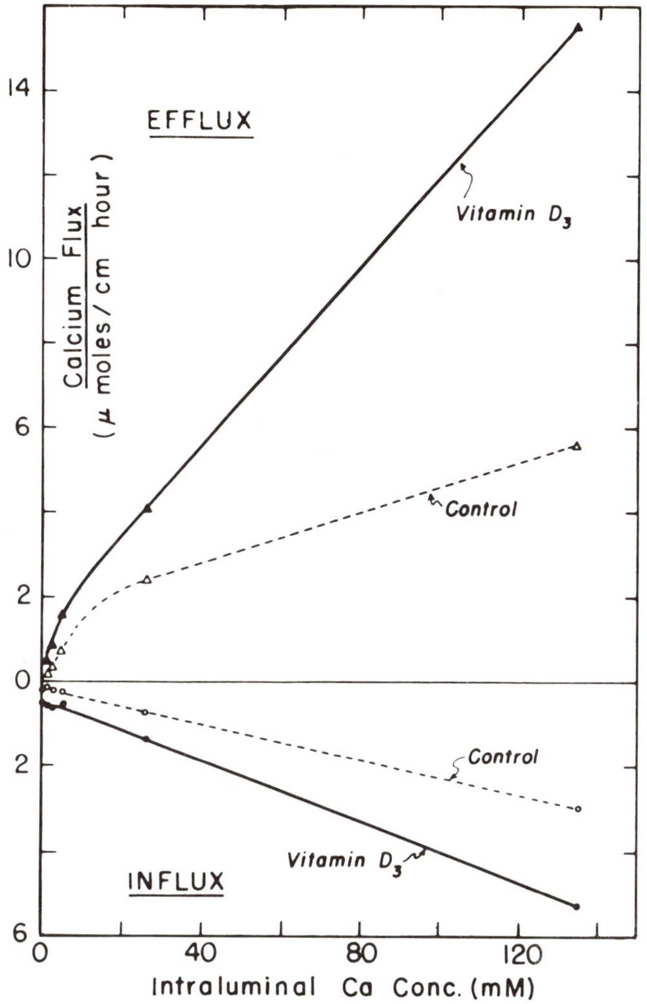

FIGURE 1. Effect of vitamin D_3 and intraluminal calcium concentration on the unidirectional fluxes of calcium across the chick duodenum. Radiocalcium (^{47}Ca) was placed in the ligated duodenum for 10 min for efflux (lumen to plasma) determinations. Net flux was determined from ^{40}Ca movement; influx (plasma to lumen) was derived by difference. Note change in slope of efflux at low intraluminal calcium concentrations as active transport system became saturated. There was no evidence of a further change in slope, indicating that the passive transport system did not become saturated. The control chicks were vitamin D-deficient; the treated birds received vitamin D_3 (500 IU orally) 24 hr before the experiment. (From Wasserman, R. H. and Kallfelz, F. A., *Am. J. Physiol.*, 203, 222, 1962. With permission.)

forces such as chemical (concentration or *activity*) gradient, electrical gradient, solvent drag, or any combination of these forces. It is to be expected as a first approximation that the concentration or *activity* ratio (serosal/mucosal) will equal unity or less at equilibrium, or approach unity with time in a non-equilibrium situation. A more precise approach is that of measuring flux ratios as discussed (see Section II.A).

The mechanism or mechanisms of passive transport of calcium across the gut are unknown. Two major possibilities exist: simple diffusion or facilitated (carrier-mediated) diffusion. Functionally, these would express themselves as either a nonsaturable or a saturable system, respectively. Using the balance approach in rats, Bronner and his associates[281,283,284] found that, as the calcium intake (v_i)* was increased, the true calcium absorption (v_a) tended to plateau; they suggested the mathematical relationship: $v_a = 84.0\ (1 - e^{-0.011}v_i)$. These data can be interpreted as indicating that the "downhill" transport system becomes saturated as v_i is increased. Acute in vivo preparations have failed to show any saturation of the calcium efflux (lumen to plasma) with intraluminal concentrations as high as 25 m*M* in the rat[297] or 135 m*M* in the chicken.[319] On the other hand, chronic in vivo preparations (Thiry-Vella loop) exhibited saturation at 12.5 m*M* in the dog[290] and around 40 m*M* in the sheep.[293] Whether these different findings (saturable in dog and sheep; nonsaturable in rat and chicken) have their origins in the differences between the species or in the difference between the preparations (acute *vs.* chronic) is uncertain.

C. Sites of Absorption

In a discussion of the sites of absorption of calcium in the gut several aspects require consideration. These include:

1. The existence of active transport and its importance relative to passive transport in the particular segment
2. The time of passage through the segment
3. The calcium concentration of the gut contents which obviously changes as it passes down the intestine
4. The chemical state of the calcium as it is influenced by changes in pH and the addition of secretory products (e.g., bile)
5. Where the bulk of the calcium is absorbed

The last factor is a composite of the preceding factors. Much is known about the existence and location of active transport, particularly in the rat. There is some knowledge about where the bulk of the calcium is absorbed. Little information exists with regard to the other parameters.

1. *Sites of Absorption: Rodents*

Active transport of calcium has been studied in all major segments of the gut in the rat from duodenum to the colon.[299,325,332,334,341,342,344,346,390] It is exhibited by the duodenum to the greatest extent and decreases as the distance from the pylorus increases.[334] These findings are in accord with those of Waldron-Edward et al.[302,391] who observed absorption to the greatest extent in the proximal areas; these studies utilizing the in vivo ligated loop techniques did not differentiate between active and passive transport. Some authors find little or no active transport in the jejunum and ileum in rats on a normal diet,[334,341,342,348,349,352] but are able to demonstrate it in all segments of the small intestine in calcium-deprived rats.[334] Others have been able to demonstrate its existence under normal conditions in all segments of the small intestine[299,346] as well as in the colon.[332] The latter observation is interesting in the

* Here, and subsequently, the terminology of Aubert et al.[389] is used to denote: v_i, Ca intake; v_a, true Ca absorption; v_f, endogenous fecal Ca; v_F, total fecal Ca; v_o, bone resorption; and a, fractional absorption (v_a/v_i).

light of the finding of Kimberg et al.[334] that active transport begins to increase again in the distal ileal region as the contents approach the colon.

A similar situation exists in the rabbit, mouse, and guinea pig; transport decreases as the distance from the pylorus increases.[323,352] Among the rodents studied to date, the hamster and the newborn rat are exceptions; active transport is greatest in the ileum in the hamster[343] and is more evenly distributed in the newborn rat.[355]

2. Sites of Absorption: Dogs

Cramer,[288] using Thiry-Vella loops in dogs, found that the greatest rate of calcium absorption was in the duodenum (0.35 mg Ca/cm). The rates in jejunum and ileum (0.2 mg Ca/cm) were only 57% of the duodenal rate. However, when other factors, such as length of segment and the amount of dietary calcium found in the segment, are considered, the *bulk* of the calcium is estimated to be absorbed in the ileum. These experiments were not designed to determine the role of active transport.

3. Sites of Absorption: Sheep

The sheep appears to be different from other mammalian species in that secretion of calcium into the gut (plasma to lumen flux) often outweighs the translocation from the gut (lumen to plasma flux). Phillipson and Storry[294] could not demonstrate net absorption in either the duodenum or the ileum using Thiry-Vella loops with re-entrant cannulae (see Section I.A.2). Net absorption did occur in the upper jejunum and in the middle of the small intestine even at intraluminal calcium concentrations as low as 1.9 m*M*. In those areas of the intestine where they could find net absorption (duodenum and lower ileum) the highest calcium concentration used was 10.5 m*M*. Care and van't Klooster,[293] on the other hand, found net absorption of calcium in the ileum at intraluminal calcium concentrations of 10 m*M* and above; in agreement with Phillipson and Storry[294] they observed a net secretion at levels below 10 m*M*.

4. Sites of Absorption: Chickens

Active transport has been demonstrated in both the duodenum[319] and the ileum.[388] There is disagreement on the most effective site of calcium absorption in the chicken. Wasserman,[303] Hurwitz, et al.,[392] and Harmeyer and DeLuca[314] have found the duodenum to have the highest rate of absorption. Others[301,317,320,393,394] are not in accord with this observation. Bar et al.[395] have also shown in the Japanese quail that the duodenum has the highest rate of calcium absorption.

5. Sites of Absorption: Humans

Two reports in this area have appeared[382,384] using two different techniques (see Section I.C.2). Both studies found that in normal human subjects calcium absorption occurred at a much greater rate in the proximal small intestine.

D. Miscellaneous Aspects of Calcium Transport

There have been reports of various phenomena purported to be associated with intestinal transport of calcium. Some of these are of historical interest only, while some remain isolated reports with little further development. These phenomona include:

1. The role of a calcium-dependent adenosine triphosphatase[396–401]
2. The sodium dependence of calcium transport[338,402]
3. The role of alkaline phosphatases[311,403,404]

Table 4
PROPERTIES OF CHICKEN CALCIUM-BINDING PROTEIN (CaBP)[411]

Molecular weight	28,000
Sedimentation coefficient (S_{20})	2.96 S
Affinity constant for Ca	$2 \times 10^6\ M^{-1}$
Binding capacity	4 mol Ca/mol protein

4. The role of a vitamin D-dependent protein with a molecular weight of 42,000[405]
5. The role of phospholipids[406]

III. CALCIUM-BINDING PROTEIN

In 1966, Wasserman and his associates reported the existence of a protein in chicken intestinal tissue which preferentially bound calcium and was increased by vitamin D administration.[407] Subsequently, this protein, designated calcium-binding protein (CaBP), was purified and its chemical properties defined.[353,408,409] The properties of chicken intestinal CaBP are summarized in Table 4. Since the discovery of CaBP, there has been a considerable amount of work performed in attempting to define its species and tissue distribution, its cellular and intracellular location, its properties, its regulation, and its physiological function.

A. Calcium-Binding Protein: Tissue Distribution

In addition to its existence in the gut, calcium-binding protein has been shown to be present in the kidney cortex,[408,410–412] chicken brain,[413,414] rat placenta,[416] and the shell gland of the chicken.[417] It has not been found in the following bovine tissues: salivary glands; cardiac ventricular muscle; skeletal muscle; thyroid; parathyroid; aorta; adrenal medulla; adrenal cortex; liver; gall bladder; pancreas; spleen; bladder; brain; esophagus; rumen; reticulum; omasum; abomasum; terminal ileum; colon; rectum; or mammary glands.[411] The distribution of calcium-binding protein within the intestine has been examined in the cow,[411] the chicken,[418] the hamster,[321] and the pig,[419] and found to be highest in the duodenum with less and less present as the ileum is approached.

B. Calcium-Binding Protein: Species Distribution

The presence of calcium-binding protein has been demonstrated in several avian and mammalian species. Its presence in the chicken intestine has been amply confirmed[192,420–428] and it has been identified in another avian species, the Japanese quail.[429]

Mammalian species in which calcium-binding protein has been demonstrated include the rat,[416,432–438] the guinea pig,[423–440] the pig,[423,441,442] the hamster,[321] the horse,[423,443] the cow,[423,443–445] the dog,[446,447] the monkey,[448] and man.[449,450]

C. Calcium-Binding Protein: Cellular Location

The first attempts to pinpoint the cellular location of calcium-binding protein in the intestine were made by Taylor and Wasserman in the chicken.[451] These investigators, using the technique of indirect fluorescent antibody, claimed that calcium-binding protein was located in the goblet cells and in the surface coat-microvillar region of all intestinal epithelial cells. Other investigators have examined its location

Table 5
CALCIUM-BINDING PROTEIN (CaBP) LOCALIZATION IN THE INTESTINE[454]

	Localization Results					
Species	Goblet cells	Brush border	Basal and/or lateral membranes	Cytoplasm	Nucleus	Ref.
Chick	+	+	–	–	–	451
	–	?	+	+	+	453
Hen	+	+	–	–	–	452
Human	?	+	+	–	–	450
	–	?	+	–	–	458
	+	+	+	–	–	459
Pig	–	?	+	+	+	455
Rat	–	–	+	+	+	456

in the chicken,[452–454] as well as in the pig,[455] in the rat,[456] and in the human,[450,456,459] with conflicting results. Morrissey et al.,[454] who find no evidence for the presence of calcium-binding protein in goblet cells, have summarized the evidence (Table 5). Marche et al.[456] claim that it is mainly a cytoplasmic protein in the rat. Hence there is no agreement yet concerning the localization of the protein in either the goblet cells, the brush border, the basal or lateral membranes, the cytoplasm, or the nucleus.

D. Calcium-Binding Protein: Purification and Properties

Calcium-binding protein has been purified from various species, including the cow,[411,423,443,444] horse,[411] pig,[411,441] rat,[430,433] guinea pig,[411] and its original source, the chicken.[411] Molecular weight determinations (Table 6) indicate the avian molecule (27,100[a]) is much larger than that obtained from mammalian sources (8800 to 9100). There is no evidence that the avian protein contains subunits.[411] The calcium-binding proteins from all five species, avian and mammalian, which have been analyzed for amino acid content,[411,423,444,460] consist of a high percentage of dicarboxylic acids, which may be the basis for their calcium-binding properties.

E. Regulation of Calcium-Binding Protein

1. Vitamin D

By definition, the main regulator of vitamin D-dependent calcium-binding protein is vitamin D. Early work had established an association between vitamin D and calcium-binding protein.[311,407,461] A dose-response relationship exists between vitamin D_3 dose in rachitic chicks and duodenal calcium-binding protein content as indicated in Figure 2 which is based on the work of Bar and Wasserman.[462] This relationship exists whether the dose was presented as a single dose administered 48 hr before (Figure 2A) or incorporated in the feed for 1 week (Figure 2B). The hormonal form of vitamin D_3 also increases duodenal calcium-binding protein content.[424,463] As to be expected, the response to the hormonal form was exhibited much more rapidly than that to the prohormone, vitamin D_3. Injection of 1,25-dihydroxyvitamin D_3 into vitamin D-deficient immature chickens initiates calcium-binding protein synthesis within 2 hr.[463] The mRNA for the binding protein has been isolated and shown to stimulate calcium-binding synthesis by a wheat germ cell-free system.[463]

Table 6
MOLECULAR WEIGHTS OF INTESTINAL CALCIUM-BINDING PROTEIN (CaBP) FROM VARIOUS SPECIES

Species	Molecular weight (approx.)	Ref.
Bovine	8,900	423
Equine	9,100	423
Porcine	8,800	423
Guinea pig	8,900	423
Chicken	27,100	423
Rat	8,000—13,000	430
	27,000[a]	433
	12,500[b]	

[a] Low affinity for Ca; found mainly in jejunum and ileum.
[b] High affinity for Ca; found mainly in duodenum and jejunum.

2. Other Regulatory Factors

Deficiencies in dietary calcium or phosphorus lead to increases in the intestinal content of calcium-binding protein in the chicken.[192,353,420,421,428,461,464–466]

Using an in vitro preparation of embryonic chicken duodenum, Parkes and Reynolds[425] claim that parathyroid hormone directly stimulates an increase in calcium-binding protein content in the presence of either vitamin D_3, 25-hydroxyvitamin D_3, or 1,25-dihydroxyvitamin D_3. No effect of parathyroid hormone was recorded in the absence of vitamin D_3 or its hydroxylated metabolites.

Strontium, when incorporated in a low-calcium, normal vitamin D_3 diet, leads to decreased levels of calcium-binding protein in the duodenum of the immature chicken.[308,467–469] This effect of strontium can be understood in terms of its known suppressive effect on renal 25-hydroxyvitamin D_3-1-hydroxylase activity (see Chapter 4.V.C).

The effect of cortisol on calcium-binding protein is controversial in rats. There have been reports of increased,[470] decreased,[471] or unaltered[472] synthesis. In the chicken, cortisol decreases synthesis.[312]

A study of the effect of age on the calcium-binding protein content of the intestine in rats revealed that, whereas the content of the protein remained steady between 4 and 9 weeks of age, a rapid decline occurred after that period.[437] By 20 weeks of age the content of calcium-binding protein had fallen to a level which was 30% of that at 2 months. Fasting the rats for a period of less than 24 hr produced a marked decline in the intestinal content of the specific protein.

Egg-laying in the chicken leads to a significant increase in intestinal content of calcium-binding protein,[422] a response which is probably secondary to increased production of 1,25-dihydroxyvitamin D_3 first noted by Kenny.[72]

Cattle eating the plant *Solanum malocoxylon* may develop a disease characterized by extensive soft tissue calcification. The active principle of the plant has vitamin D-like properties and has been shown by Wasserman[469] to increase the calcium-

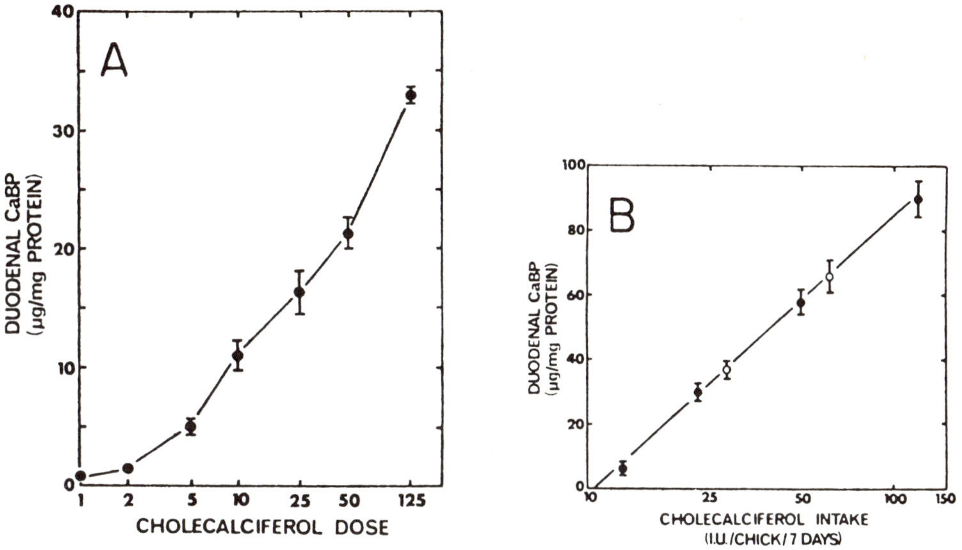

FIGURE 2. The effect of (A) *acute* and (B) *chronic* oral administration of different doses of cholecalciferol (vitamin D_3) on duodenal calcium binding protein (CaBP) in rachitic chicks. Each value represents the mean ± standard error of the mean of six chicks. (A) Cholecalciferol (1 to 125 IU) given orally 48 hr prior to killing. (B) Cholecalciferol (80 to 640 IU/kg diet) incorporated in the diet for 1 week.

binding protein levels in strontium-treated immature chickens, indicating that renal 1-hydroxylation was not required for the action of the plant material.

F. Physiological Significance of Calcium-Binding Protein

Much is now known concerning the distribution, properties, and regulation of calcium-binding protein in the intestine. Nevertheless, the question whether or not this protein plays a physiological role in the response of the intestine to vitamin D stimulation remains to be answered. Wasserman and his associates have labored long and hard in attempting to answer this question, as have others, but have modestly refrained from claiming physiological importance beyond what the data permit. In 1974, Wasserman et al.[411] stated that the "molecular role of CaBP in the calcium translocation process remains unknown although theories and hypotheses are rampant." What is the evidence for and against a physiological role in the action of vitamin D in stimulating intestinal transport of calcium?

The following evidence supports the concept of a primary role for calcium-binding protein as a carrier protein in calcium transport. First, whenever calcium transport in the gut is modified, the level of calcium-binding protein is changed in the same direction. This observation applies to:

1. Its location in the gut (duodenum > jejenum > ileum)[408]
2. Its response to dietary calcium intake[353,461,464,465]
3. Its response to vitamin D[311,407,461]
4. Its response to actimonycin D[364,366,368,474]
5. Its relationship to age and egg-laying[353,422,437,461]
6. Its relationship to uremia[326]
7. Its response to strontium feeding[308,467–469]
8. Its response to extracts of *S. malacoxylon*[469]

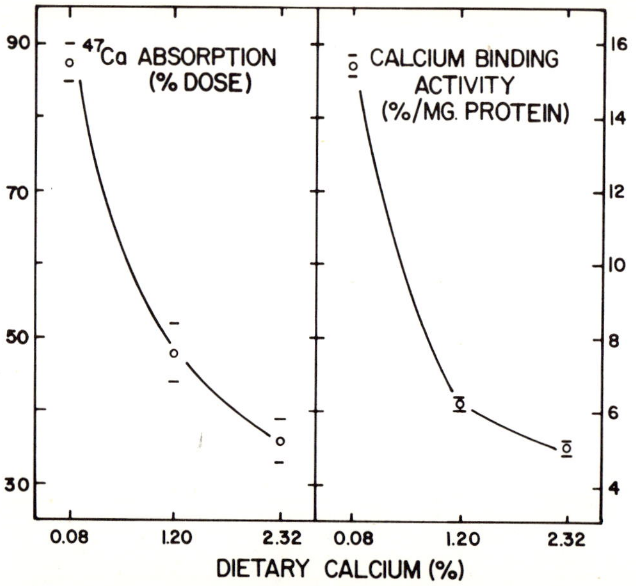

FIGURE 3. Comparison of calcium absorptive capacity and calcium binding protein (CaBP) content of duodenum in chicks adapted to varying levels of dietary calcium. ^{47}Ca absorption determined with ligated loop and calcium binding activity determined by Chelex resin method. (From Taylor, A. N. and Wasserman, R. H., *Fed. Proc. Fed. Am. Soc. Exp. Biol.*, 28, 1834–1838, 1969. With permission.)

The correlation between the binding affinity of calcium-binding protein for the alkaline earths (Ca > Sr > Ba > Mg) and the relative absorption of these ions is also impressive.[465] An example of one of these correlations, namely the response of calcium-binding protein to dietary calcium intake and its relationship to calcium absorption, is presented in Figure 3 with data taken from Taylor and Wasserman.[465] Secondly, there is general agreement that an important component, if not the whole, of the mechanism of vitamin D is the induction of synthesis of a carrier protein through stimulation of nuclear transcription and ribosomal translation. To date, calcium-binding protein is the only specific protein so synthesized which has been identified.[475]

Evidence which does not support a primary role for calcium-binding protein in vitamin D-stimulated calcium transport is not insignificant. The time relationship between the initiation of enhanced calcium transport and the first detectable increase in calcium-binding protein levels presents difficulties in acceptance of the primary role concept. If calcium-binding protein is an essential carrier protein for calcium transport, then it should be detectable before or at least simultaneously with the increase in calcium transport. DeLuca and others have never been able to observe this condition; enhanced intestinal absorption of calcium is always detectable *before* an increase in calcium-binding protein levels.[314,396,424,476] Data taken from the work of Spencer et al.[424] and representative of this counter-argument is presented in Figure 4. Active transport of calcium, measured by the everted gut sac technique, increased within 2 hr of administering 1,25-dihydroxyvitamin D_3 intracardially in vitamin D-deficient, 4-week old chickens. The rise in calcium-binding protein was not detectable until 7 hr after injection. This lag in appearance of calcium-binding protein was

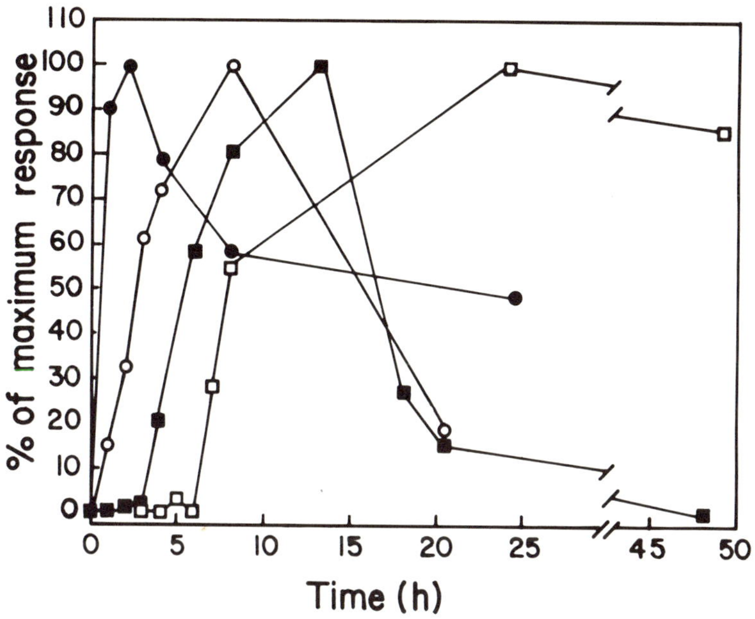

FIGURE 4. Stimulation of calcium transport, measured in vitro, and calcium binding protein synthesis by 1,25-dihydroxyvitamin D_3. For each experiment, rachitic chicks were dosed intracardially with 125 ng of 1,25-dihydroxyvitamin D_3 and killed at the indicated times. Calcium transport (○) was measured in vitro each time by using everted intestinal sacs. Each point is the mean of a group of seven to ten chicks; vertical bars indicate ±S.E.M. Calcium-binding protein (□) was measured in the pooled duodenal cytosols obtained from six chicks by immunoelectrophoresis. Polyribosomes were prepared at each time from the pooled duodenal mucosa of groups of four chicks, and were incubated in the protein-synthesizing system in vitro. Duplicate 20 μℓ-portions of the post-ribosomal supernatants were removed for the determination of acid-precipitable radioactivity. The remainder were immunoprecipitated with antiserum to calcium-binding protein. The dissociated immunoprecipitates were electrophoresed and the gels sliced and processed for radioactivity counting. ^3H radioactivity (dpm) in the calcium-binding protein area of the gels (■) is expressed as a percentage of the total acid-precipitable incorporation into released proteins (corrected up to the maximal value obtained, i.e., 1.4×10^6 dpm/mℓ). The accumulation of the tritiated 1,25-dihydroxyvitamin D_3 is also depicted (●). (From Spencer, R., Charman, M., Wilson, P. W., and Lawson, D. E. M., *Biochem. J.*, 170, 93, 1978. With permission.)

present in the early report from Wasserman's laboratory.[407] Wasserman and his colleagues responded to this criticism by suggesting that the difficulty is satisfying this criterion is due to the insensitivity of the method for detecting calcium-binding protein. Using a more sensitive detection method (immunodiffusion and gel electrophoresis rather than chelation with Chelex 100), they were able to show an increase in calcium-binding protein levels occurring *simultaneously* with the enhanced calcium absorption in the chicken duodenum following administration of vitamin D_3.[311,318,353] This was confirmed by Emtage et al.[477] who used an even more sensitive detection method, namely radioimmunoassay. A later study from the laboratory[424] used a more precise method for measuring calcium transport; the data, presented in Figure 4, forced the investigators to reverse their position. There the matter rests at time of writing.

Table 7
TRANSPORT RATE AND CALCIUM ABSORPTION IN THE RAT GASTROINTESTINAL TRACT

	Transport rate[a] (cm/hr)		Transit[a] half-time (min)		Calcium absorbed[b] (% of total absorbed in all segments)	
Segment	**Solid[c]**	**Liquid[d]**	**Solid[c]**	**Liquid[d]**	**Solid[c]**	**Liquid[d]**
Stomach	—	—	60	36	0	0
Duodenum (21 cm)	220	210	6	6	8	15
Jejunum						
Upper (21 cm)	73	70	18	18		
Lower (21 cm)	18	55	72	24	4	23
Ileum (21 cm)	13	11	102	120	88	62

[a] Determined using ^{91}Y; adapted from Reference 481.
[b] From Reference 482.
[c] Solid diet given in form of single 10-min meal of ground diet (2 g).
[d] Liquid diet, 1 mℓ given by gavage.

Other barriers to acceptance of a carrier-protein role for calcium-binding protein also exist. First, the decay of the calcium-binding protein response to 1,25-dihydroxyvitamin D_3 is much slower than that of the calcium transport response (Figure 4) indicating a lack of correlation between these two parameters. Secondly, cortisol-injected rats consistently exhibit decreased calcium transport but variable responses in calcium-binding protein.[470–472]

In summary, it appears that calcium-binding protein is necessary for *sustaining*, but not for initiating, enhanced rates of calcium transport by acting as a buffer for intracellular calcium in its transport across the mucosal cell as suggested by Spencer et al.[424]

IV. OVERVIEW OF CALCIUM TRANSPORT

At this point in time the information available does not permit a complete understanding of the phenomenon of calcium transport across the intestinal barrier. Nevertheless, a consensus is emerging at the tissue level concerning certain aspects of calcium absorption. These include the existence and relative contributions of active and passive transport, and the relative contributions of the various segments of the small intestine to the overall absorption of calcium. The picture is less clear at the cellular and molecular levels.

A. Tissue Level

Only one species, the rat, has been studied in sufficient depth to allow meaningful conclusions. In this species it is well documented that active transport decreases as the distance from the pylorus increases,[334] whereas the calcium concentration of the gut contents increases with the distance.[478] It is obvious that passive or "downhill" transport must play a greater role as the contents pass down the gut. If to this fact we add the observation that the *bulk* of the calcium is absorbed in the lower rather than the upper small intestine due to differences in transit times,[288,479–482] then we must conclude that under *normal* dietary conditions active transport probably plays a minor role in calcium absorption. Table 7 presents data taken from Marcus and

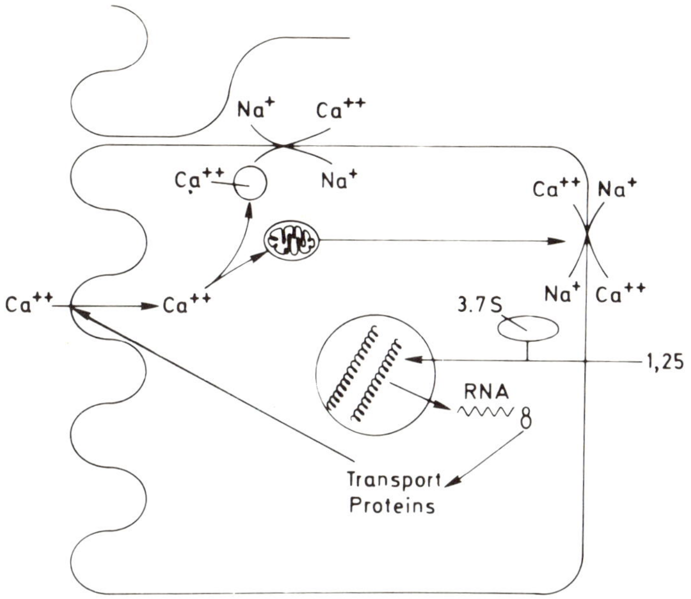

FIGURE 5. Diagrammatic representation of the expected mechanism whereby 1,25-dihydroxyvitamin D_3 initiates intestinal calcium transport in chick intestinal mucosa. Note that 1,25-dihydroxyvitamin D_3 is believed to interact with a 3.7S cytosol receptor that is then transferred to the nucleus where in some unknown manner it initiates transcription of genes that code for calcium transport proteins. These proteins appear presumably at the brush border surface, permitting calcium to enter the intestinal epithelium absorption cells. Calcium is then either packaged in vesicles at the terminal web region, or is taken up by mitochondria. Calcium is expelled from the cell by a sodium-dependent process. (From DeLuca, H. F., *Vitamin D. Metabolism and Function*, Springer-Verlag, New York, 1979, 46. With permission.)

Lengeman[481,482] showing estimated transit times and relative contributions of the segments to the bulk calcium absorption in the rat. In addition, the observation that in the rat duodenum the active transport mechanism may become saturated at 3 m*M* calcium, further minimizes the contribution of the active or "uphill" process. The situation is different in a period of calcium deprivation. First, it is known that the rat adapts to this stress by increasing the efficiency of its active transport system in all segments of the small intestine.[334,346] Secondly, under conditions of calcium deprivation the calcium contents of the gut would probably remain below the level (3 to 5 m*M*) at which the active transport process becomes saturated. Support for this contention may be found in the work of Sernka and Borle,[478] who determined the gut content of the ultrafilterable calcium in rats on a "tolerable" calcium diet. No analytical data were reported for this diet but it was estimated to contain 0.15% calcium, a level which approaches one tenth that of normal commercial laboratory chows, and therefore can be considered a low calcium diet. The ultrafilterable calcium increased from a value of 0.19 m*M* in the duodenum to a maximum of 1.1 m*M* in the ileum, levels significantly lower than the saturation point of active transport. It is very likely that calcium deprivation switches the active transport system from a minor to a major role.

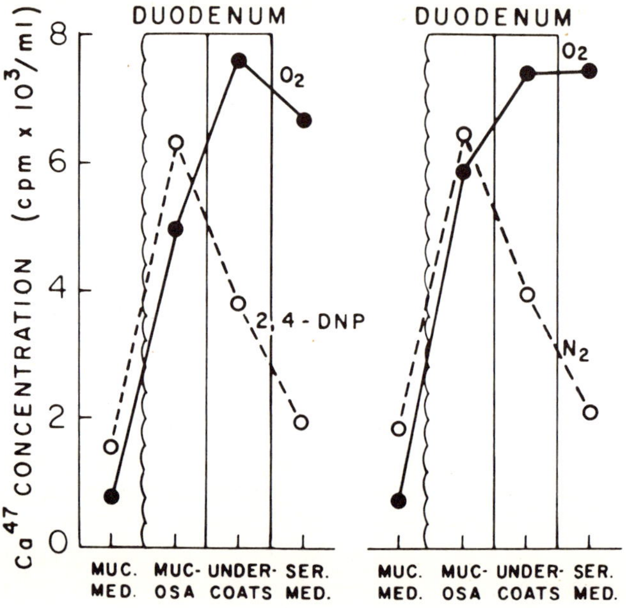

FIGURE 6. Effects of incubation under N_2 or with 2,4-dinitrophenol (DNP) on ^{47}Ca gradients across duodenal sacs prepared from six 80- to 90-g rats. Half the sacs were incubated under O_2 and the remainder under N_2 for 2 hr at 37°C. Duodenal sacs were also prepared from each of twelve rats and were incubated in the presence or absence of 1 m*M* DNP for 2 hr at 37°C under O_2. Net movement of ^{47}Ca to the serosal surface was observed only under O_2 or in the absence of DNP. (From Schachter, D., Kowarski, S., Finkelstein, J. D., and Ma, R. I. W., *Am. J. Physiol.*, 211, 1133, 1966. With permission.)

B. Cellular and Molecular Levels

It is not possible yet to sketch a clear picture of calcium transport at the cellular and molecular levels. Certain facts have emerged, but much is still in the realm of speculation. It is speculated that calcium enters the brush border of the intestinal epithelial cell by passive uptake, is transported across the cell by means of a carrier protein—with mitochondria and/or calcium-binding protein serving a buffer function—and extruded at the basal or basal-lateral pole of the cell by a sodium-dependent process (Figure 5). It is assumed that the active transport component lies in the basal or basal-lateral membrane and is associated with the sodium-dependent process which has been reported.[338,402]

There is a considerable body of evidence to indicate that a specific step in the translocation of calcium from lumen to plasma involves the uptake and concentration of calcium in mucosal tissue. This uptake phenomenon was first studied by Schachter et al.[358,483] in vitro, using slices of rat intestine; the technique was also used by Avioli.[484] Subsequent studies have employed different approaches. These include:

1. In vitro incubation of the everted gut sac with radiocalcium followed by analysis of either the whole tissue,[301,338] mucosal scrapings,[301,342,343,353,485] or muscle layer[301,342,343]

2. In vitro incubation of isolated intestinal loops, either with radiocalcium[317] or with stable calcium,[344] followed by analysis of the whole tissue
3. In vitro incubation of a sheet of intestinal tissue in an apparatus which permitted exposure of only the mucosal side to the fluid containing radiocalcium[356]

Different conclusions have been drawn by different groups depending upon the approach used. Some claim that this uptake phenomenon is partially energy-dependent.[356,358,359,483] However, the energy-dependence of the uptake step has not been emphasized in later publications from Schachter's group[342,343] in which mucosal scrapings rather than whole tissue were analyzed. Figure 6 is taken from the work of Schachter et al.[342] and diagrammatically represents their later findings. Other investigators, who also separated mucosal epithelial uptake from whole tissue uptake, support the concept that calcium uptake by mucosal epithelium, although apparently "uphill" in terms of *total* calcium concentration, is not energy-dependent.[301,353,485,486] It is obvious that the calcium taken up by the mucosal epithelium cannot be in the ionic form. First, such concentrations would be deleterious to the integrity of the cell. Secondly, if this calcium were ionic it would have to be transported against the gradient (Figure 6) and therefore would require energy but, as discussed above, the consensus of opinion is that the *uptake* process is not dependent upon energy. It may be assumed then that most of this calcium pool is chemically bound, perhaps to a protein similar to calcium-binding protein.

Chapter 6

EFFECTS OF AGE ON CALCIUM ABSORPTION

Only two experimental species, the rat and the bovine, have been studied in any depth with respect to the effects of age on calcium absorption by the intestine. More limited studies have been conducted in man.

I. EXPERIMENTAL ANIMALS

A. Rats

It has been known for decades that the efficiency of absorption, expressed as a percentage of the calcium intake, decreases with increasing age. These early observations were arrived at using the balance method and culminated in the classical studies of Henry and Kon[271,487] in the rat (Table 1). Two major developments have occurred since the early 1950s which have allowed the phenomenon to be studied more precisely and in greater depth. One development was the recognition of, and the ability to determine, the endogenous component of fecal calcium. The other was the development of the everted gut sac technique and its application to studies of calcium absorption. Using the balance method, coupled with radiocalcium techniques for determining the endogenous component of fecal calcium, Hansard and Crowder[278] and Lemaire[488] have confirmed the observation of Henry and Kon[271,487] that the percentage of calcium absorbed decreases with age (Table 1). Others have found that the percentage of calcium absorbed increases with age.[489,490] Before further discussing the effects of age on calcium absorption it would be well to sound a note of caution concerning the interpretation of the data. Absorption may be expressed in at least two ways: (1) the efficiency of absorption or, in other words, either the fraction (α) or the *percent* absorbed of the intake as determined by the balance method with or without correction for the endogenous component of fecal calcium; or (2) the absolute amount absorbed (mg/day) or the v_a in the terminology of Aubert et al.[389] The former is more common; neither is ideal. At a given age both are influenced by the calcium concentration in the diet and in fact have opposite relationships to the dietary calcium level. As the latter is increased the absolute intake (v_a) increases, but the percent absorbed decreases (Table 1, Chapter 5, and Bronner[283]). The question to be resolved is what parameters should be used in order to make comparisons of calcium absorption at different ages? As mentioned above, the data of Hansard and Crowder[278] suggest that calcium absorption decreases with increasing age if percent absorption is used as the criterion (Table 1). No such conclusion can be drawn from the consideration of the v_a data, the values being 27, 24, 30, 33, and 20 mg/day, respectively, with increasing age (Table 1). On the other hand Lemaire[488] found a decrease in both percent absorbed and v_a with age, but he studied only two age groups (4 and 10 months). The commonly accepted fact that calcium absorption decreases with advancing ages has been based in the past largely on the criterion of percent absorption rather than absolute intake.

Within the past decade, the everted gut sac technique has given information with respect to the active transport component of calcium absorption and its relationship to age, supplying a third criterion of the efficiency of absorption. In some respects this measurement is ideal but its physiological importance is not known with certainty (see Chapter 5.IV.A). The first observation that active transport in rats declines as age increases was made by Schachter et al.;[341] the data are presented in Table 2.

Table 1
GROWTH AND CALCIUM ABSORPTION IN RATS

Age (months)	Ca intake v_i (mg/day)	Ca absorbed v_a (mg/day)	Ca Absorption: Apparent[a] (%)	Ca Absorption: True[b] (%)	Ref.
1	16.4	—	95	—	271
3	26.0	—	92	—	271
6	24.7	—	53	—	271
9	26.7	—	21	—	271
12	28.4	—	16	—	271
15	30.3	—	15	—	271
18	32.2	—	14	—	271
24	29.6	—	10	—	271
1	28	27	93	98	278
3	42	24	40	57	278
6	65	30	28	46	278
11—17	80	33	22	41	278
24	85	20	—	24	278
4	57.0	37.8	59	62	488
10	68.4	31.0	35	41	488

[a] $(v_i - v_F)100/v_i$.
[b] $(v_i - v_F + v_f)100/v_i$ or $v_a \times 100/v_i$, where v_F = total fecal Ca.

Table 2
EFFECT OF AGE ON ACTIVE TRANSPORT OF CALCIUM IN RATS

Age (months)	Weight (g)	Serosal/mucosal ratio[a] (mean ± SE)[b]
1—1½	50—90	4.8 ± 0.36
2—4	150—250	3.7 ± 0.25[c]
>12	400—500	1.9 ± 0.30[d]

[a] Everted duodenal sac technique.
[b] SE: Standard error of the mean.
[c] Significantly different from 1—1½ months ($p < 0.025$).
[d] Significantly different from 1—1½ months and 2—4 months ($p < 0.001$).

From Schacter, D., Dowdle, E. B., and Schenker, H., *Am. J. Physiol.*, 198, 263, 1960.

Confirmatory evidence exists in the reports of Finkelstein and Schachter,[330] Schachter et al.,[343] and Walling and Rothman.[362]

B. Bovine

Hansard et al.[491] found in cattle that the percent absorbed decreased with advancing age, being 95% at 1 month and declining to a value of 23% at 12 to 16 years.

II. MAN

The picture concerning the effects of age on calcium absorption in man is less clear. Bronner[373] has summarized much of the data in subjects ranging from 11 to 72 years of age. First, it should be pointed out that these data are composite, having been assembled from reports not one of which studied a wide range of ages. Secondly, the experience with experimental animals indicates that the large decline in percent absorption occurs between birth and puberty (Table 1), an age range not included by Bronner[373] in his summary. A recent preliminary report claims that elderly subjects have decreased calcium absorption and a loss of adaptation.[492]

Chapter 7

ADAPTATION TO REPRODUCTIVE STATES

I. MAMMALIAN REPRODUCTION

It is obvious that pregnancy must impose an increased demand for calcium on the mother, particularly during the third trimester when the bulk of the fetal calcium stores are being laid down. Species differ in this demand: on a body weight basis the relative demands of the rat are greater than those of the human.[493] The question is: from where does this extra calcium come? Does it come from the maternal bones, the diet, or both? If it comes from the diet and the dietary intake remains the same, then an increased efficiency of absorption must be postulated. The same remarks would apply to other reproductive states demanding extra calcium, such as lactation and egg laying. This discussion will concern itself mainly with the question whether or not increased efficiency of absorption results from a particular reproductive state.

A. Adaptation to Pregnancy

What is the evidence, if any, which supports the concept that pregnancy is associated with an increased efficiency of intestinal calcium absorption? The rat and the bovine are the only species which have been adequately studied. Precise information in the human is particularly lacking in this area, presumably due to a natural reluctance to use radioisotopes which might endanger the development of the fetus.

1. Rat Studies

In the rat, the in vivo studies of Fournier and Susbielle[494,495] remain the definitive work in spite of the approach used (balance technique). No correction was made for the endogenous loss of fecal calcium (v_f); the work was done before the methods for determining this component of the total fecal calcium were fully developed. Hence estimates of the amount of calcium absorbed will necessarily be lower than the true value. With this reservation in mind, the data of Fournier and Susbielle lead to a cautious conclusion that whether the rats were on a diet rich in clacium (0.83%) or low in calcium (0.225%) there was no significant increase in absorptive efficiency $\{(v_i - v_f)100/v_i\}$. All rats were fed a constant intake of 12 g of diet per day. Therefore, if it is assumed that there was no change in v_f,* it can be claimed that pregnancy in rats does not result in an increased efficiency of absorption of calcium (Table 1).

Opposed to this observation are the findings of Schachter and his associates.[341,343] Using the everted duodenal sac, this group has shown that active transport is enhanced during the third week of gestation in rats (Table 2). Reconciliation of these apparently opposed findings is needed. The disagreement may have its origins in one or more of the following points. First, Schachter et al.[341,343] observed the increased active transport during the third week, but did not specify the day of gestation. Thus their observations could have been made anytime during the third week and may in fact have been close to the end of the third week. If this were so, it is to be expected that the balance method, even though Fournier and Susbielle[494,495] collected urinary and fecal samples daily, would not detect such a change until the

* This is a reasonable assumption as changes in v_f tend to correlate best with changes in either v_F (total fecal calcium) or $\dot{v}_i$ (calcium intake) as discussed by Bronner.[373] Presumably, neither of these parameters changed in the study under discussion.

Table 1
EFFECT OF PREGNANCY AND LACTATION ON CALCIUM ABSORPTION IN RATS MAINTAINED ON A LOW OR HIGH CALCIUM INTAKE[494,495]

Period	Duration of experiment (days)	Ca intake v_i (mg/day)	Ca absorbed $v_i - v_F$ (mg/day)	Ca absorption $(v_i - v_F)100/v_i$ (%)
Low Ca Diet Study (0.22% Ca)				
Control	1—12	27	7.41	27
Pregnancy	14—34	27	8.1	30
Lactation	35—56	27	23.6	87
Post-lactation				
1st (4 Days)	57—60	27	22.9	85
2nd (10 Days)	61—70	27	22.6	84
3rd (8 Days)	71—88	27	12.7	47
High Ca Diet Study (0.83% Ca)				
Control	1—17	100	7.9	8
Pregnancy	18—37	100	7.5	8
Lactation	38—62	100	39.2	39
Post-lactation				
1st (3 Days)	63—65	100	33.9	34
2nd (3 Days)	66—68	100	11.4	11
3rd (4 Days)	69—72	100	8.0	8

Note: Based on seven (low-Ca diet) and five (high-Ca diet) rats given 12 g food per day.

beginning of the lactation period, when indeed a very marked increase in absorptive efficiency did occur (Table 1). Second, it is not necessarily predictable on the basis of present knowledge that a marked change in active transport will result in a marked change in absorptive efficiency. It will depend on the relative importance of the active and passive transport system as discussed in Chapter 5.IV.A. If, for example, an increase in active transport was accompanied by a decrease in transit time in the gastrointestinal tract, the effect of the latter would negate that of the former. Third, the lack of sensitivity of the balance method, particularly in the absence of endogenous fecal calcium determinations, may not allow detection of small but significant changes in efficiency of absorption.

Plasma 1,25-dihydroxyvitamin D levels are elevated in the pregnant rat (see Chapter 4.III.B and Table 1, Chapter 2). It would be expected that this would lead to enhanced calcium absorption.

2. *Bovine Studies*

Absorptive efficiency of calcium in bovine pregnancy has received little attention. The major definitive study is that of Plumlee[496] quoted by Comar.[497] Pregnancy had no significant effect on the efficiency of absorption as measured by the balance method coupled with radiocalcium techniques. However, Ramberg et al.[498] found during the latter part of pregnancy that the intestinal absorption of calcium (v_a) is much more important quantitatively in meeting the demand for calcium than in resorption (v_{o-}) of the maternal bones.

Table 2
ADAPTIVE RESPONSE TO PREGNANCY OF THE ACTIVE TRANSPORT SYSTEM FOR CALCIUM ABSORPTION IN THE RAT

Parameter	Serosal/mucosal ratio mean ± SE[a]		Probability level (p)
	Nonpregnant	Pregnant	
^{45}Ca	2.0 ± 0.38	4.6 ± 0.38	<0.001
Ionized ^{40}Ca	1.4	2.0	<0.02

[a] SE: standard error of the mean.

3. *Human Studies*

The response of the human female with respect to calcium absorption during pregnancy has been studied only by the classical balance method with no correction for endogenous fecal loss. Simkiss[493] has summarized balance data taken from the early work of Coons and Blunt[499] and of Macy et al.[500] In four of the five patients there was an increase in the extent of the positive balance and in the efficiency of absorption $\{(v_i - v_f)100/v_f\}$ as pregnancy progressed. However, it is difficult to draw this conclusion with any degree of conviction.

The fact that plasma 1,25-dihydroxyvitamin D levels are elevated in pregnancy (see Chapter 4.III.B, and Table 1, Chapter 2) would lead to a conclusion that calcium absorption would be increased as a consequence.

B. Adaptation to Lactation

Whereas pregnancy imposes a mild strain on calcium metabolism, lactation causes a much more severe stress often resulting in a prolonged period of negative calcium balance. As in pregnancy, species differ in this demand. However, perhaps of more importance in the case of lactation is the difference between individuals within a particular species; this difference can be as much as tenfold in cows.[501] It is surprising how little information there is on the subject of adaptation to lactation with respect to intestinal absorption of calcium.

1. *Rat Studies*

The only definitive study is in rats and again in the work of Fournier and Susbielle.[494,495] In contrast to the response to pregnancy, rats responded to lactation by a marked increase in absorptive efficiency $\{(v_i - v_F)100/v_i\}$ whether the rats were on a diet rich in calcium (0.83%) or low in calcium (0.225%). On the low calcium diet the absorption of calcium increased from 30% of the intake during gestation to 87% during lactation; on the high calcium diet the figures were 8% and 39%, respectively (Table 1). There is no evidence available to indicate whether or not this increase in the efficiency of absorption is due to endogenous changes in the active and passive transport systems. This point needs to be studied with the everted gut sac and ligated loop techniques.

Lactation in the rat is associated with increased plasma levels of 1,25-dihydroxyvitamin D (see Chapter 4.III.C, and Table 1, Chapter 2), a phenomenon which could account for the increased calcium absorption.

2. Bovine Studies

Lactation in the bovine species has been studied with more precise methods using calcium kinetics and systems analysis.[498,502] It is possible to conclude from the data that the initial adaptive response to lactation is an increase in both calcium absorption (v_a) and efficiency of absorption $\{(v_a/v_i) \times 100\}$. In the data presented by Mayer et al.[502] the efficiency rose from 22.6% during the 6 days immediately prior to parturition to 34% during the 8- to 14-day post-partum period. Later, as lactation proceeds, the gut response declines as bone resorption takes over to meet the increased demand.

3. Human Studies

Little information exists to permit acceptable conclusions with respect to adaptation to lactation in the human female. No studies with radiocalcium are readily available. All information is based on the classical balance approach. There does not seem to be any major adaptation in the form of increased efficiency of absorption of calcium. In many cases the total fecal calcium (v_f) exceeds the calcium intake (v_i), making it difficult to entertain the existence of increased efficiency (see Table 10.3 in Simkiss[493]). More precise work is badly needed in this area. This is a situation which calls for the application of the stable tracer, ^{48}Ca, which can be subsequently converted outside the body to the gamma-emitting ^{49}Ca, by neutron activation. The background for such an application lies in the rat bone studies of Conaway et al.[503] The plasma 1,25-dihydroxyvitamin D levels have been reported to be elevated in the lactating woman (see Chapter 4.III.C, and Table 1, Chapter 2). This would predictably result in enhanced absorption of calcium by the intestine.

II. AVIAN REPRODUCTION

Egg laying exposes the calcium metabolism of birds to an extraordinary calcium stress. A chicken with total calcium stores amounting to 20 g can lay an egg containing 2 g of calcium every day.* How does the laying hen adapt to this stress with respect to calcium absorption from the gut? There are three aspects of this question. The first concerns itself with the larger picture of laying *vs.* immature female birds. The second relates to laying *vs.* nonlaying days (ovulation pauses) once the mature hen has begun egg laying. The third aspect is the situation within the egg-laying cycle, i.e., the interval between consecutive ovulations, which is approximately 26 hr in the chicken and 24 hr in the Japanese quail.

Most mature female chickens immediately enter a state of negative calcium balance at the onset of egg production in spite of a prompt increase in food intake and, therefore, in calcium intake.[273] Much of the negative calcium balance is accounted for by the loss in the egg of approximately 2 g Ca/day, an amount which usually by itself exceeds the total calcium absorbed (v_a). Bar and his associates[206,504] have noted that egg-laying Japanese quail exhibit a much higher rate of calcium absorption (50%) than immature quail (21%), a phenomenon which may be attributed to a greater rate of synthesis of 1,25-dihydroxyvitamin D_3 in the former.[203,206,504] A similar situation exists in the chicken; laying hens have a much greater rate of calcium absorption than that observed in nonlaying pullets.[392]

Is there a difference in calcium absorption between laying and nonlaying birds once egg production has begun? Mueller et. al.[505] found that the v_a equaled 1.81 g Ca/day on a laying day, a value which was only 3% higher than the mean value (1.76

* Production rates for individual birds might vary between 75 and 100% of a daily rate.

Ca/day) for a nonlaying day. Thus it appears that the laying hen does not regulate its calcium absorption rate during ovulation pauses, assuming that the calcium intake remained unchanged. This finding is difficult to reconcile with the well-documented fact, first observed by Kenny and his associates,[63,72,202–204] that 1,25-dihydroxyvitamin D_3 production is decreased during ovulation pauses both in the chicken and in the Japanese quail (see Chapter 4.III.A above).

Is calcium absorption regulated during the 26- (chickens) or 24-hr (Japanese quail) egg-laying cycle? Hurwitz and Bar[506] studied the interval between ovipositions and obtained results which are not easy to reconcile with those of Mueller et al.[505] Hurwitz and Bar[506] measured absorptive efficiency in the laying hen at three different periods during the egg-laying cycle: at the time of no shell calcification, early in the calcification period, and later in the same period. The approach used was to:

1. Label uniformly two diets (1.90% and 3.56% Ca, respectively) with a nonabsorbable marker, ^{91}Y
2. Feed the diets for 4 days
3. Kill the hens at each of the three periods of the egg-laying cycle
4. Calculate the degree of calcium absorption from the Ca/^{91}Y ratios in the distal intestine.

Absorption increased from 40% during the no-calcification period to values between 68 and 77% during the period of calcification. The overall response was relatively independent of the dietary calcium level (1.90% *vs.* 3.56%). It appears from these data that the hen responds to the stress of calcification by an increase in the efficiency of calcium absorption. Similar results have been observed by the same laboratory using the Japanese quail.[395] During periods of eggshell formation (egg in shell gland; 12 to 17 hr after oviposition), intestinal calcium absorption (49.1%; using the ^{91}Y unabsorbed marker technique) was increased over that seen (22.1%) in birds with an ovum in the magnum of the oviduct (105 to 120 min after oviposition), i.e., prior to initiation of calcification of the egg. In spite of this finding, these investigators observed no difference in the calcium-binding protein content of the duodenum during these two periods in the 24-hr egg-laying cycle. The finding of a sharp difference in calcium absorption (22.1% and 49.1%) between the early and late phases of the ovulatory cycle needs to be reconciled with the report of Kenny[72] who found very little difference in 1,25-dihydroxyvitamin D_3 production between these two phases in the egg-laying Japanese quail (Figure 3, Chapter 4). In fact, 1,25-dihydroxyvitamin D_3 production tended to decline, if anything, during the later phases. Kenny's finding is supported by the plasma 1,25-dihydroxyvitamin D data of Castillo et al.[210] who found that the 1,25-dihydroxyvitamin D levels in chickens were high throughout the cycle but were higher during the earlier phase. Wasserman and Combs[429] offered an explanation of the discrepancy between the calcium absorption data of Bar et al.[395] on the one hand and their own calcium-binding protein data, and the renal 1-hydroxylase[72,210] and plasma 1,25-dihydroxyvitamin D[210] data of others on the other hand. Wasserman and Combs[429] found no difference in either calcium absorption (using *in situ* ligated loop technique) or in calcium-binding protein content of the duodenum between the early (1 to 2 hr after oviposition) and later (12 to 17 hr after oviposition) phases of the ovulatory cycle. They suggest that the fundamental difference in the calcium absorption data may be due to an artifact arising from the use of the ^{91}Y technique by Bar et al.,[395] which measures *net* calcium absorption rather than unidirectional absorption as measured by the *in situ* ligated loop technique. The technique of Bar et al. depends upon determining the Ca/^{91}Y

ratio of the lower small intestine following 4 days of feeding a diet labeled with ^{91}Y. Wasserman and Combs suggest that the difference, interpreted by Bar et al.[395] as a difference in calcium absorption, may be due to a difference in *secretion* of calcium into the intestinal lumen rather than due to a difference in *absorption* of calcium. The conclusion may be drawn that calcium absorption, at least in the Japanese quail, remains elevated but varies little during the 24-hr egg-laying cycle. If it does change then it tends to decline during the calcification phase. Calcium-binding protein content of the duodenum exhibits a similar pattern without a tendency to decline. The data supporting these conclusions are presented in Table 3.

Table 3
DUODENAL CALCIUM ABSORPTION AND CALCIUM BINDING PROTEIN (CaBP), RENAL 1-HYDROXYLASE AND PLASMA 1,25-DIHYDROXYVITAMIN D IN JAPANESE QUAIL DURING THE 24-HR OVULATORY CYCLE

Phase of cycle	Eggshell calcification	Ca absorption[429] (ligated duodenal loop) (%)	CaBP in duodenum		Renal 1-hydroxylase activity[210] ($pmol\ 200\ mg^{-1}\ 10\ min^{-1}$)	Plasma $1,25\text{-}(OH)_2D$[210] (pg/ml)
			(μg/mg protein)[429]	(mg/g)[395]		
Early[a]	Inactive	52.1 ± 6.8	32.8 ± 3.2	2.33 ± 0.12	100—200	100—250
Late[b]	Active	46.1 ± 3.0	32.5 ± 2.3	2.70 ± 0.24	50—120	80—120

Note: Data represent mean ± S.E.

[a] Ovum in upper oviduct (infundibulum, magnum, or isthmus); less than 6 hr after ovulation; no calcification of eggshell in progress.
[b] Ovum in shell gland (uterus); greater than 6 hr after ovulation; active calcification of eggshell in progress.

Chapter 8

ADAPTATION TO CALCIUM DEPRIVATION

I. EXPERIMENTAL ANIMALS

Mammals adapt to calcium deprivation by a more efficient absorption of calcium (defined as the amount of calcium absorbed as a percent of the intake) and thereby remain in positive balance.[507] This phenomenon had been well documented by the late 1950s in rats[271,279,508–510] and in dogs.[274] In adapted dogs, Gershoff et al.[274] were unable to observe a negative calcium balance even on a diet containing only 0.034% calcium. Adapted rats also remain in satisfactory balance on 0.04% and 0.1% calcium diets.[509]

The maintenance of a positive balance in the face of calcium deprivation is not necessarily indicative of increased efficiency of absorption only. Other factors such as decreases in the endogenous loss of calcium in the urine and feces also contribute to this phenomenon. The problem is identifying whether or not there has been an increase in the efficiency of absorption. Put another way, the question is which parameter or parameters can be accepted as representing efficiency of absorption. Balance data coupled with radiocalcium techniques can generate the two parameters: percent absorbed and absolute amount absorbed (v_a) per day. As discussed previously, neither is satisfactory. For example, Hansard and Plumlee,[279] Bronner and Aubert,[284] and Sammon et al.[281] have studied the effects of different levels of dietary calcium, ranging from 0.01% to 1.5% calcium, on various parameters generated by the balance approach. Some of the relevant data have been presented earlier in Table 1, Chapter 5, and indicate that as the dietary calcium level is decreased the percent absorption increases while the absolute amount absorbed (v_a) decreases. Others have shown a similar relationship between percent absorption and dietary levels both in rats[272] and in laying hens.[506,511] However, Shah and Draper[280] studied three levels of dietary calcium (0.3, 0.6, and 1.2% Ca) and found the relationship to hold only at the two higher levels. Are we to conclude then on the basis of the percent absorption data that an endogenous adaptation had occurred with a concomitant increase in the efficiency of calcium absorption? Surely such data could be interpreted in exogenous and less mysterious terms. Perhaps, as the calcium intake is increased from a low to a high level, the only events occurring are the following, in roughly the order listed:

1. Active transport playing a major role
2. Active transport becoming saturated
3. "Downhill" transport playing a major role
4. "Downhill" transport becoming saturated

These events could occur with no endogenous change in the transport systems themselves. From these considerations we can claim only that balance data per se are confirmatory but not conclusive evidence of increased efficiency of absorption. We know from other studies that the systems themselves can undergo endogenous changes; for example, active transport decreases with age, and vitamin D enhances "downhill" transport. Do endogenous changes occur in the phenomenon of adaptation or is this phenomenon explicable completely in terms of the relative roles of "uphill" and "downhill" transport and their saturation kinetics?

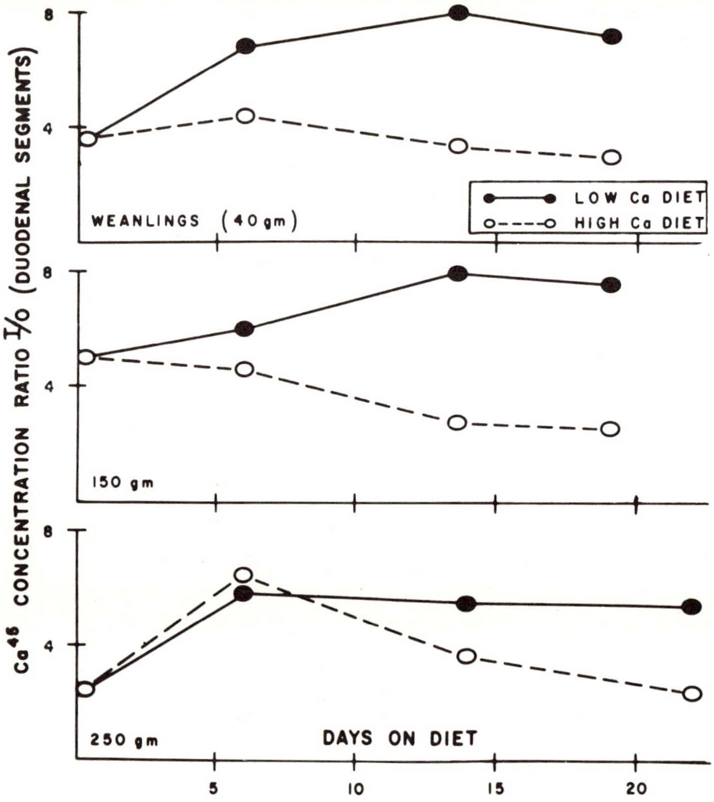

FIGURE 1. Effect of age on response of duodenal segments to dietary calcium. At the appropriate intervals, duodenal sacs were prepared and incubated in vitro for 3 hr at 37°C under oxygen. I/O ratio represents the ratio of radiocalcium (^{45}Ca) concentrations in the inside (serosal) and outside (mucosal) compartments, respectively (S/M ratio). (From Kimberg, D. V., Schachter, D., and Schenker, H., *Am. J. Physiol.*, 200, 1258, 1961. With permission.)

The in vitro everted gut sac technique could be used to indicate an adaptation in the active component of calcium transport. In many respects, though, the ligated segment technique (see Chapter 5.I.A.4) is ideal as it reflects both the active and passive components, is not subject to exogenous influences of the dietary calcium level such as obviously affect percent absorption or absolute amount (v_a), and can be used to identify the sites of increased efficiency of absorption. With these remarks in mind let us proceed to discuss some of the developments in this area, particularly those concerning the mechanisms of adaptation to deprivation.

A. Effects of Calcium Deprivation on Calcium Transport

In 1960 Wasserman,[346] using the everted gut sac preparation, first demonstrated that calcium deprivation leads to an enhancement of the active transport system in rats. This initial observation was rapidly followed by a confirmatory and more extensive report by Kimberg et al.,[334] from which the data presented in Figure 1 are taken. Kimberg et al. reported that the increased active transport was seen in both the duodenum and the jejunum and that it was seen to a greater extent and appeared earlier (within 7 days) in younger (40 g) than in older (250 g) rats. After 14 days on a low calcium diet (0.02% Ca) the serosal/mucosal (S/M) ratios were around 8, double those obtained from rats maintained on a normal calcium diet (1.2% Ca). These initial observations have been adequately confirmed by others who have measured various parameters associated with calcium absorption including:

1. S/M ratios in the in vitro everted gut sac preparation of the rat[231,343,346–512]
2. Calcium absorption in vivo from ligated duodenal and jejunal loops in rats[231,306,513]
3. Calcium absorption in vivo from ligated duodenal loops in chickens[186,318,464,465,514]
4. In vitro calcium flux ratio measurements using the Ussing and Zerahn[360] technique with rat duodenum[362,515,516]
5. In vivo Thiry-Vella jejunal loops in the pig[517]
6. Balance method in the rat[518]
7. Indirectly, calcium-binding protein determinations in chicken duodenum[192,308,318,401,420,421,428,464–466]

No effect of calcium deprivation was seen on intestinal calcium adenosine triphosphatase in chickens.[401] A selection of these data is presented in Table 1.

It is therefore well established that calcium deprivation does lead to endogenous changes, such as in the active transport system, which can be interpreted unequivocally as increased efficiency of absorption. The repeated finding that active transport is enhanced by calcium deprivation[231,334,343,346,362] is of great significance in view of the fact that in periods of calcium deprivation the active transport system probably plays a major role in calcium absorption (see Chapter 5.IV.A).

B. Mechanisms of Adaptation

What are the links in the pathway between dietary calcium level and increased efficiency of calcium absorption by the intestine? Over 35 years ago, Nicolaysen[508] proposed the existence of an "endogenous factor" which linked the body stores of calcium with intestinal absorption of calcium; "endogenous factor" required vitamin D for its action. Nicolaysen suggested that, as the amount of skeletal calcium fell, the endogenous factor was released, perhaps from bone itself, and transported to the gut where it increased the efficiency of calcium absorption. During the intervening decades a search for the endogenous factor has continued.

There is no question that the final link in the pathway is the renal hormone, 1,25-dihydroxyvitamin D_3. Its production is markedly stimulated by calcium deprivation (see Chapter 4.I.A) and it stimulates intestinal transport of calcium (see Chapter 10.I) 1,25-Dihydroxyvitamin D_3 qualifies as the endogenous factor, but this association is of historical interest only. The question now becomes: what are the links in the pathway between calcium deprivation and activation of the renal 25-hydroxyvitamin D_3-1-hydroxylase enzyme? Various potential physiological regulators of the renal 1-hydroxylase enzyme have been discussed elsewhere in this monograph (see Chapter 4). Those potential regulators which are most relevant to the matter under current discussion include calcium deprivation (Chapter 4.I.A) plasma calcium (Chapter 4.II.A), parathyroid hormone (Chapter 4.IV.A), and certain pituitary hormones (Chapter 4.IV.E and Chapter 4.IV.F). Let us now examine one of these factors, parathyroid hormone, with respect to its potential role in the intestinal calcium absorption response to calcium deprivation.

Table 1
EFFECT OF CALCIUM DEPRIVATION ON VARIOUS PARAMETERS ASSOCIATED WITH CALCIUM ABSORPTION

Species	Preparation	Days on diet	Parameter	Dietary calcium[a]		p	Ref.
				High	Low		
Rat	Everted duodenal sac	7	S/M	1.7	3.2	< 0.02	346
	Everted duodenal sac	7	S/M	6.2	12.5	< 0.01	231
	Everted duodenal sac	14	S/M	5.7	11.9	< 0.01	231
	Ligated duodenal loop	7	%[b]	36	55	< 0.01	231
	Ligated duodenal loop	14	%[b]	46	60	< 0.001	231
	Ligated duodenal loop	21	%[b]	67	79	< 0.001	231
	Balance		%[c]	61	92	< 0.001	518
	In vitro Ussing[d]	7	MS	17.1	29.9	< 0.001	362
			SM	7.9	7.1	NS	
			MS/SM	2.16	4.21	< 0.001	
Chicken	Ligated duodenal loop	10	%[b]	48	87	< 0.001	465
	Duodenum	10	CaBP	6.1	15.1	< 0.001	465
Pig	Thiry-Vella jejunal loop	4—6	mmol[e]	0.21	0.35	p < 0.001	517

Note: *p*: probability level; NS: not significant ($p > 0.05$); S/M: serosal/mucosal ratio; MS: mucosal to serosal flux (nmols/cm^2 and 10 min); SM: serosal to mucosal flux (nmols/cm^2 and 10 min); CaBP: Calcium-binding protein (%/mg protein).

[a] The figures in this column represent the values of the parameters indicated in the preceding column under either high or low dietary Ca conditions.
[b] % absorption from ligated loop.
[c] % absorption of intake calculated from balance data.
[d] Apparatus of Ussing and Zerahn.[360]
[e] mmol Ca absorbed from Thiry-Vella loop during each perfusion period (30—60 min).

Table 2
EFFECT OF THYROPARATHYROIDECTOMY ON THE ADAPTIVE RESPONSE TO CALCIUM DEPRIVATION OF THE ACTIVE TRANSPORT SYSTEM FOR CALCIUM IN THE RAT[334]

	Serum calcium[a] (mg/100 mℓ)		Serosal/mucosal ratio (mean ± SE)		
Operation	HCD	LCD	HCD	LCD	p
Sham	6.9	7.4	2.8 ± 0.58	6.6 ± 0.22	<0.001
TPTX	4.4	3.5	2.6 ± 0.22	5.5 ± 0.36	<0.001

Note: HCD: high-Ca diet (1.2% Ca); LCD: low-Ca diet (0.02% Ca); SE: standard error of the mean; *p:* probability level of significance between HCD and LCD responses; TPTX: thyroparathyroidectomy.

[a] Median values given.

1. *Parathyroid Hormone*

In 1960, Kenny[507] and Dowdle et al.[329] suggested independently that parathyroid hormone might be Nicolaysen's endogenous factor. This concept was generated by the following facts: (1) calcium deprivation causes hypertrophy of the parathyroid glands[519] and, therefore, presumably release of parathyroid hormone; and (2) calcium absorption is enhanced by parathyroid hormone administration (see Chapter 10.II.B). The following year Kimberg et al.[334] produced evidence which did not support the involvement of parathyroid hormone in the adaptive response to calcium deprivation. They found that thyroparathyroidectomy did not abolish the adaptive response, as measured by increased active transport (S/M ratios) in the everted duodenal sac in rats, to an 18-day period of calcium deprivation (Table 2). Three aspects of this study led our laboratory to reinvestigate the problem. First, the fact that Kimberg et al.[334] had used thyroparathyroidectomized rats and thus were studying the effect of eliminating three different types of hormones (parathyroid hormone, iodinated thyroid hormones, and calcitonin, which had been discovered since the study of Kimberg et al. had been completed), all of which are known to influence calcium metabolism in general, if not gut calcium absorption in particular. The second aspect was the fact that it did not appear that the food intake was controlled by pair feeding. The third aspect was the unusually low serum calcium levels which ranged from 6.4 to 7.4 mg/dℓ in normal rats on a normal calcium diet (1.2% Ca) as can be seen in Table 2 where the median values are given*.

Data from our laboratory have indicated that the noninvolvement of parathyroid hormone in the adaptive response is not clear-cut. Pento et al.[231,520,521] found that parathyroidectomy did abolish the adaptive response to a 7-day but not a 21-day period of calcium deprivation. Calcium deprivation for 14 days gave equivocal results. Both the in vitro everted duodenal sac (7- and 14-day data) and in the in vivo ligated loop technique (7-, 14-, and 21-day data) were used in conjunction with quad feeding.** In the latter technique absorption indexes were obtained by measuring

* In response to an inquiry, Dr. Daniel V. Kimberg was kind enough to comment that he had no explanation for the unusually low serum calcium levels.

** The term "quad feeding" is used to describe the situation in which three groups of rats (intact-high Ca diet; intact-low Ca diet; and PTX-high Ca diet) are fed that quantity of diet consumed by the fourth group (PTX-low Ca diet) the previous day.

both the disappearance of ^{45}Ca from the loop and the appearance of ^{45}Ca in the plasma. This study led Pento et al. to conclude that parathyroid hormone appears to be necessary for short-term (7-day), but not for long-term (21-day), adaptation to calcium deprivation. This finding is in accord with that of Kimberg et al.[334] who used an 18-day adaptation period. Nevertheless, this conclusion must remain tentative until more information is available, particularly whether or not *accessory* parathyroid tissue is implicated. Such tissue is a common occurrence in rats;[522,523] 65% of the rats were found by Casewell and Fennell[522] to contain ectopic parathyroid tissue in the thymus. Nevertheless, if accessory tissue is invoked to explain the breakthrough of the adaptive response in parathyroidectomized rats at longer time intervals, it is necessary to postulate that the gut response is more sensitive to parathyroid hormone action than the blood calcium response; the blood calcium remained low in calcium-deprived, parathyroidectomized group at 21 days. Such a postulate meets with little favor. But it is certain from the work of both Kenny[524] and Casewell and Fennell[522] that the accessory tissue, known to be present in the latter work and assumed to be present in the former, was unable to restore the blood calcium levels to normal following ablation of the regular parathyroid glands. Casewell and Fennell[522] did find that parathyroidectomized rats with accessory tissue in the cervical region were able to maintain slightly but significantly higher levels of serum calcium (7.9 mg/dℓ) than those with no accessory tissue (6.6 mg/dℓ). Kenny[524] also found that rats subjected to the stress of calcium deprivation survived to a much higher degree if the stress were applied at 7 days, rather than immediately, after parathyroidectomy; this could be interpreted as evidence for the gradual development of functional accessory tissue. Is it possible that with the passage of time and with the constant hypocalcemic stimulus sufficient parathyroid hormone is released from accessory tissue to enhance calcium absorption without any gross effects on the blood calcium levels?

Since the publication of these early reports of Pento and his associates discussed above, there have been other studies confirming the parathyroid independence of long-term adaptation to calcium deprivation in rats. Kemm[518] used the balance method and Favus et al.[516] employed the Ussing-Zerahn flux technique in studies of periods of calcium deprivation lasting 4 to 6 weeks and 20 days, respectively. Parathyroidectomy performed several weeks after instigating the low calcium diet did not prevent the adaptive response.[518] Pento et al.[231] had reported a similar experience with rats parathyroidectomized after 11 days. In the pig, Fox et al.[517] found that the adaptive response was independent of the parathyroid glands even after only 4 to 6 days of calcium deprivation.

A study of the plasma 1,25-dihydroxyvitamin D levels in the parathyroidectomized rat, deprived of calcium for several weeks, has yet to be reported. In the absence of such important information, which undoubtedly will be forthcoming in the near future, it may be assumed that the plasma 1,25-dihydroxyvitamin D levels are elevated in the parathyroidectomized, calcium-deprived rat relative to the parathyroidectomized calcium-replete animal; the data of Larkins et al.[230] would support this contention. If this assumption is granted, what is the link between low dietary calcium and activation of the renal 1-hydroxylase enzyme in long-term adaptation if it is not parathyroid hormone? Is one of the pituitary hormones, prolactin or growth hormone, or both, involved? Is the ionic calcium level in extracellular fluid directly playing a role? The author's feeling is that prolactin should be examined closely as a potential messenger in long-term adaptation. Let us review the evidence for these possibilities however sparse it is.

2. *Other Pathways*

Nearly 2 decades ago, Kimberg et al.[334] reported that neither hypophysectomy nor adrenalectomy abolished the adaptive response to calcium deprivation in the rat. This finding essentially eliminated from serious consideration either the pituitary or the adrenal hormones as candidates for Nicolaysen's endogenous factor. Since the more recent discovery that prolactin and growth hormone are each capable of stimulating renal production of 1,25-dihydroxyvitamin D_3 (see Chapter 4.IV.E and 4.IV.F, respectively), the pituitary has been reexamined as a link in the pathway.

Intestinal calcium absorption is increased in lactating rats when compared with that in nonlactating females. Bromocriptine, a dopamine agonist known to inhibit prolactin release, reduced calcium absorption by 44% as well as the plasma 1,25-dihydroxyvitamin D levels.[249] Plasma concentrations of parathyroid hormone remained unchanged by the treatment. Yet to be demonstrated is whether or not prolactin administration has any effects on calcium absorption by the intestine.

The hypophysectomy experiments of Kimberg et al.,[334] although removing the pituitary hormones from consideration as endogenous factors, did reveal that calcium absorption was reduced by the endocrinectomy. Later, the same laboratory reported that growth hormone could restore the deficit in calcium absorption.[330] More recently James et al.[249] have shown that hypophysectomy in rats leads to a fall in plasma 1,25-dihydroxyvitamin D levels from 160 p*M* in sham-operated controls to 72 p*M*. Injection of growth hormone into the hypophysectomized animals restored the level to 184 p*M*.

The pituitary must remain a viable candidate as a link in the adaptive response to calcium deprivation in spite of the earlier hypophysectomy experiments of Kimberg et al.[334] Badly needed are data such as the plasma levels of prolactin and growth hormone in the chronically calcium-deprived, compared with calcium-replete, animal before a more definitive conclusion can be reached. Prolactin has great appeal as the candidate for a role in long-term adaptation. It is better known as a slowly acting hormone rather than a rapidly acting, minute-to-minute regulator. It is a known hypercalcemic agent in lower vertebrates.[69,247] It can stimulate renal production of 1,25-dihydroxyvitamin D_3 in certain species (see Chapter 4.IV.E). Intriguing in this context is the little known fact that calcium deprivation in the laying chicken leads to cessation of *ovulation*.[525] Is this response mediated by prolactin release?

It is of course possible that the ionic calcium milieu may be the controlling factor in long-term adaptation. Although acute control of renal 1-hydroxylase activity by ionic calcium is controversial (see Chapter 4.II.A), *chronic* deprivation may lead to changes in membrane or intracellular calcium content which may assume a dominant role in control. Such changes must be subtle; the adaptive response appears to become independent of the parathyroids even when intact animals are placed on a low calcium diet for extended periods and then parathyroidectomized.[231,581] During such periods of depletion intact rats maintain essentially normal plasma calcium concentrations.[231]

Is calcitonin a link in the adaptive response pathway? Although a definitive answer to this question cannot be made in the light of available data, the author believes that it is highly unlikely. It has been reported that calcitonin inhibits renal 1,25-dihydroxyvitamin D_3 synthesis, although this response remains controversial (see Chapter 4.IV.B). Whether or not calcitonin influences calcium absorption by the intestine is also controversial[526] (see Chapter 10.III). Is it possible that calcium deprivation suppresses calcitonin release and thereby eliminates calcitonin's inhibitory effect on calcium absorption?

II. MAN

That man adapts to calcium deprivation by eventually going into zero or positive balance has been well documented.[527,529] However, the evidence that this adaptive response is due to increased efficiency of absorption is incomplete. Malm[527] notes in his studies that when men were shifted from an intake of 940 mg Ca/day to a lower one of 463 mg Ca/day, the main change in the excretory loss occurred in the fecal calcium; there was no significant fall in urinary calcium. This was interpreted as indicating an increased efficiency of absorption. Malm assumed that the endogenous fecal loss (digestive juice calcium) remained relatively constant at a level of 750 mg Ca/day. These assumptions may be questioned. Estimates of endogenous fecal loss of calcium made with radiocalcium techniques subsequent to Malm's report indicate that the normal loss is considerably lower, ranging between 80 and 180 mg Ca/day, and the loss is not necessarily constant.[282,373,530,531] In fact, Heaney and Skillman[531] found that the endogenous fecal calcium (v_f) was positively correlated with the dietary calcium intake (v_f) as follows: $v_f = 0.0343\ v_i + 103$ (in terms of mg Ca/day). Nevertheless, if we assume this relationship to be correct then the endogenous fecal calcium should be 135 mg Ca/day when the intake was 940 mg Ca/day and 118 mg Ca/day at the lower intake of 463 mg Ca/day. This fall in endogenous fecal calcium from 135 to 118, or 17 mg Ca/day, is insufficient to account for Malm's observed fall in total fecal calcium (v_F) from 338 to 266 mg Ca/day. These considerations do permit the conclusion from Malm's data that increased efficiency of absorption had occurred as a result in adaptation. Whether this response in humans is due to endogenous changes in the transport mechanisms or whether it is completely explicable in terms of the relative roles of the transport systems and their saturation kinetics (as discussed in Chapter 7.I) is not known with certainty at this time. The fact that the adaptive response is not immediate but often takes time to develop favors the former endogenous explanation. If adaptation in humans were due to the latter explanation, in which the response is dependent entirely on an exogenous factor (dietary calcium level), one would expect the adaptive response to be immediate.

As yet, there is no data in humans which permits a conclusion concerning the mechanism of the adaptive response in man.

Chapter 9

NUTRITIONAL ASPECTS OF CALCIUM ABSORPTION

There are many dietary constituents, other than calcium, which can affect intestinal calcium absorption. These include minerals, such as phosphate and magnesium, cereal phytates, lactose, and amino acids. In addition, there are factors endogenous to the intestine, such as bile and pH, which may be affected by dietary manipulation.

I. MINERALS

A. Phosphate

It is a widely accepted maxim that addition of inorganic phosphate to the diet suppresses the absorption of calcium by the intestine, in spite of informed denials of this generalization.[373,532] This conclusion is based largely on early and extensive rat studies with the balance method in which extremes of Ca:P ratios were often used. It is unfortunate that these findings are frequently extrapolated to other species and to more moderate Ca:P ratios. By the mid-1950s it became generally recognized that, in the presence of adequate levels of dietary calcium and vitamin D, changing the Ca:P ratio over a fairly wide range had little or no effect on calcium absorption either in man[373,532,533] or in other species.[373,534] Spencer and her associates[535] have found that varying the Ca:P ratio from 2:1 through 1:8 by the addition of glycerophosphate to both a low-calcium diet (200 mg/day intake) and a high-calcium diet (1500 mg/day intake) had no consistent effects on calcium absorption in human patients except possibly to *enhance* absorption in the low-calcium diet study. Similarly, in rats Clark,[536] using the balance method, found that addition of phosphate to a diet adequate in calcium *enhanced* calcium absorption.

All of the studies quoted above used the balance method approach. As other methods became available they were applied to an examination of the influence of dietary phosphate on intestinal calcium absorption with confusing results. In the dog, using the Thiry-Vella loop, Cramer[289] studied various Ca:P ratios, including the addition of no phosphate. He found that addition of phosphate enhanced calcium absorption but, once phosphate was present, varying the Ca:P molar ratio from 0.5:2.0 had no effect on the calcium absorption rate. In vitro studies in the rat led to similar findings. Addition of phosphate, in situations where the solubility product of calcium phosphate was not exceeded, either had no effect,[356] slightly depressed calcium transport,[362] or greatly enhanced calcium transport.[361] In the ligated loop of the chicken Wasserman[303] found that addition of a chemically equivalent amount of phosphate (presumably around 25 m*M*), in the form of either orthophosphate or glycerophosphate to the loop contents containing 25 m*M* of calcium, depressed calcium absorption. However, this inhibition can be explained on the basis of precipitation of calcium phosphate;[537] Helbock et al.[361] observed precipitation with concentrations of 3.0 and 10.7 m*M* for calcium and phosphate, respectively.

The past decade saw the emergence of the concept of the endocrine nature of vitamin D; this prompted a reexamination of the influence of dietary phosphate on calcium absorption. It appears that, in contrast to the confusion existing earlier, a consensus has emerged: dietary phosphate deprivation leads to enhanced calcium transport by the intestine. This is the reported finding in rats using either the everted gut sac,[512,538] the *in situ* ligated loop,[513] or the balance method.[539] Similar findings have been reported for the chicken, using the *in situ* ligated loop.[192,420] Only in man were the data not supportive of this concept. Little change in calcium absorption (measured by following the plasma ^{47}Ca levels after a single oral dose of ^{47}Ca) was noted when the patients were subjected to two levels of dietary phosphate intake (800 and 2000 mg P/day) at calcium intakes of 200, 800, 1500, 2000, and 2700 mg Ca/day. This essentially confirmed the earlier report from the same laboratory.[535]

The mechanism of the stimulating effect of phosphate depletion on calcium absorption in experimental animals is not known with certainty. It differs importantly from that of calcium deficiency in that the enhanced calcium absorption, unlike that following calcium deprivation, persists when large doses of vitamin D_3 or 25-hydroxyvitamin D_3 are administered to phosphate-deprived rats.[538] Ribovich and DeLuca[538] suggest that in addition to stimulating 1,25-dihydroxyvitamin D_3 production, phosphate deficiency must have an unknown effect on gut calcium absorption.

B. Magnesium

The effect of magnesium on calcium absorption is not consistent and is dependent upon many factors.[353] There are reports which conclude that addition of magnesium to the diet can either enhance, depress, or have no effect on calcium absorption.[540–548] There appear to be few points of agreement. In some laboratories magnesium deficiency leads to increased transport whether this was measured by the everted duodenal sac in the rat,[333,350,540] or by the ligated loop in the rat[549] or in the chicken.[550] This response was abolished by prior parathyroidectomy,[350] indicating that it might be secondary to stimulation of the parthyroid glands. In the Harrisons' laboratory no effect due to magnesium deficiençy was seen in the same preparation.[335,336] Addition of magnesium to the fluid used in the everted duodenal sac has been shown either to decrease[323,551],* or to have no effect[333,335] on active transport of calcium. In the Thiry-Vella loop preparation, magnesium depressed calcium absorption in both the dog[290] and the sheep.[293] The picture is far from clear and must await further work for clarification.

II. PHYTATES

Since Mellanby's first discovery in 1925 of a rachitogenic factor present in cereals, later identified as phytic acid or inositol hexaphosphoric acid, a considerable controversy has raged in nutritional circles as to its importance. There is no question, as was later shown, that phytic acid can inhibit calcium absorption from the diet.[373,532,534,552] This action has in fact been applied therapeutically in man in cases of sarcoidosis and hypercalciuria.[553] Its therapeutic effectiveness was not dramatic; diarrhea was the only side effect. In the human, however, adaptation occurs; the initial fall in calcium absorption following phytate ingestion is eventually overcome.[529]

By the mid-1950s, Harris[554] and Bronner et al.[555] were led to conclude that "when the intake of unrefined cereals is relatively low and that of calcium relatively high nutritional problems due to phytate ingestion are negligible."[373] The nutritional controversy has subsided and interest in phytate and calcium absorption has waned to insignificant levels.

III. LACTOSE

It has been known for over 40 years that lactose, when incorporated into experimental diets, will enhance the intestinal absorption of calcium in many species. The

* See Table 2, Chapter 5, for Schachter and Rosen[323] data.

effect of lactose in the rat is directly on the gut.[340,537,553–560] Other sugars (mannose, cellobiose, raffinose, D- and L-xylose, D- and L-arabinose) and polyalcohols (mannitol, sorbitol, and inositol) have a similar effect. Glucose and sucrose are effective in vitro but ineffective in vivo due to their rapid absorption in the upper part of the small intestine.[559]

In man, lactose gave only a slight enhancement of calcium absorption from the intestine.[561] On the other hand, Pansu et al.[562] have recently made the interesting observation that osteoporotic patients, intolerant to lactose with respect to the hyperglycemic response to ingested lactose, show a more dramatic response in calcium absorption.

IV. AMINO ACIDS AND PROTEIN

The fact that certain amino acids directly and immediately enhance the intestinal absorption of calcium in the rat was first documented by Wasserman's group.[563–565] The relative effectiveness of the amino acids is as follows:

1. Highly effective: L-lysine, and L-arginine
2. Moderately effective: L-tryptophan, L-leucine, L-histidine, L-methionine, L-aspartic acid, hydroxyl-L-proline, L-glutamic acid, and DL-tryosine
3. Relatively ineffective: glycine, L-isoleucine, L-valine, and L-phenylalanine

In the chicken, Wasserman et al.[565] found that lysine inhibited calcium absorption. Sallis and Holdsworth,[317] on the other hand, found no effect of either L-lysine or L-arginine in the ligated loop preparation of the rachitic chick. The effect of lysine in man is not dramatic.[566] In addition, varying protein intakes (0.5, 1.0, and 2.0 g/kg) had little effect on intestinal calcium absorption in man.[567]

V. HYDROGEN ION

Two factors make the relationship between pH and intestinal absorption of calcium worthy of study:

1. The pH of the small intestine varies from the proximal to the distal regions
2. The solubilities of calcium salts generally decrease as pH rises

The pH of the rat small intestine varies from around 6.5 in the duodenum, decreases to a minimum of 6.0 in the proximal jejunum, and increases to a maximum of 7.2 in the terminal ileum.[302] In the chicken the pH increases progressively from a value of 6.55 in the duodenum to a value of 7.83 in the distal region of the small intestine.[310] Earlier work reviewed by Irving[532] had led to the conclusion that intestinal pH under normal conditions was relatively unimportant. In a study using the ligated duodenal loop of the rat, Sallis and Holdsworth[317] found no difference in calcium absorption from the loop whether the contents of the loop were at pH 4 or 6. In the chicken, Wasserman[485] tested the effect of pH 1.8, 4.0, and 6.9 on calcium absorption from ligated duodenal loops in both normal and rachitic chicks. There was no dramatic effect of pH on absorption in the normal chick. However, there were sharp differences between the normal and the rachitic chicks at pH 4.0 and 6.9 (the rachitic absorption was suppressed relative to the normal); there was no difference between the two nutritional states at pH 1.8. In the dog, Cramer[289] found no differences in calcium absorption rates from Thiry-Vella loops between pH 3.3, 5.2, and 7.4.

VI. BILE AND BILE ACIDS

The chronic effects of bile and the bile acids are complicated by the fact that in the rat, and presumably in other species, bile is normally required for the optimal absorption of vitamin D.[568] However, bile does have an immediate and direct effect on calcium absorption in the rat[568–570] and in the chicken.[310,320,570] Rachitic bile was just as effective and the response was rapid, indicating that the effect was not due to the vitamin D or active metabolite content of the bile. Three observations in the rat cloud this picture. Vaughan and Filer[571] found no positive effect of bile added to ligated duodenal and ileal sacs. Cholestryamine resin is an anion exchange resin which binds bile acids in the lumen and prevents their absorption; therefore its administration to rats would predictably decrease calcium absorption. However, the resin has been found both to increase calcium absorption[572] and to have no effect.[573] The positive effects of bile acids are also seen with other materials of an anionic detergent nature, such as sodium lauryl sulfate, whereas cationic (benzalkonium chloride) and neutral (Polysorbate 80, U.S.P., or Tween 80®) detergents were ineffective.[320] This generalization does not necessarily hold, as a cationic detergent (cetyltrimethylammonium bromide) enhances calcium absorption from ligated duodenal loops of rachitic chicks but depresses calcium absorption in normal chicks.[353]

Chapter 10

ENDOCRINE ASPECTS OF CALCIUM ABSORPTION

I. VITAMIN D

The first recognition of a dietary factor which could cure experimental rickets, enhance calcium absorption from the gut, and was related to exposure to sunlight, dates back to the early 1920s in the classical studies of Mellanby, McCollum, Steenbock, and Hess, and their respective associates. Fourman et al.[552] and DeLuca[574,575] present an excellent review of the early history of vitamin D. Subsequently, two provitamins, ergosterol and 7-dehydrocholesterol, and the active forms to which they are converted by ultraviolet irradiation, vitamin D_2 and vitamin D_3, respectively, have been identified. Vitamin D has actions on the bone and kidney but its main physiological and pharmacological actions are on calcium absorption by the intestine.

The vitamin D terminology needs some explanation. Vitamin D itself is generic, there being no particular molecule associated with the term. A compilation of the terms for the provitamins, the vitamins and their active metabolites, and the respective synonyms, is presented in Table 1. Selected chemical structures are given in Figure 1.

This is not the place to launch into a general review of the physiology and pharmacology of vitamin D. Details of its actions on bone and kidney, its therapeutic uses, its toxicity, and its dosage forms may be found elsewhere.[574,575] In the discussion which follows, only studies on its mechanism of action on the gut will be emphasized.

A. Mechanism of Vitamin D Action

That vitamin D is an essential factor for the optimal absorption of calcium from the gut had been solidly documented by the early 1950s when Nicolaysen and his associates reviewed the material.[528,576] Most of the early work was done with the classical balance approach and therefore could not supply answers to the mechanism of the essentiality of vitamin D for optimal calcium absorption. Was the action of vitamin D due to decreased excretion of endogenous fecal calcium or was it due to increased efficiency of absorption? If the latter, did it enhance active transport, passive transport, or both?

By the mid-1950s it was possible to conclude that vitamin D enhances the efficiency of absorption.[313,577–579] As the vitamin will cause this effect in the absence of any change in calcium intake, we may further conclude that the increased efficiency must be due to an endogenous change in the transport systems, assuming that the vitamin has no effect on transit time. Questions to be answered are

1. In which segment or segments of the intestine does vitamin D act?
2. Does vitamin D enhance active transport, passive transport, or both?
3. How does it influence the transport mechanisms?
4. Which parameters play the most important role in the overall effect of the vitamin on calcium absorption?

These questions will be discussed one by one.

Table 1
VITAMIN D TERMINOLOGY

Natural occurrence	Vitamin	Provitamin	Hydroxylated metabolites[a]: Metabolite	Major tissue source
Animals	Vitamin D_3 (Cholecalciferol)	7-Dehydrocholesterol (Provitamin D_3)	25-Hydroxyvitamin D_3 (25-Hydroxycholecalciferol) [25-(OH) D_3]	Liver
			1,25-Dihydroxyvitamin D_3 (1,25-Dihydroxycholecalciferol) (Calcitriol) (Rocaltrol®) [1,25-$(OH)_2D_3$]	Kidney
			24,25-Dihydroxyvitamin D_3 (24,25-Dihydroxycholecalciferol) [24,25-$(OH)_2D_3$]	Kidney
			25,26-Dihydroxyvitamin D_3 (25,26-Dihydroxycholecalciferol) [25,26-$(OH)_2D_3$]	Unknown
			1,24,25-Trihydroxyvitamin D_3 (1,24,25-Trihydroxycholecalciferol) [1,24,25-$(OH)_3D_3$]	Kidney
			25-Hydroxyvitamin D_3-26,23-lactone (Calcidiol lactone) [25-(OH) D_3-26,23-Lactone]	Unknown
			Calcitroic acid[b] (1-Hydroxy-24,25,26,27-tetranor-vitamin D_3-23-carboxylic acid) [1-(OH)-24,25,26,27-Tetranor-23-(COOH) D_3]	Gut/liver
			Cholacalcioic acid[c] (25,26,27-Trinorvitamin D_3-24-carboxylic acid) [25,26,27-Trinor-24-(COOH) D_3]	(Kidney?)

Plants	Vitamin D_2 (Ergocalciferol) (Calciferol)	Ergosterol (Provitamin D_2)	25-Hydroxyvitamin D_2 (25-Hydroxyergocalciferol) [25-(OH) D_2]	Liver
			1,25-Dihydroxyvitamin D_2 (1,25-Dihydroxyergocalciferol) [1,25-$(OH)_2$ D_2]	Kidney
			24,25-Dihydroxyvitamin D_2 (24,25-Dihydroxyergocalciferol) [24,25-$(OH)_2$ D_2]	Kidney
			(It may be assumed that other metabolites of vitamin D_2, analogous to the vitamin D_3 series, are produced)	

[a] This list contains the major known metabolites and is by no means exhaustive; other metabolites are known to exist and remain to be identified, Synonyms and abbreviations are given below each metabolite in parentheses.
[b] Water-soluble metabolite formed from 1,25-$(OH)_2$ D_3 by side-chain oxidation to form a 23-carboxylic acid.
[c] Water-soluble metabolite formed from 24,25-$(OH)_2$ D_3 by side-chain oxidation to form a 24-carboxylic acid.

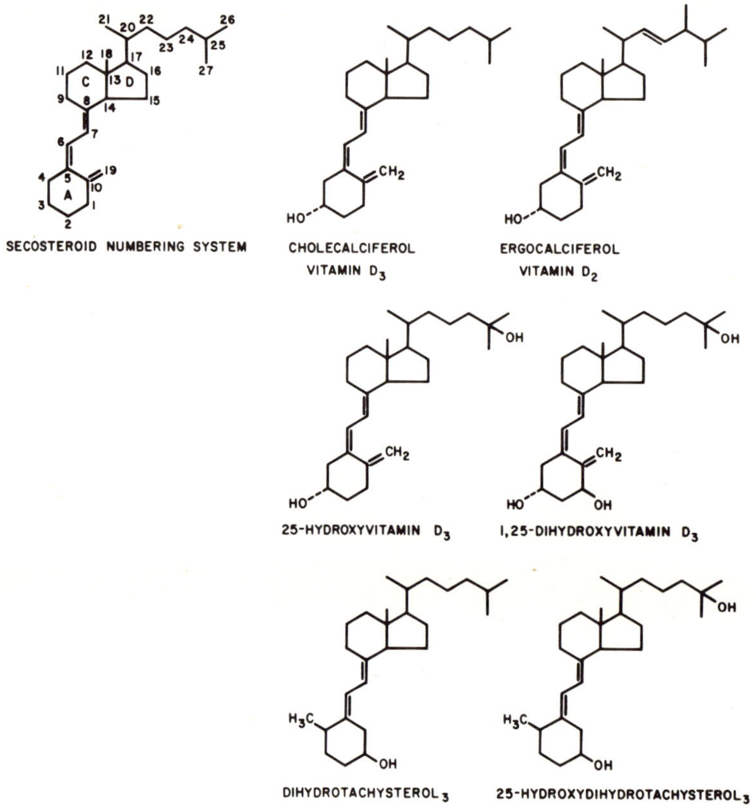

FIGURE 1. Chemical structures and numbering system of selected secosteroids related to vitamin D.

1. Sites of Vitamin D Action: In Vivo Studies

Vitamin D has been shown to enhance calcium absorption in all segments of the small intestine of the chicken using the in vivo ligated loop.[303,315,320] Others have reported similar findings in the duodenum[317,580] and in the ileum[301,316,317] of the chicken, and in the duodenum of the rat.[344] The observation that the rat ileum does not respond to vitamin D[344,581] is not in accord with the in vivo experiments of Harrison and Harrison,[582] nor with in vitro experiments described below.

2. Sites of Vitamin D Action: In Vitro Studies

The action of vitamin D on the intestinal transport of calcium has been much more extensively studied in vitro, particularly in the rat and the chicken. All segments of the rat small intestine respond to vitamin D as measured by the in vitro everted gut sac technique.[325,483,583–585] Oswald and Binswanger[325] made the important observation that the everted *ileal* sac, prepared from nephrectomized, thyroparathyroidectomized rats, did not respond to administration of 1,25-dihydroxyvitamin D_3 as did that prepared from rats which had been nephrectomized only. The response of the *duodenal* everted sac was not parathyroid dependent. Others have also shown in vitro that specific segments of the rat small intestine respond; these segments include the duodenum,[326,328,329,334–336,338,343–345,348,390,396,586–591] the jejunum,[587] and the ileum.[325,334,390] In addition, Harrison and Harrison[332] and Petith et al.[592] have

Table 2
EFFECT OF VITAMIN D ON PASSIVE PERMEABILITY IN ALL SEGMENTS OF THE RAT SMALL INTESTINE

Conditions			Passive permeability[a]					
			Proximal 1/6 (Segment)		Middle 3/6 (Segment)		Terminal 2/6 (Segment)	
Gas phase	Temp. (°C)	Inhibitor (0.5 m*M*)	–D[b]	+D[c]	–D[b]	+D[c]	–D[b]	+D[c]
O_2	37	—	0.163	0.519	0.100	0.230	0.157	0.280
N_2	37	—	0.186	0.464	0.153	0.285	0.173	0.338
O_2	25	—	0.147	0.403	0.096	0.138	0.080	0.163
O_2	5	—	0.099	0.155	0.072	0.095	—	—
O_2	37	KCN	0.136	0.600	0.105	0.269	0.122	0.274

[a] Data represent diffusion rate constants (*k*) in $(\text{min})^{-1}$; ^{45}Ca was placed on mucosal side of everted segment and rate of transfer to serosal side was determined, total Ca being equal on both sides. All effects of vitamin D are significant.
[b] –D: vitamin D-deficient rats.
[c] +D: vitamin D-deficient rats treated with vitamin D.

From Harrison, H. E. and Harrison, H. C., in *The Transfer of Calcium and Strontium Across Biological Membranes*, Wasserman, R. H., Ed., Academic Press, New York, 1963, 229. With permission.

shown that the rat colon responds to vitamin D. A similar situation exists in the hamster and the chicken; all segments of the small intestine respond to the vitamin using in vitro techniques.[315,343,593,594]

3. Vitamin D and Active Transport

It has been frequently demonstrated that vitamin D enhances active transport in the rat duodenum as measured by the in vitro gut sac technique.[325,326,328,329,332,334–336,338,343–345,348,349,390,483,585,586,588–591,595] The question to be resolved is whether or not this response represents a primary effect of the vitamin; this will be discussed below.

4. Vitamin D and Passive Transport

There is a considerable body of evidence to support the concept that vitamin D enhances passive transport by increasing permeability of the mucosal cells to calcium. Two main approaches have been made: (1) the use of in vitro techniques under conditions (anaerobiosis, cold, and metabolic inhibitors) in which active transport is presumably inhibited; and (2) in vivo experiments using the flux ratio approach.

Harrison and his associates have used the former approach. In their first reports they demonstrated that vitamin D enhanced the mucosal to serosal transport in everted loops prepared from all segments of the rat intestine.[583,596] This enhanced transport was seen in the presence of potassium cyanide, under anaerobiosis, and at both 5°C and 25°C incubation temperatures (Table 2). Subsequent work from the same laboratory has confirmed these findings and contributed additional observations.[315,332,584,585,587] These include:

1. Demonstration of the vitamin D response in the rat in the presence of N-ethyl maleimide which blocks active transport of calcium, sodium, and associated water movements[584,585]

Table 3
EFFECT OF VITAMIN D ON CALCIUM ABSORPTION IN THE CHICKEN DUODENUM: FLUX RATIO METHOD

Infused Ca (m*M*)	Efflux, lumen to plasma (μmols/cm/hr)		Influx, plasma to lumen (μmols/cm/hr)		Flux ratio (efflux/influx)			
					Observed[a]		Theoretical[b]	
	−D[c]	+D[d]	−D[c]	+D[d]	−D[c]	+D[d]	−D[c]	+D[d]
1.3	0.22	0.47	0.14	0.53	1.6	0.9	0.5	0.5
2.7	0.37	0.82	0.19	0.60	1.9	1.4	1.1	1.0
5.2	0.72	1.54	0.24	0.52	3.0	3.0	1.7	1.6
26	2.43	4.08	0.71	1.40	3.4	2.9	9.1	7.0
135	5.6	15.5	3.0	5.3	2.4	2.9	41.2	43.2

Note: ^{47}Ca placed in ligated duodenum for 10 min for efflux determination; net flux was determined from ^{40}Ca movement; influx was derived by difference.

[a] Vitamin D treatment had no significant effect on observed flux ratios.
[b] Calculated from diffusion equation of Ussing;[387] the fact that the observed exceeded the theoretical flux ratios at 1.3 and 2.7 m*M* infused Ca was interpreted as evidence for active transport.
[c] −D: vitamin D-deficient chicks.
[d] +D: vitamin D-deficient chicks treated with vitamin D (500 IU orally) 24 hr prior to experiment.

From Wasserman, R. H. and Kallfelz, F. A., *Am. J. Physiol.*, 203, 221, 1962. With permission.

2. Absence of the response in rat intestinal preparations stripped of their mucosal epithelium[584]
3. Presence of the response in rat colon[332]
4. Presence of the response in the chicken intestine.[315]

The use of the flux ratio approach to demonstrate an effect of vitamin D on passive transport of calcium in both the chicken and the rat is largely attributable to Wasserman and his associates;[319] the data are presented in Figure 1, Chapter 5. The efflux (lumen to plasma) was measured by ^{47}Ca disappearance from the loop over a short time period of 10 min. The net calcium flux was determined from ^{40}Ca disappearance. The influx (plasma to lumen) was not specifically measured; it was derived from the difference between the efflux and the net flux. The most important observation was that vitamin D had no effect on the flux ratio (efflux/influx) over a range of intraluminal calcium concentrations between 1.3 and 135 m*M* (Table 3). Secondly, the vitamin increased the individual fluxes, notably the influx (plasma to lumen). This latter point was confirmed in a later publication with actual measurement of the influx (intravenous injection of ^{47}Ca) rather than by deriving it from the efflux and net flux data.[485] Subsequently, Wasserman et al.[305] measured flux ratios in the chick ileum and rat duodenum and have come to a similar conclusion: that vitamin D enhances calcium transport by increasing bidirectional permeability.

5. Vitamin D and Calcium Uptake

There is a considerable body of evidence to indicate that a specific step in the translocation of calcium from lumen to plasma involves the uptake and concentration of calcium in mucosal tissue. This uptake phenomenon was first studied by Schachter et al.[358,483] in vitro using slices of rat intestine; the technique was also used by Avioli[484] and by Ziporin et al.[357] Subsequent studies have employed different approaches; these include:

1. In vitro incubation of the everted gut sac with radiocalcium, followed by analysis of either the whole tissue,[301,338] mucosal scrapings,[301,342,343,353,485] or muscle layer[301,342,343]
2. In vitro incubation of isolated intestinal loops, either with radiocalcium[317,597] or with stable calcium,[344] followed by analysis of the whole tissue
3. In vitro incubation of a sheet of intestinal tissue in an apparatus which permitted exposure of only the mucosal side to the fluid containing radiocalcium[356,598]
4. In vitro cultures of embryonic chicken duodenum.[363,364,366,367,369,370]

Different conclusions have been drawn by different groups depending upon the approach used. Some claim that this uptake phenomenon is partially energy-dependent.[356,358,359,483] However, the energy-dependence of the uptake step has not been emphasized in subsequent publications from Schachter's group[342,343] in which mucosal scrapings rather than whole tissue were analyzed. Figure 6 in chapter 5 is taken from the work of Schachter et al.[342] and diagrammatically represents their later findings. Other investigators, who also separated mucosal epithelial uptake from whole tissue uptake, support the concept that calcium uptake by mucosal epithelium, although apparently "uphill" in terms of *total* calcium concentration, is not energy dependent.[301,353,485,486]

Two questions immediately present themselves. First, does vitamin D influence this uptake of calcium by the mucosal epithelium? Secondly, what is the chemical state of the calcium taken up by the mucosa? Most investigators agree that vitamin D enhances calcium uptake by intestinal tissue.[301,343,353,356,358,363,364,366,367,369,370,483,485,486] These include those who isolated and measured uptake in mucosal epithelium following incubation of the whole tissue with radiocalcium. Only in those studies in which mucosal cells were isolated first and then incubated with radiocalcium was there no effect of vitamin D on calcium uptake.[301,359]

With respect to the second question it is obvious that the calcium taken up by the mucosal epithelium cannot be in the ionic form. First, such concentrations would be deleterious to the integrity of the cell. Secondly, if this calcium were ionic it would have to be transported against the gradient and therefore would require energy but, as discussed before, the consensus is that the uptake process is not dependent upon energy. It may be assumed then that most of this calcium pool is chemically bound, perhaps to calcium-binding protein, which itself is increased as a result of vitamin D action (following in this Section).

6. *Vitamin D and Protein Synthesis*

That protein synthesis is a vital step in the mechanism of action of vitamin D on the intestine has been demonstrated with the aid of actinomycin D. One of the main pharmacodynamic actions of actinomycin D is to inhibit protein synthesis by preventing DNA-directed mRNA synthesis in the nucleus. It has been repeatedly shown that this agent will inhibit the action of vitamin D on calcium transport or uptake by the intestine of both the rat[390,396,585,590,591,599,600] and the chicken.[364,366,368,474,601–604] Such observations support only the hypothesis that vitamin D stimulates protein synthesis in the mucosal epithelial cells as a prerequisite to enhancing calcium absorption; they by no means prove it.

These findings led to further studies aimed at demonstrating that vitamin D has a primary action on the nucleus of the intestinal mucosal cell. First, it was shown that vitamin D enhanced the incorporation of ^{3}H-orotic acid into the nuclear RNA of intestinal mucosa of the rat[396,603,605–607] and that actinomycin D inhibited this incorporation.[607] Secondly, it was observed that in both rats and chickens the nucleus of the intestinal mucosal cell is a major intracellular site of accumulation of vitamin D metabolites following administration of a *physiological* dose (10 IU) of ^{3}H-labeled vitamin D.[4,396,604,608,609]

In 1971, 1,25-dihydroxyvitamin D_3 was isolated and identified as the most active metabolite of vitamin D_3 with respect to its action in the intestinal transport of calcium (see Chapter 2). It was natural, then, that subsequent research in this area focused on the relationship between 1,25-dihydroxyvitamin D_3 and protein synthesis rather than on the prohormone. It is now accepted that the secosteroid 1,25-dihydroxyvitamin D_3 binds to a cytosolic receptor and the secosteroid-receptor complex moves to the nucleus where DNA-directed mRNA synthesis is initiated. The mRNA or mRNAs move to the endoplasmic reticulum where polyribosomal translation and protein synthesis is initiated. It is assumed that the protein or proteins so synthesized are directly involved in calcium transport and that calcium-binding protein is one such protein. The evidence supporting this concept embraces the following observations. A receptor preparation, which exhibits high-affinity binding characteristics for 1,25-dihydroxyvitamin D_3, has been isolated from the cytoplasm of intestinal mucosal cells of the chicken,[121,149,150,156,610,611] of the rat,[612] and of Japanese quail.[151] Dissociation constants for the secosteroid-receptor complex have been reported as 37 p*M*[121] and 71 p*M*[152] in the chicken and as 730 p*M*[151] in the Japanese quail. The intestinal cytosolic receptor has a Svedberg constant of 3.7 S and binds to nuclear chromatin at 37°C but not at 4°C. The transfer of the receptor to nuclear chromatin is specific for intestinal cytosol; cytosolic preparations from other tissues will not so transfer. The cytosolic protein is highly specific for 1,25-dihydroxyvitamin D_3 in the chicken,[439,613] as indicated in Figure 2, in the rat,[612] and in the Japanese quail.[151] More recently, Spencer et al.[475] have demonstrated that administration of 1,25-dihydroxyvitamin D_3 to vitamin D-deficient chickens leads to the production of a mRNA which has the ability to code specifically for calcium-binding protein in the cell-free, wheat-germ system.

7. *Vitamin D and Calcium-Binding Protein*

It is well established that vitamin D stimulates the formation of calcium-binding protein in the intestine of the chicken,[308,311,314,318,353,363–370,407,408,461,465,424,474,475,614] of the rat,[314,326,592,615] and of the dog.[447] The chicken data of Spencer et al.[424] are presented in Figure 4, Chapter 5. As mentioned above, 1,25-dihydroxyvitamin D_3 administration leads to the appearance of a mRNA which is specific for calcium-binding protein.[475]

8. *Vitamin D and Calcium-Dependent Adenosine Triphosphatase*

A strong case exists for the association of certain adenosine triphosphatases (ATPases) with the phenomenon of cation transport across membranes.[616] The association between sodium-potassium transport and a particular magnesium-dependent, sodium-potassium-activated, ouabain-sensitive ATPase (transport-ATPase) has been delineated to the greatest extent.

Attempts to link gut transport of calcium to a calcium-ATPase have been reported from several laboratories. The first reports came from DeLuca and his associates,[396–400] who claimed that a calcium-ATPase was present in the proximal small intestine of both the chicken and the rat, and that the levels of intestinal

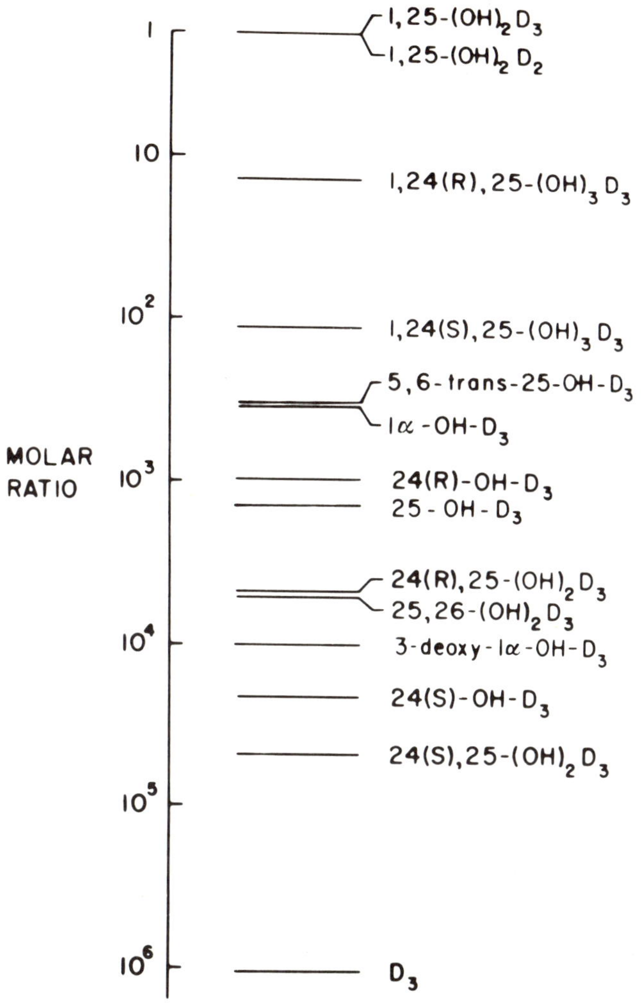

FIGURE 2. Diagrammatic representation of the binding affinity of chick intestinal cytosol for the various vitamin D metabolites and analogs. In this study, ^{3}H-labeled 1,25-dihydroxyvitamin D_3 in approximately saturating amounts was added to chick intestinal cytosol 3.7S receptor. Varying amounts of unlabeled metabolite or analog were added, and, following incubation, the protein-bound and -free tritium were separated. The molar ratio of unlabeled metabolite or analog to the labeled 1,25-dihydroxyvitamin D_3 required for 50% displacement of the label from the receptor was calculated and is plotted. Note that 1,25-dihydroxyvitamin D_2 and 1,25-dihydroxyvitamin D_3 are equally competent, whereas the nearest other competitor is 1,24(R),25-trihydroxyvitamin D_3. Note that approximately 1000-fold excess of 25-hydroxyvitamin D_3 is required to product a 50% displacement. (From DeLuca, H. F., *Vitamin D. Metabolism and Function*, Springer-Verlag, New York, 1979. With permission.)

calcium-ATPase were increased by administration of vitamin D_3. These findings have been confirmed in the rat,[617–619] and in the chicken.[620] However, Wasserman's group has failed to show any effects on intestinal calcium-ATPase levels in the chicken following treatments (vitamin D, low-calcium diet) which increased calcium absorption, calcium-binding protein levels, and certain other enzymatic activities.[401] The evidence marshalled by Melancon and DeLuca[400] in support of a role for calcium-ATPase in gut transport of calcium in the chicken is impressive. The enzyme was located in the mucosal brush border and the time-course of the increase in calcium absorption and calcium-ATPase levels following vitamin D_3 was similar. The latter finding is in sharp contrast to the experience of DeLuca's group with the time-course of calcium-binding protein levels.[314,396]

9. Vitamin D and Adenosine 3′,5′-Cyclic Monophosphate

Reports have appeared linking intestinal calcium absorption with adenosine 3′, 5′-cyclic monophosphate (cAMP). Neville and Holdsworth[316] noted that vitamin D increased adenylate cyclase activity in the intestine of the chicken. They further reported that the dibutyryl derivative of cAMP (DB-cAMP) increased calcium transport both in vivo from ligated ileal loops and in vitro using everted ileal sacs. In the latter experiments, DB-cAMP was added in vitro and caused the effect only in sacs removed from rachitic chicks. Neville and Holdsworth suggested that cAMP is the second messenger through which vitamin D acts. Harrison and Harrison[587] studied the effects of DB-cAMP on calcium absorption in a different species, the rat, and came to somewhat different conclusions. They were able to demonstrate an enhancement of passive transport of calcium by the rat duodenum but, in contrast to the experience of Neville and Holdsworth[316] in the chicken, they observed this effect only in the vitamin D-replete animal. No effect of DB-cAMP was seen in the jejunum. Harrison and Harrison[587] concluded that the effect of cAMP is dependent upon a vitamin D-induced factor, and suggested that these observations may have more relevance to the mechanism of the action of parathyroid hormone on calcium absorption. Delling et al.[621] injected DB-cAMP into both intact and parathyroidectomized rats and found that ^{47}Ca retention, after feeding 1 g of food labeled with ^{47}Ca, was increased by the treatment. Corradino[622] reported that DB-cAMP increased calcium uptake and transport in embryonic chicken intestine organ cultures. In addition, he found that both vitamin D_3 and 1,25-dihydroxyvitamin D_3 increased the intestinal content of cAMP as well as that of calcium-binding protein. There has been little additional work of note in this area so that until more information is available, it is hazardous to offer any firm conclusions concerning the role of cAMP in vitamin D-induced gut calcium transport.

10. Effects of Metabolites other than 1,25-Dihydroxyvitamin D_3

The hormonal and most potent form of vitamin D_3 is the dihydroxylated renal metabolite, 1,25-dihydroxyvitamin D_3. Do the other metabolites of vitamin D_3, such as the monohydroxylated metabolite 25-hydroxyvitamin D_3, the dihydroxylated metabolites 24,25-dihydroxyvitamin D_3 and 25,26-dihydroxyvitamin D_3, and the trihydroxy derivative 1,24,25-trihydroxyvitamin D_3, have any *direct* effect on gut calcium transport? Some of these derivatives have been found to circulate at a much higher level than that of 1,25-dihydroxyvitamin D (Table 1, Chapter 2). When this fact is taken into consideration, is it possible that even though they are less potent than 1,25-dihydroxyvitamin D_3, they may exert physiological effects on the intestinal absorption of calcium?

The effectiveness of 24,25-dihydroxyvitamin D_3, which circulates in man at concentrations of 1 to 5 ng/nℓ (Table 1, Chapter 2), in stimulating gut calcium transport has been studied in the rat,[52,623–625] in the chicken,[626] and in uremic man.[627] When injected into the *intact* animal, the natural isomer 24R,25-dihydroxyvitamin D_3 stimulates transport of calcium. This has been demonstrated in the rat duodenum using either the everted sac preparation[52,623,624] or the flux ratio method,[623] both of which measure active transport. It has also been observed in the chicken duodenum using the *in situ* ligated loop approach.[626] Walling et al.[625] and Miravet et al.[623] examined the response to the dihydroxy derivative in the *nephrectomized* rat and found that the response was completely abolished by the surgery. They concluded that 24,25-dihydroxyvitamin D_3 per se is inactive with respect to gut calcium transport and must be converted first to the trihydroxy metabolite, 1,24,25-trihydroxyvitamin D_3, by the renal 1-hydroxylase enzyme to render it active. The observation that 24,25-dihydroxyvitamin D_3 has little or no activity in uremic man supports this contention.[627]

The trihydroxy metabolite, 1,24,25-trihydroxyvitamin D_3, on the other hand, appears to possess inherent activity with respect to stimulating active transport of calcium in the duodenum of the rat. The response was seen both in intact[59,625] and in nephrectomized rats;[625] the trihydroxy metabolite was found to be less potent than 1,25-dihydroxyvitamin D_3[59].

The dihydroxy metabolite 25,26-dihydroxyvitamin D_3, when injected into intact rats also stimulates active transport of calcium by the rat duodenum.[52,623] Nephrectomy abolishes this response,[623] indicating that 1-hydroxylation is necessary for activation of 25,26-dihydroxyvitamin D_3.

It is interesting to compare the inherent biological activities of the various metabolites with their respective affinities for the intestinal cystolic receptor presented in Figure 2. Whereas 1,25-dihydroxyvitamin D_3 and 1,24R,25-trihydroxyvitamin D_3 have high affinities, 24R,25-dihydroxyvitamin D_3 and 25,26-dihydroxyvitamin D_3 have much lower affinities which are close to each other in value.

11. Summary of Vitamin D Mechanism

The following presents a summary of the action of vitamin D on intestinal absorption of calcium. It represents a simplification of the problem and ignores some findings which remain inadequately confirmed or in a state of confusion. For a more extensive review of the subject the reader is referred to the review of DeLuca.[575]

Vitamin D_3, through its active renal metabolite 1,25-dihydroxyvitamin D_3, has the following actions on the gut in facilitating the translocation of calcium from intestinal lumen to plasma:

1. 1,25-Dihydroxyvitamin D_3 enters the intestinal mucosal cell, presumably by passive diffusion, and binds to the cytosolic receptor (3 to 4 S).
2. The secosteroid-receptor complex is translocated to the nucleus where it binds to nuclear chromatin and initiates DNA-directed synthesis of one or more mRNAs which are coded for the synthesis of a protein or proteins associated with calcium transport.
3. Following transcription the mRNAs move out of the nucleus to the free polyribosomes of the cytoplasm where the synthesis of at least one protein associated with calcium transport, namely calcium-binding protein, is initiated.
4. The transport protein or proteins so synthesized gravitate to the brush border of the cell where they are involved in calcium uptake and intracellular translocation of calcium to the basal-lateral membrane where calcium is transported out of the cell by an active process.
5. In addition, 1,25-dihydroxyvitamin D_3 increases, by an unknown mechanism,

the bidirectional permeability of intestinal mucosal epithelial cells in all segments of the small intestine by a passive process not requiring energy.

6. This increase in permeability *indirectly* increases the unidirectionally oriented (lumen to plasma) and the basal-laterally located active transport system.

Many of these actions of vitamin D are depicted in Figure 5, Chapter 5.

II. PARATHYROID HORMONE

Historically, it was always assumed that the parathyroid glands had no direct influence on calcium absorption from the intestine.[507] Statements to this effect were made in the review literature in the mid-1950s.[528,532] Today it is generally recognized that parathyroid hormone does exercise some influence on calcium absorption; the disagreement is over the degree and importance of its *direct* influence. For decades since its discovery in 1925 parathyroid hormone was available only in very crude preparations. The commercially available pharmaceutical product, Parathyroid Injection, U.S.P. (100 USP units/mℓ), more often than not was used as a source of the hormone; this preparation in terms of units/mg protein was less than 1% pure. For this and other reasons many early investigators often preferred to rely on the endocrinectomy approach, using either parathyroidectomy or the less satisfactory thyroparathyroidectomy. The latter was usually selected in those species, such as the dog, where removal of the parathyroid glands only is a more difficult surgical procedure. More recently, pure parathyroid hormone, either as the intact 84-amino acid polypeptide isolated from natural, usually bovine, sources or as the synthetic 1–34 N-terminal polypeptide, has been available from commercial sources. Unfortunately, neither of these pure forms is inexpensive.

The following discussion will outline the relationships between parathyroidectomy, parathyroid hormone, vitamin D, and intestinal absorption of calcium. The rapid developments in our understanding of vitamin D metabolism which occurred over the past decade, coupled with the fact that parathyroid hormone exercises some control over vitamin D metabolism, have necessitated a reevaluation of our concept of the relationship between parathyroid hormone and intestinal absorption of calcium. In addition, the recent confirmation of Pang and his associates[628,629] of the original observations of Charbon[630–634] that parathyroid hormone has potent vasoactive properties which influence hemodynamics, requires consideration of the possibility that parathyroid hormone may influence gut calcium absorption by influencing blood flow through the intestine. In spite of this new knowledge, particularly in vitamin D metabolism, there remain certain enigmatic areas. One such area is the role of parathyroid hormone in the gut calcium response to calcium deprivation.

A. Parathyroidectomy and Calcium Absorption

A survey of the literature reveals a degree of confusion concerning the effects of parathyroidectomy on calcium absorption by the small intestine. The discrepancies do not appear to have their origins either in the species or in the techniques used. For example, from studies using the everted gut sac of the rat there have emanated reports of parathyroidectomy (or thyroparathyroidectomy) leading both to a decrease in calcium absorption[324,325,337,352] and to no effect.[304,331,334,350] Similar discrepancies exist in those studies using the balance method in the rat. Aubert et al.,[635] Milhaud and Moukhtar,[636] and Shah and Draper[280] found decreased calcium absorption following parathyroidectomy (or thyroparathyroidectomy), whereas Sammon et al.,[281] Kemm,[518] Clark and Rivera-Cordero,[637] and Clark[544] found no consistent effects.

The in vivo ligated loop method in the rat has also led to discordant findings. Wasserman and Comar[304] and Cramer et al.[638] were not able to demonstrate an effect of parathyroidectomy on calcium absorption. Winter et al.[307] obtained different effects depending upon the dietary levels of calcium, while Talmage and Elliott[639] and Kodicek et al.[640] reported a fall in calcium absorption. Cramer et al.[638] studied the absorption of oral dose of ^{45}Ca in rats and found that it was decreased by thryroparathyroidectomy, whereas Larsson and Ahlgren[641] using a similar approach found no such response. Other species have been studied less thoroughly. Nelson et al.[642] claimed no effect of thyroparathyroidectomy in the sheep using the balance technique although the data are not clear cut. On the other hand, both the dog[286] and the goat[643] respond to thyroparathyroidectomy by a decrease in calcium absorption. In man, hypoparathyroid patients have decreased calcium absorption relative to normal subjects[382] and parathyroidectomy in patients with primary hyperparathyroidism resulted in a significant lowering of the elevated rate of intestinal calcium transport.[644]

Is it possible to bring a semblance of order to these apparently discordant findings? The apparent chaos is not due to differences between parathyroidectomy and thyroparathyroidectomy as no correlation can be found in these terms. The reports emanating from our own laboratory[231,520,521] pointed in the direction of a possible explanation. The relevant data are summarized in Table 4. First, parathyroidectomy had no effect on gut calcium absorption if the rats were maintained on a diet containing adequate calcium (1.5%). This was the finding whether the rats were maintained on this diet for 7 or for 21 days, or whether the technique used to measure gut transport was the everted duodenal sac or the *in situ* ligated loop. Secondly, in those rats placed on a low calcium (0.01%) diet the effect of parathyroidectomy was dependent upon the number of days on the diet. At 7 days, parathyroidectomy resulted in a significant fall in gut calcium transport, whereas at 21 days no such response was observed. At 14 days Pento et al.[231] found the response to be equivocal (data not shown in Table 4).

If all the rat studies mentioned above, with only five exceptions,[281,352,638–640] are arranged in descending order of calcium content of the diet a pattern develops (Table 5). A sharp division takes place at about 0.65% Ca; all studies using dietary calcium levels above this value report no significant effect of parathyroidectomy on calcium absorption by the intestine. The studies using diets below 0.65% Ca are not as clear-cut. However, if, in those studies using either the ligated loop or duodenal sac, a separation is made depending upon the length of time on the special diet, a pattern again develops. If, guided by the experience of Pento et al.,[231] we divide the low-calcium diet series (less than 0.65% Ca) into two categories — less than or greater than 2 weeks of dietary treatment, remembering that Pento et al.[231] found the data at 2 weeks to be equivocal — we find significant effects of parathyroidectomy in short-term* and no effects in the long-term dietary treatment. At least this concept reconciles the negative data of Wasserman and Comar,[304] which have often been explained by others in terms of the acuteness of the parathyroidectomy (24 hr) who at the same time ignored the fact that a positive effect was seen by Rasmussen[324] only 4 hr after. It may be concluded from the above discussion that, in order to demonstrate an effect of parathyroidectomy on calcium absorption from the rat intestine with either the ligated loop or duodenal sac, certain conditions must be met. The rats must be placed on a diet which is moderately or markedly low in

* The one exception is that of Winter et al.[307] who report a significant effect in one experiment and no effect in a second experiment at the same level of dietary calcium (0.6%) where, close to the crossover point, a variable response might be expected.

Table 4
EFFECTS OF PARATHYROIDECTOMY ON DUODENAL CALCIUM TRANSPORT[231]

Experiments	Surgical[a] status	Diet	Number of rats	Body Weight (final) (g)	Plasma Ca (mg/dℓ)	In vitro gut sac (S/M ratio)	*In situ* ligated duodenal loop: Plasma ^{45}Ca (cpm)	*In situ* ligated duodenal loop: Absorption (%)
7-Day Adaptation Period								
TP111[b,c]	Sham	HCD	10	70	11.3 ± 0.14	6.2 ± 0.90		
	Sham	LCD	10	68	11.3 ± 0.10	12.5 ± 0.86[d]		
	PTX	HCD	9	61	6.1 ± 0.28	5.2 ± 0.75		
	PTX	LCD	10	44[e]	5.9 ± 0.14	5.3 ± 0.47		
PT2[f,g]	Sham	HCD	8	110	9.8 ± 0.20		6,217 ± 518	35.9 ± 1.5
	Sham	LCD	8	110	9.7 ± 0.30		11,030 ± 939[e]	54.6 ± 5.1[d]
	PTX	HCD	8	111	5.1 ± 0.10		7,231 ± 802	44.7 ± 3.8
	PTX	LCD	8	109	5.7 ± 0.10		9,066 ± 798	54.6 ± 5.5
21-Day Adaptation Period								
V170[f,g]	Sham	HCD	9	130	9.5 ± 0.15		6,936 ± 346	67.2 ± 0.9
	Sham	LCD	10	136	9.5 ± 0.11		14,924 ± 726[e]	79.4 ± 2.1[e]
	PTX	HCD	8	133	5.2 ± 0.10		5,318 ± 715	66.8 ± 1.2
	PTX	LCD	9	128	5.4 ± 0.14		13,294 ± 1,299[e]	75.4 ± 1.9[e]

Note: Values in the last four columns are means ± S.E.; S/M ratio: serosal ^{45}Ca/mucosal ^{45}Ca; LCD: low-Ca diet containing 0.01% Ca; HCD: high-Ca (or normal) diet containing 1.54% Ca as $CaCO_3$ added to LCD.

[a] Sham: sham operated at time of PTX; PTX, parathyroidectomized 3 days prior to starting adaptation period.
[b] The results of *experiment TP111* are a combination of two individual experiments.
[c] *Ad libitum* feeding routine.
[d] $P < 0.01$.
[e] $P < 0.001$, when compared with HCD control in surgically similar rats.
[f] Quad-feeding: all four groups pair-fed to PTX-LCD group as pacesetter.
[g] Ca (0.2%) added to drinking water of the HCD groups as Ca lactate.

Table 5
RELATIONSHIP BETWEEN DIETARY CALCIUM LEVEL AND EFFECT OF PARATHYROIDECTOMY (PTX) OR THYROPARATHYROIDECTOMY (TPTX) ON CALCIUM ABSORPTION

Dietary Ca (%)	Technique	Parameter	Response[a] *p* level	Ref.
		High Ca Series		
2.0	In vivo ligated loop	% absorbed	N.S.	304
2.0	In vitro duodenal sac	S/M	N.S.	304
1.5	In vitro duodenal sac	S/M	N.S.	231
1.5	In vivo ligated loop	% absorbed	N.S.	231
1.2	In vitro duodenal sac	S/M	N.S.	334
1.2	Balance method	v_a	N.S.	280
0.8	Balance method	a	N.S.	544
0.76	In vitro duodenal sac	S/M	N.S.	331
0.68	In vitro duodenal sac	S/M	N.S.	350
		Low Ca Series: Short-Term Studies[b]		
0.6	In vivo ligated loop	% absorbed	N.S.	307
0.6	In vivo ligated loop	% absorbed	<0.001	307
0.6	Balance method	v_a or a	<0.001	415
0.6	Balance method	v_a	<0.001	280
0.54	In vitro duodenal sac	S/M	<0.025	337
0.44	Balance method	a	<0.001	635
0.3	Balance method	v_a	<0.001	280
0.1	In vivo ligated loop	% absorbed	<0.001	307
0.01	In vivo ligated loop	% absorbed	<0.01	231
0.01	In vitro duodenal sac	S/M	<0.05	231
Low	In vitro duodenal sac	S/M	<0.001	324
		Low Ca Series: Long-Term Studies[c]		
0.4	In vivo ligated loop	% absorbed	N.S.	638
0.2	In vivo ligated loop	% absorbed	N.S.	304
0.2	In vitro duodenal sac	S/M	N.S.	304
0.02	In vitro duodenal sac	S/M	N.S.	334
0.01	In vivo ligated loop	% absorbed	N.S.	231

Note: N.S.: not significant ($p > 0.05$); S/M: serosal/mucosal ratio; v_a: amount absorbed; a: v_a/dietary intake (v_i)

[a] Fall in Ca absorption following PTX on TPTX.
[b] Rats were 2 weeks or less on diet.
[c] Rats were 2 weeks or more on diet.

calcium and ideally they should be on this diet for no more than 7 days, assuming that the rats were maintained previously on a normal commercial laboratory chow which usually contains more than 1.0% Ca. Under the right conditions there appears to be no doubt that parathyroidectomy results in a suppression of calcium absorption from the intestine.

A word about the exceptions and why they were eliminated from Table 5: Cramer et al.,[638] Kodicek et al.,[640] Schachter,[352] and Talmage and Elliott[639] did not report their dietary calcium levels.* Only the data of Sammon et al.[281] cannot be fitted into the scheme; no explanation can be offered. It is obvious that in presenting this simplified scheme only the dietary calcium level has been taken into consideration. Dietary phosphorus level is of significance too and therefore caution must be exercised in extrapolating this scheme too indiscriminately.

If the pattern presented in Table 5 is accepted there is a logical explanation for it: that the dietary calcium level influences parathyroid hormone secretion rate, such that the higher the dietary calcium level the lower will be the plasma parathyroid hormone concentration. If this is so then one would expect that at high dietary calcium levels the difference between plasma parathyroid hormone levels of the intact and parathyroidectomized rats would be negligible, at least with respect to the gut calcium response. At low dietary calcium levels the difference is presumably great enough to be reflected in the gut response.

B. Parathyroid Hormone and Calcium Absorption

Since Rasmussen's first report of a suppressing effect of parathyroidectomy on active transport of calcium in the everted duodenal sac of the rat,[324] there have been several attempts to demonstrate an enhancing effect of parathyroid hormone on gut calcium transport in this species. The majority of the studies had a successful outcome.[332,638,645–647] Nevertheless, a significant number of other investigators have reported either no response,[330] equivocal responses,[352] or even a decrease in calcium absorption.[637] Harrison and Harrison[332] used the commercially available impure parathyroid extract at a subcutaneous dose of 1000 USP units/kg 5 hr before the intestines were removed for preparation of everted duodenal sacs. In thyroparathyroidectomized rats the hormone increased the S/M ratios significantly back to control levels. However, no effect was seen in intact rats. Addition of parathyroid extract in vitro had no effect, confirming the former observation of Rasmussen.[324] Robinson et al.[645] found highly significant increases in calcium absorption measured by the ligated loop technique in parathyroidectomized rats following administration of parathyroid hormone. This study is important for two reasons. First, a highly purified preparation (900 USP units/mg) of parathyroid hormone was used; it was administered subcutaneously in a total dose of 600 USP units in eight divided doses over a period of 48 hr. Secondly, all segments of the small intestine were studied; all responded, but the jejunum gave the greatest response. This latter point is interesting in view of the fact that Birge et al.[382] concluded that in humans the more distal segments of the small intestine were more sensitive to controlling factors such as parathyroid hormone. In an earlier study Cramer et al.,[638] using the balance method, observed a definite enhancement of calcium absorption following a subcutaneous injection of 50 USP units per rat twice daily for 3 days. Birge et al.[647] reported that injection of 30 USP units of commercial parathyroid extract into parathyroidectomized rats 4 hr prior to removal of the duodenum, enhanced the release of ^{45}Ca from mucosal cells prepared from the gut sample and prelabeled with ^{45}Ca. They concluded that parathyroid hormone stimulates a sodium-dependent mechanism of calcium transport across the basal-lateral membranes. Parsons et al.,[646] using a double isotope method (oral ^{47}Ca and intravenous ^{45}Ca), a purified preparation of bovine parathyroid hormone (200 USP units subcutaneously and daily for 3 days) enhanced gut calcium absorption in the rat. Schachter[352] obtained equivocal results after par-

* In the studies of Cramer et al.[638] and of Schachter,[352] stock diets of unstated calcium content were used in the relevant experiments.

athyroid extract treatment. In everted gut preparations removed from hypophysectomized rats, Finkelstein and Schachter[330] have found no response to injection of parathyroid extract at a subcutaneous dose of 30 USP units per rat given daily for 7 days prior to the experiment. Clark and Rivera-Cordero,[637] using the balance method, found that injection of 20 to 80 USP units of a commercial parathyroid extract decreased calcium absorption in parathyroidectomized rats.

There have been several attempts to demonstrate an effect of parathyroid hormone on intestinal absorption of calcium in the human. Birge et al.[382] used a partially purified preparation of parathyroid hormone and a kinetic approach. Although no response was seen following a 4-hr infusion of 400 USP units they did observe a twofold increase in calcium absorption following treatment with 200 USP units in gelatin given intramuscularly twice daily over a 3-week period. In addition, they found that calcium absorption was greatly enhanced in hyperparathyroid patients. Wensel et al.[384] found no effect in humans with a low dose of parathyroid extract (a single dose of 120 to 200 USP units) given intravenously, whereas Wills et al.[648] reported positive effects with higher doses (400 USP units daily for 3 to 4 days) of commercial parathyroid extract.

It thus appears that parathyroid hormone does have a definite effect opposite to that of parathyroidectomy on intestinal transport of calcium. It does not seem to be consistently observable and its physiological importance may be questioned. Whether or not parathyroid hormone acts directly or indirectly on the gut will be discussed next.

C. Mechanism of Action of Parathyroid Hormone on Calcium Absorption

Prior to the explosive developments in vitamin D research during the past decade, there was an interest in the question of the vitamin D dependency of parathyroid hormonal action on gut calcium absorption. Toverud[649] used the balance method and found that the regulatory effect of parathyroid hormone on gut calcium transport was independent of vitamin D. Parathyroidectomy and treatment of parathyroidectomized rats with parathyroid extract resulted in significant responses in the face of vitamin D deficiency. In contrast to this observation Dowdle et al.[329] and Winter et al.,[307] using in vitro and in vivo methods, respectively, found no effect of parathyroidectomy on calcium in the vitamin D-deficient rat.

This question has been reinvestigated recently in the light of our recognition of the renal-vitamin D endocrine system. Parathyroid hormone is a known regulator of this system, stimulating 1,25-dihydroxyvitamin D_3 production (see Chapter 4.III.A). Is the action of parathyroid hormone on intestinal absorption of calcium entirely indirect, mediated by the release of 1,25-dihydroxyvitamin D_3 from the kidney? Garabedian et al.[650] examined this specific question in the rat. A hypercalcemic dose of a commercial parathyroid extract failed to increase active transport of calcium as measured by an everted duodenal sac when administered to thyroparathyroidectomized, nephrectomized rats. Administration of 1,25-dihydroxyvitamin D_3 to this animal preparation had its usual marked stimulatory effect on active transport of calcium. These authors concluded that the findings strongly support the concept that parathyroid hormone has no direct action on *duodenal* calcium transport. The reports of Bonjour et al.[513] and of Oswald and Binswanger[325] are in accord with this conclusion; the former used the diphosphonate, ethane-1-hydroxy-1,1-diphosphonate (EHDP), and the latter used nephrectomy to eliminate 1,25-dihydroxyvitamin D_3 involvement. Nevertheless, Oswald and Binswanger[325] concluded that parathyroid hormone does have a direct effect on calcium transport in the *ileum* in contrast to its lack of a direct effect on the upper part of the small intestine. The organ culture preparation of the embryonic chicken duodenum fails to respond directly to parathyroid hormone.[651]

In summary, it appears that parathyroid hormone has no direct effect on the *duodenal* absorption of calcium in the rat. Its effect, when observed, is most likely mediated through the stimulation of 1,25-dihydroxyvitamin D_3 production by the kidney. There is an unconfirmed report that parathyroid hormone might have a direct effect on *ileal* transport of calcium.

III. CALCITONIN

Calcitonin has no consistent acute effects on gut calcium transport. The early studies in this area were indirect. Hirsch and his associates observed that the hypocalcemic response to a single injection of calcitonin in the rat was not affected if the rat had been previously subjected to a low calcium diet[652] or to a complete removal of the gastrointestinal tract;[653] they concluded that the gut was not involved in the response. Kenny and Heiskell[654] came to a similar conclusion after showing that fasting for 48 hr did not impair the response. Wase et al.[655] found that repeated administration of calcitonin to intact rats increased the positive calcium balance significantly. Interpretation of these data is not simple. The authors claim that this response is largely due to decreased endogenous calcium excretion; a single dose of calcitonin had no effect on the absorption of an oral dose of ^{45}Ca.

Subsequent reports have been concerned more directly with gut calcium transport, with the almost consistent finding of no acute effect of calcitonin on this parameter. The negative findings in the rat have included the use of

1. Perfusion of an isolated loop in vivo and the determination of flux ratios[298,656]
2. In vivo ligated loops in parathyroidectomized rats with and without parathyroid hormone treatment[645]
3. Balance method coupled with radiocalcium techniques[636]
4. Everted duodenal sacs[331,520]
5. Disappearance of ^{45}Ca from the gastrointestinal tract 4 hr following administration of ^{45}Ca by stomach tube[657]
6. Flux measurement in vitro using the Ussing and Zerahn technique.[658]

In one rat study, purified porcine calcitonin was found to inhibit calcium transport (measured during in vitro perfusion of the small intestine) when the hormone was infused into the superior mesenteric artery at low doses (10 MRC m units). At high doses (500 MRC m units) calcium transport was enhanced.[526] The inhibitory response to calcitonin was not observed in vitamin D-deficient rats.

Negative responses of gut calcium transport to calcitonin have been observed in the dog using Thiry-Vella loop preparations[292,659] and in the rabbit using flux techniques.[660] A study of *acute* injections of calcitonin in the sheep resulted in equivocal data.[661] Chronic administration of calcitonin in the sheep results in a definite fall in calcium absorption within 2 or 3 days.[662]

IV. GLUCOCORTICOIDS

It has been consistently reported, with few exceptions, that glucocorticoids, directly or indirectly, inhibit the intestinal transport of calcium.

Divergence of opinion has developed over the question whether this response represents a direct or indirect effect of the adrenomimetic steroids. In other words, do glucocorticoids effect this response *indirectly* by affecting either the production of 1,25-dihydroxyvitamin D_3 or its availability at the intestinal site of action, or do they act *directly* by inhibiting calcium transport across the intestinal wall with or without the mediation of vitamin D?

The majority of studies which have examined this question favor an inhibitory action of glucocorticoids which is independent of any possible indirect effects of the adrenomimetic steroids on vitamin D metabolism in at least three species: the rat,[258,663–665] the chicken,[366] and the pig.[666] Two reports in man suggest that the response to glucocorticoids is indirect, being mediated by effects on vitamin D metabolism.[667,668] This conclusion was also reached by Sallis and Holdsworth[597] using the chicken prior to the discovery of the renal-vitamin D endocrine system.

The overwhelming evidence in favor of an inhibitory effect of glucocorticoids on gut calcium transport has been assembled largely in the rat,[258,330,348,349,583,663–665,669] but studies in other species such as the chicken,[366,597] the pig,[666] and man,[667] have also contributed to the evidence. These studies have used a variety of approaches. The latter have included *in situ* perfusion of the rat small intestine,[665] the everted duodenal sac of the rat,[258,669] flux ratio technique in the rat,[664] in vivo double isotope ($^{45}Ca/^{47}Ca$) technique in the pig[666] and in man,[667] the *in situ* ligated loop of the chicken,[597] and calcium uptake in embryonic chicken duodenum maintained in organ culture.[366]

A few studies found no effect of the glucocorticoids on intestinal absorption of calcium in the rat; techniques used included the *in situ* ligated loop,[306] the balance method,[349] and the absorption of an oral dose of ^{45}Ca.[670]

V. THYROID HORMONES

Most of the earlier studies of thyroid dysfunction in man, particularly in cases of hyperthyroidism, had led to the conclusion that the iodinated thyroid hormones, thyroxine (T_4) and triiodothyronine (T_3), depress calcium absorption from the intestine.[552] During the 1960s this relationship received greater attention in experimental animals with very clear-cut results. The thyroid hormones definitely suppress calcium absorption from the intestine of the rat. The relevant studies include

1. Suppression of active transport in the everted duodenal sac following subcutaneous administration of either thyroid-stimulating hormone (TSH) at a dose of 1 USP unit/day for 2 weeks, or triiodothyronine at a dose of 10 mg/day for either 7, 14, or 28 days[671]
2. Suppression of both active and passive transport in the everted duodenal, jejunal, or ileal sac following subcutaneous administration of thyroxine at a dose of 1 mg/kg daily for 7 days[339]
3. Suppression of active transport in the everted duodenal sac removed from hypophysectomized rats after subcutaneous treatment with thyroxine at a dose of 10 mg daily for 6 days[330]
4. Suppression of calcium absorption as measured by the balance method after addition of thyroxine to the diet at a concentration of 0.008%.[546]

The suppression was immediate (1 day) and showed no evidence of escape even after 98 days of treatment.[671]

The effects of the thyroid hormones have been studied in other species. The calcium balance data of Jones et al.[672] in human hypothyroid and hyperthyroid patients treated with triiodothyronine and propylthiouracil, respectively, are in agreement with the rat data. Propylthiouracil given to hyperthyroid patients moved them from negative to positive balances, while triiodothyronine treatment of hypothyroid individuals moved the balances in the opposite direction. In goats, on the other hand, replacement with thyroxine (1 mg/day or 5 mg/week intramuscularly in arachis oil) had no effect on calcium absorption following an oral dose of ^{45}Ca in either thyroparathyroidectomized or thyroidectomized animals.[643] In addition, no effect was seen on the calcium balance of the goats.

VI. GROWTH HORMONE

Clinical experience has led to the general conclusion that administration of growth hormone in humans leads to increased calcium absorption from the intestine.[552] The only studies of the relationship between growth hormone and calcium absorption in the rat have emerged from Schachter's laboratory. The first observation was that of Kimberg et al.[334] who found that hypophysectomy was followed by a decrease in the active transport system in the everted duodenal sac in both calcium-depleted and calcium-replete rats. The pituitary hormone responsible was identified as growth hormone in a subsequent publication.[330] Growth hormone given subcutaneously to hypophysectomized rats at a dose of 0.5 mg daily for 7 days restored the impaired active transport system (everted duodenal sac) to 70 to 100% of normal. No such effect was seen with adrenocorticotropin (ACTH), TSH, or the gonadotropins, with the exception of prolactin. The latter finding could not be explained on the basis of contamination with growth hormone. Examination of the time course of the effect of hypophysectomy revealed that the initial response (4 to 5 days) was an enhancement of active transport followed by a decline which was seen at 7 days and persisted through 21 days, the last time interval studied. The fall in S/M ratios seen at 14 days is very impressive, reaching well below 50% of control levels. Equally impressive is the ability of replacement therapy with growth hormone to restore the *status quo*. These observations of Schachter's group are important and merit further and more extensive study. A recent preliminary report claims that the action of growth hormone on intestinal calcium absorption is mediated by activation of the renal-vitamin D endocrine system at least in rats.[248] The effect of growth hormone on this endocrine system has been discussed (see Chapter 4.IV.F).

VII. GONADAL STEROID HORMONES

In spite of the well-documented effect of estrogens on 1,25-dihydroxyvitamin D_3 production (see Chapter 4.IV.D), there is little information concerning their effects on intestinal absorption of calcium. The negative data of Finkelstein and Schachter[330] is representative of the limited data in experimental animals. They found that neither estradiol, progesterone, nor testosterone had any effect on active transport of calcium in everted duodenal sacs removed from hypophysectomized rats.

A preliminary report of a study in man claims that cyclic administration of conjugated estrogens (1.25 to 2.5 mg/day for 6 months) increased intestinal absorption of calcium as well as plasma levels of 1,25-dihydroxyvitamin D in postmenopausal osteoporotic women.[673]

VIII. GASTRIN

There appears to be no direct effect of gastrin polypeptides on calcium absorption by the intestine of rats using the *in situ* ligated loop technique.[674,675] Although Fujita, using synthetic tetragastrin, did find an enhancing effect in intact rats, this response was abolished by prior parathyroidectomy.

Chapter 11

PHARMACOLOGICAL ASPECTS OF CALCIUM ABSORPTION

I. DIPHOSPHONATES

Diphosphonates are a series of compounds that contain phosphorus-carbon-phosphorus bonds. They are known to be potent inhibitors of the formation and dissolution of bone mineral in vitro[676–680] and to decrease bone turnover in vivo.[681] The compound which has received the most attention is disodium ethane-1-hydroxy-1,1-diphosphonate (EHDP).

With few exceptions, all of the reports describing the effects of EHDP on intestinal absorption of calcium have emanated from Fleisch's laboratory. Fleisch and his associates have consistently found in the rat that high subcutaneous doses of EHDP (10 mg P $kg^{-1}day^{-1}$ for 7 days) lead to a decrease in gut calcium transport whether the latter was measured by the *in situ* ligated loop technique,[513,682,683] by in vivo perfusion of an intestinal segment,[619] or by in vitro everted duodenal sac technique.[683] Another laboratory, using the latter technique, has also shown the inhibitory effect of high doses of EHDP.[684]

Lower doses of EHDP (1 mg P kg^{-1} day^{-1} for 7 days) led to stimulation of gut calcium transport in the *in situ* ligated loop,[263] confirming an earlier observation of Gasser et al.[681] who used the balance method in the rat.

Trechsel et al.[683] studied the effects of 13 other diphosphonates and related compounds, each given subcutaneously at a dose of 10 mg P kg^{-1} day^{-1} for 7 days. EHDP was one of the most effective inhibitors of gut calcium transport. Methane diphosphonic acid (MDP) was much less effective, whereas dichloromethane diphosphonic acid (Cl_2MDP) slightly stimulated, rather than inhibited, absorption.

The mechanism of EHDP action on gut calcium transport lies in the effect of the drug on the renal-vitamin D endocrine system; EHDP inhibits the production of 1,25-dihydroxyvitamin D_3 (see Chapter 4.V.B).

II. ANTICONVULSANTS

Chronic anticonvulsant therapy consisting of either phenytoin (4 to 6 mg kg^{-1} day^{-1}) and phenobarbital (2 to 3 mg kg^{-1} day^{-1}), or of phenobarbital alone, resulted in calcium balances which were significantly negative relative to control patients receiving no anticonvulsant therapy.[685] As the vitamin D_3 intake was increased, the patients receiving anticonvulsant therapy went into positive calcium balance but always remained in less positive balance than the control patients receiving the same dose of vitamin D_3. The inhibitory effect of anticonvulsants on calcium absorption by the intestine has been more clearly demonstrated in the everted duodenal sac[686–688] of the rat using either phenytoin alone or a conbination of phenytoin and phenobarbital. Corradino[365] has demonstrated a direct inhibitory effect of phenytoin on ^{45}Ca uptake by organ cultures of embryonic chicken duodenum in vitro. Conflicting with these findings is the report that *acute* doses of phenytoin lead to *enhanced* absorption of calcium in the rat.[617]

The mechanism of the effect of chronic administration of anticonvulsants on intestinal transport of calcium is not known. At first it was suggested that the lower plasma levels of 25-hydroxyvitamin D seen in these patients might be the basis for the effect.[689] However, the subsequent report of Jubiz et al.[47] that plasma 1,25-

dihydroxyvitamin D levels are normal or even slightly elevated eliminates interference with renal vitamin D metabolism as a major contributing factor. The report of Corradino[365] indicates that, at least in the chicken, there is a direct effect on gut calcium transport but this observation remains to be more widely confirmed.

III. *SOLANUM MALACOXYLON* AND RELATED PLANTS

A cattle disease found in Argentina, where it is known as "enteque seco", is characterized by extensive soft tissue calcification. It has been demonstrated that the etiological agent is the plant, *Solanum malacoxylon*, which was being ingested by the grazing animal.[690] O'Donnell and Smith[691] verified the similarity between the action of the administration of *S. malacoxylon* leaf and that of vitamin D_3 on the in vitro ^{45}Ca uptake by duodenal segments removed from vitamin D-deficient rats. The report of Wasserman[469] that the plant, incorporated in the diet, can reverse the inhibitory effect of dietary strontium with respect to calcium absorption in chickens, supported the contention that the active principle of the plant mimics 1,25-dihydroxyvitamin D_3. Strontium is known to inhibit endogenous production of 1,25-dihydroxyvitamin D (see Chapter 4.V.C). Further work in Wasserman's laboratory led to the identification of one of the plant water-soluble factors as a conjugated glycoside of 1,25-dihydroxyvitamin D_3.[692] Other related plants, *Cestrum diurnum* and *S. glaucophyllum* contain similar 1,25-dihydroxyvitamin D_3-like principles.[693–696] Miravet et al.[669] have confirmed the effects of an aqueous extract of *S. malacoxylon* on active transport of calcium in the rat using the everted duodenal sac technique.

IV. ANTIBIOTICS

Certain antibiotics, such as penicillin, chloramphenicol, and neomycin, have been shown to increase calcium absorption from the intestine.[560,697,698] Whether or not this response is related to the fact that germ-free rats absorb calcium more efficiently[699] is not known.

V. STRONTIUM

Strontium, when incorporated in the diet, leads to inhibition of calcium absorption by the *in situ* ligated loop of the chicken.[264,467,468] The mechanism of this effect lies in the fact that strontium inhibits the production of 1,25-dihydroxyvitamin D_3 (see Chapter 4.V.C).

References

REFERENCES

1. **Haussler, M. R.**, Vitamin D: Metabolism, drug interactions and therapeutic applications in humans, in *Nutrition and Drug Interrelations,* Hathcock, J. N. and Coon, J., Eds., Academic Press, New York, 1978, chap. 26.
2. **Blunt, J. W., DeLuca, H. F., and Schnoes, H. K.**, 25-Hydroxycholecalciferol. A biologically active metabolite of vitamin D_3, *Biochemistry*, 7, 3317, 1968.
3. **Ponchon, G., Kennan, A. L., and DeLuca, H. F.**, "Activation" of vitamin D by the liver, *J. Clin. Invest.*, 48, 1273, 1969.
4. **Haussler, M. R., Myrtle, J. F., and Norman, A. W.**, The association of a metabolite of vitamin D_3 with intestinal mucosa chromatin in vivo, *J. Biol. Chem*, 243, 4055, 1968.
5. **Fraser, D. R. and Kodicek, E.**, Unique biosynthesis by kidney of a biologically active vitamin D metabolite, *Nature (London)*, 228, 764, 1970.
6. **Holick, M. F., Schnoes, H. K., DeLuca, H. F., Suda, T., and Cousins, R. J.**, Isolation and identification of 1,25-dihydroxycholecalciferol. A metabolite of vitamin D active in intestine, *Biochemistry*, 10, 2799, 1971.
7. **Lawson, D. E. M., Fraser, D. R., Kodicek, E., Morris, H. R., and Williams, D. H.**, Identification of 1,25-dihydroxycholecalciferol, a new kidney hormone controlling calcium metabolism, *Nature (London)*, 230, 228, 1971.
8. **Lund, J. and DeLuca, H. F.**, Biologically active metabolite of vitamin D_3 from bone, liver and blood serum, *J. Lipid Res.*, 7, 739, 1966.
9. **Holick, M. F., DeLuca, H. F., and Avioli, L. V.**, Isolation and identification of 25-hydroxycholecalciferol from human plasma, *Arch. Int. Med.*, 129, 4253, 1972.
10. **Ponchon, G. and DeLuca, H. F.**, The role of the liver in the metabolism of vitamin D, *J. Clin. Invest.*, 48, 1273, 1969.
11. **Horsting, M. and DeLuca, H. F.**, *In vitro* production of 25-hydroxycholecalciferol, *Biochem. Biophys. Res. Commun.*, 36, 251, 1969.
12. **Olson, E. B., Jr., Knutson, J. C., Bhattacharyya, M. H., and DeLuca, H. F.**, The effect of hepatectomy on the synthesis of 25-hydroxyvitamin D_3, *J. Clin. Invest.*, 57, 1213, 1976.
13. **Tucker, G., Gagnon, R. E., and Haussler, M. R.**, Vitamin D_3-25-hydroxylase: tissue occurrence and apparent lack of regulation, *Arch. Biochem. Biophys.*, 155, 47, 1973.
14. **Bhattacharyya, M. H. and DeLuca, H. F.**, The regulation of calciferol-25-hydroxylase in the chick, *Biochem. Biophys. Res. Commun.*, 59, 734, 1974.
15. **Holick, S. A., Holick, M. F., Tavela, T. E., Schnoes, H. K., and DeLuca, H. F.**, Metabolism of 1α-hydroxyvitamin D_3 in the chick, *J. Biol. Chem.*, 251, 1025, 1975.
16. **Rojanasathit, S. and Haddad, J. G.**, Hepatic accumulation of vitamin D_3 and 25-hydroxyvitamin D_3, *Biochim. Biophys. Acta*, 421, 12, 1976.
17. **Hahn, T. J., Scharp, C. R., and Avioli, L. V.**, Effect of phenobarbital administration on the subcellular distribution of vitamin D_3-^3H in rat liver, *Endocrinology*, 94, 1489, 1974.
18. **Norman, A. W. and DeLuca, H. F.**, The preparation of H^3-vitamin D_2 and D_3 and their localization in the rat, *Biochemistry*, 2, 1160, 1963.
19. **Ponchon, G. and DeLuca, H. F.**, Metabolites of vitamin D and their biologic activity, *J. Nutr.*, 99, 157, 1969.
20. **Bhattacharyya, M. H. and DeLuca, H. F.**, Subcellular location of rat liver calciferol-25-hydroxylase, *Arch. Biochem. Biophys.*, 160, 58, 1974.
21. **Björkhem, I. and Holmberg, I.**, Assay and properties of a mitochondrial 25-hydroxylase active on vitamin D_3, *J. Biol. Chem.*, 253, 842, 1978.
22. **Madhok, T. C., Schnoes, H. K., and DeLuca, H. F.**, Incorporation of oxygen-18 into the 25-position of cholecalciferol by hepatic cholecalciferol 25-hydroxylase, *Biochem. J.*, 175, 479, 1978.
23. **Delvin, E. E., Arabian, A., and Glorieux, F. H.**, Kinetics of liver microsomal cholecalciferol 25-hydroxylase in vitamin D-depleted and -repleted rats, *Biochem. J.*, 172, 417, 1978.
24. **Steenbock, H., Kletzien, S. W. F., and Halpin, J. G.**, The reaction of the chicken to irradiated ergosterol and irradiated yeast as contrasted with the natural vitamin D of fish liver oils, *J. Biol. Chem.*, 97, 249, 1932.
25. **Chen, P. S., Jr. and Bosman, H. B.**, Effect of vitamins D_2 and D_3 on serum calcium and phosphorus in rachitic chicks, *J. Nutr.*, 83, 133, 1964.
26. **Jones, G., Schnoes, H. K., and DeLuca, H. F.**, An *in vitro* study of vitamin D_2 hydroxylases in the chick, *J. Biol. Chem.*, 251, 24, 1976.
27. **Bhattacharyya, M. H. and DeLuca, H. F.**, The regulation of rat liver calciferol-25-hydroxylase, *J. Biol. Chem.*, 248, 2969, 1973.

28. **Fukushima, M., Nishii, Y., Suzuki, M., and Suda, T.,** Comparative studies on the 25-hydroxylations of cholecalciferol and 1α-hydroxycholecalciferol in perfused rat liver, *Biochem. J.*, 170, 495, 1978.
29. **Mawer, E. B. and Reeve, A.,** The use of an isolated perfused liver to study the control of cholecalciferol-25-hydroxylase activity in the rat, *Calcif. Tissue Res.*, 22 (Suppl.), 24, 1977.
30. **Horsting, H. and DeLuca, H. F.,** Feed-back control of 25-hydroxycholecalciferol production, *Fed. Proc. Fed. Am. Soc. Exp. Biol.*, 29, 542, 1970.
31. **Clark, M. B. and Potts, J. T., Jr.,** 25-Hydroxyvitamin D_3 regulation, *Calcif. Tissue Res.*, 22 (Suppl.), 29, 1977.
32. **Haddad, J. G. and Stamp, T. C. B.,** Circulating 25-hydroxyvitamin D in man, *Am. J. Med.*, 57, 57, 1974.
33. **Seino, Y., Shimotsuji, T., Kai, H., Ikehara, C., and Yabuuchi, H.,** The plasma levels of 25-hydroxyvitamin D in patients with various liver diseases and the response of 25-hydroxyvitamin D to vitamin D treatment, *Acta Paediatr. Scand.*, 67, 39, 1978.
34. **Nicholson, R., Akhtar, M., and Taylor, T. G.,** Oestradiol as a regulator of the metabolism of vitamin D_3 in the liver of Japanese quail, *J. Endocrinol.*, 68, 16P, 1976.
35. **Kehayoglou, A. K., Agnew, J. E., Holdsworth, C. D., Whelton, M. J., and Sherlock, S.,** Bone disease and calcium absorption in primary biliary cirrhosis, *Lancet*, 1, 715, 1968.
36. **Paterson, C. R. and Losowski, M. S.,** The bones in chronic liver disease, *Scand. J. Gastroenterol.*, 2, 293, 1967.
37. **Long, R. G., Skinner, R. K., Wills, M. R., and Sherlock, S.,** Serum-25-hydroxy-vitamin-D in untreated parenchymal and cholestatic liver disease, *Lancet*, 2, 650, 1976.
38. **Skinner, R. K., Long, R. G., Sherlock, S., and Wills, M. R.,** 25-Hydroxylation of vitamin D in primary biliary cirrhosis, *Lancet*, 1, 720, 1977.
39. **Lund, B., Sørensen, O. H., Hilden, M., and Lund, B.,** The hepatic conversion of vitamin D in alcoholics with varying degrees of liver affection, *Acta Med. Scand.*, 202, 221, 1977.
40. **Hepner, G. W., Roginsky, M., and Moo, H. F.,** Abnormal vitamin D metabolism in patients with cirrhosis, *Am. J. Dig. Dis.*, 21, 527, 1976.
41. **Posner, D. B., Russell, R. M., Absood, S., Connor, T. B., Davis, C., Martin, L., Williams, J. B., Norris, A. H., and Merchant, C.,** Effective 25-hydroxylation of vitamin D_2 in alcoholic cirrhosis, *Gastroenterology*, 74, 866, 1978.
42. **Jung, R. T., Davie, M., Hunter, J. O., Chalmers, T. M., and Lawson, D. E. M.,** Abnormal vitamin D metabolism in cirrhosis, *Gut*, 19, 290, 1978.
43. **Dent, C. E., Richens, A., Rowe, D. J. F., and Stamp, T. C. B.,** Osteomalacia with long-term anticonvulsant therapy in epilepsy, *Br. Med. J.*, 4, 69, 1970.
44. **Hahn, T. J., Birge, S. J., Scharp, C. R., and Avioli, L. V.,** Phenobarbital-induced alterations in vitamin D metabolism, *J. Clin. Invest.*, 51, 741, 1972.
45. **Richens, A. and Rowe, D. J. F.,** Disturbance of calcium metabolism by anticonvulsant drugs, *Br. Med. J.*, 4, 73, 1970.
46. **Stamp, T. C. B., Round, J. M., Rowe, D. J. F., and Haddad, J. G.,** Plasma levels and therapeutic effect of 25-hydroxycholecalciferol in epileptic patients taking anticonvulsant drugs, *Br. Med. J.*, 4, 9, 1972.
47. **Jubiz, W., Haussler, M. R., McCain, T. A., and Tolman, K. G.,** Plasma 1,25-dihydroxyvitamin D levels in patients receiving anticonvulsant drugs, *J. Clin. Endocrinol. Metab.*, 44, 617, 1977.
48. **Levison, J. C., Kent, G. N., Worth, G. K., and Retallack, R. W.,** Anticonvulsant induced increase in 25-hydroxy-vitamin D_3-1α-hydroxylase, *Endocrinology*, 101, 1898, 1977.
49. **DeLuca, H. F.,** Metabolism of vitamin D: current status, *Am. J. Clin. Nutr.*, 29, 1258, 1976.
50. **Baran, D. T., Fausto, A. C., Roberts, M. L., Karl, I., and Avioli, L. V.,** Phenobarbital-induced alterations in the metabolism of ^3H-vitamin D_3 by the perfused rachitic rat liver in vitro, *J. Clin. Invest.*, 64, 1112, 1979.
51. **Holick, M. F., Schnoes, H. K., and DeLuca, H. F.,** Identification of 1,25-dihydroxycholecalciferol, a form of vitamin D_3 metabolically active in the intestine, *Proc. Natl. Acad. Sci. U.S.A.*, 68, 803, 1971.
52. **Suda, T., DeLuca, H. F., Schnoes, H. K., Ponchon, G., Tanaka, Y., and Holick, M. F.,** 21,25-Dihydroxycholecalciferol. A metabolite of vitamin D_3 preferentially active on bone, *Biochemistry*, 9, 2917, 1970.
53. **Holick, M. I., Schnoes, H. K., DeLuca, H. F., Gray, R. W., Boyle, I. T., and Suda, T.,** Isolation and identification of 24,25-dihydroxycholecalciferol, a metabolite of vitamin D_3 made in kidney, *Biochemistry*, 11, 4251, 1972.
54. **Omdahl, J. L., Gray, R. W., Boyle, I. T., Knutson, J., and DeLuca, H. F.,** Regulation of metabolism of 25-hydroxycholecalciferol by kidney tissue *in vitro* by dietary calcium, *Nature (London)*, 237, 63, 1972.

55. **Garabedian, M., Pavlovitch, H., Fellot, C., and Balsan, S.,** Metabolism of 25-hydroxyvitamin D_3 in anephric rats: a new active metabolite, *Proc. Natl. Acad. Sci. U.S.A.*, 71, 554, 1974.
56. **Haddad, J. G., Jr., Min. C., Mendelsohn, M., Slatopolsky, E., and Hahn, T. J.,** Competitive protein-binding radioassay of 24,25-dihydroxyvitamin D in sera from normal and anephric subjects, *Arch. Biochem. Biophys.*, 182, 390, 1977.
57. **Boyle, L. T., Gray, R. W., and DeLuca, H. F.,** Regulation by calcium of *in vivo* synthesis of 1,25-dihydroxycholecalciferol and 21,25-dihydroxycholecalciferol, *Proc. Natl. Acad. Sci. U.S.A.*, 68, 2131, 1971.
58. **Suda, T., DeLuca, H. F., Schnoes, H. K., Tanaka, Y., and Holick, M. F.,** 25,26-Dihydroxycholecalciferol, a metabolite of vitamin D_3 with intestinal calcium transport activity, *Biochemistry*, 9, 4776, 1970.
59. **Holick, M. F., Kleiner-Bossaller, A., Schnoes, H. K., Kasten, P. M., Boyle, I. T., and DeLuca, H. F.,** 1,24,25-Trihydroxyvitamin D_3, *J. Biol. Chem.*, 248, 6691, 1973.
60. **Kleiner-Bossaller, A. and DeLuca, H. F.,** Formation of 1,24,25-trihydroxyvitamin D_3 from 1,25-dihydroxyvitamin D_3, *Biochim. Biophys. Acta*, 338, 489, 1974.
61. **Friedlander, E. J. and Norman, A. W.,** Studies on the metabolism of calciferol, XII. Production *in vitro* of 1,24,25-$(OH)_3$-vitamin D_3 and a search for its occurrence *in vivo*, *Arch. Biochem. Biophys.*, 170, 731, 1975.
62. **Tanaka, Y., Castillo, L., and DeLuca, H. F.,** The 24-hydroxylation of 1,25-dihydroxyvitamin D_3, *J. Biol. Chem.*, 252, 1421, 1977.
63. **Baksi, S. N. and Kenny, A. D.,** Influence of reproductive status on in vitro renal production of 1,24,25-trihydroxyvitamin D_3 in Japanese quail, *J. Reprod. Fertil.*, 50, 175, 1977.
64. **Tanaka, Y., Shepard, R. A., DeLuca, H. F., and Schnoes, H. K.,** The 26-hydroxylation of 25-hydroxyvitamin D_3 in vitro by chick renal homogenates, *Biochem. Biophys. Res. Commun.*, 83, 7, 1978.
65. **Baksi, S. N. and Kenny, A. D.,** Parathyroid hormone stimulation of 1,25-dihydroxyvitamin D_3 production in antiestrogen-treated Japanese quail, *Mol. Pharmacol.*, 16, 932, 1979.
66. **Lawson, D. E., Wilson, P. W., and Kodicek, E.,** Metabolism of vitamin D. A new cholecalciferol metabolite, involving loss of hydrogen at C-1, in chick intestinal nuclei, *Biochem. J.*, 115, 269, 1969.
67. **Midgett, R. J., Spielvogel, A. M., Coburn, J. W., and Norman, A. W.,** Studies on calciferol metabolism. VI. The renal production of the biologically active form of vitamin D, 1,25-dihydroxycholecalciferol; species, tissue and subcellular distribution, *J. Clin. Endocrinol. Metab.*, 36, 1153, 1973.
68. **Henry, H. and Norman, A. W.,** Presence of renal 25-hydroxyvitamin-D-1-hydroxylase in species of all vertebrate classes, *Comp. Biochem. Physiol. B*, 50, 431, 1975.
69. **Baksi, S. N., Kenny, A. D., Galli-Gallardo, S. M., and Pang, P. K. T.,** Vitamin D metabolism in bullfrogs and Japanese quail: effects of estradiol and prolactin, *Gen. Comp. Endocrinol.*, 35, 258, 1978.
70. **Kenny, A. D., Baksi, S. N., Galli-Gallardo, S. M., and Pang, P. K. T.,** Vitamin D metabolism in amphibia and fish, *Fed. Proc. Fed. Am. Soc. Exp. Biol.*, 36, 1097, 1977.
71. **Baksi, S. N. and Kenny, A. D.,** Vitamin D metabolism in immature Japanese quail: effects of ovarian hormones, in *Vitamin D: Biochemical, Chemical and Clinical Aspects Related to Calcium Metabolism*, Norman, A. W., Schaefer, K., Coburn, J. W., DeLuca, H. F., Fraser, D., Grigoleit, H. G., and Herrath, D. V., Eds., De Gruyter, New York, 1977, 89.
72. **Kenny, A. D.,** Vitamin D metabolism: physiological regulation in egg-laying Japanese quail, *Am. J. Physiol.*, 230, 1609, 1976.
73. **Sommerville, B. A., Fox, J., and Care, A. D.,** The in vitro metabolism of 25-hydroxycholecalciferol by pig kidney: effect of low dietary levels of calcium and phosphorus, *Br. J. Nutr.*, 40, 159, 1978.
74. **Juan, D. and DeLuca, H. F.,** The regulation of 24,25-dihydroxyvitamin D_3 production in cultures of monkey kidney cells, *Endocrinology*, 101, 1184, 1977.
75. **Botham, K. M., Tanaka, Y., and DeLuca, H. F.,** 25-Hydroxyvitamin D_3-1-hydroxylase. Inhibition *in vitro* by rat and pig tissues, *Biochemistry*, 13, 4961, 1974.
76. **Botham, K. M., Ghazarian, J. G., Kream, B. E., and DeLuca, H. F.,** Isolation of an inhibitor of 25-hydroxyvitamin D_3-1-hydroxylase from rat serum, *Biochemistry*, 15, 2130, 1976.
77. **Garabedian, M., Holick, M. F., DeLuca, H. F. and Boyle, I. T.,** Control of 25-hydroxycholecalciferol metabolism by parathyroid glands, *Proc. Natl. Acad. Sci. U.S.A.*, 69, 1673, 1972.
78. **Brumbaugh, P. F., Haussler, D. H., Bressler, R., and Haussler, M. R.,** Radioreceptor assay for 1α,25-dihydroxyvitamin D_3, *Science*, 183, 1089, 1974.
79. **Baksi, S. N. and Kenny, A. D.,** Vitamin D_3 metabolism in immature Japanese quail: effects of ovarian hormones, *Endocrinology*, 101, 1216, 1977.

80. **Baksi, S. N. and Kenny, A. D.,** The effects of administration of antiestrogen (tamoxifen) *in vivo* on the metabolism of 25-hydroxyvitamin D_3 *in vitro* in the Japanese quail, *Biochem. Pharmacol.*, 26, 2439, 1977.
81. **Baksi, S. N. and Kenny, A. D.,** Vitamin D metabolism in Japanese quail: effects of gonadal hormones and dietary calcium, *Am. J. Physiol.*, 234, E622, 1978.
82. **Baksi, S. N. and Kenny, A. D.,** Acute effect of estradiol on the renal vitamin D hydroxylases in Japanese quail, *Biochem. Pharmacol.*, 27, 2765, 1978.
83. **Baksi, S. N. and Kenny, A. D.,** Effect of lead ingestion on vitamin D_3 metabolism in Japanese quail, *Res. Commun. Chem. Pathol. Pharmacol.*, 21, 375, 1978.
84. **Baksi, S. N. and Kenny, A. D.,** Vitamin D metabolism in Japanese quail: effects of lead exposure and dietary calcium, in *Vitamin D: Basic Research and its Clinical Application,* Norman, A. W., Schaefer, K., Herrath, D. V., Grigoleit, H. -G., Coburn, J. W., DeLuca, H. F., Mawer, E. B., and Suda, T., Eds., De Gruyter, New York, 1979, 503.
85. **Baksi, S. N. and Kenny, A. D.,** Acute effects of parathyroid extract on renal vitamin D hydroxylases in Japanese quail, *Pharmacology*, 18, 169, 1979.
86. **Castillo, L., Tanaka, Y., DeLuca, H. F., and Sunde, M. L.,** The stimulation of 25-hydroxyvitamin D_3-1α-hydroxylase by estrogen, *Arch. Biochem. Biophys.*, 179, 211, 1977.
87. **Tanaka, Y., Castillo, L., and DeLuca, H. F.,** Control of renal vitamin D hydroxylases in birds by sex hormones, *Proc. Natl. Acad. Sci. U.S.A.*, 73, 2701, 1976.
88. **Bar, A., Dubrov, D., Eizner, U., and Hurwitz, S.,** Calcium-binding protein and kidney 25-hydroxycholecalciferol-1-hydroxylase in turkey poults, *J. Nutr.*, 108, 1501, 1978.
89. **Lee, S. W., Haussler, M. R., and Avioli, L. V.,** Circulating 1,25-dihydroxyvitamin D (1,25$(OH)_2$D) in male and female trout, *Clin. Res.*, 27, A487, 1979.
90. **Holick, M. F., Frommer, J. E., and Potts, J. T., Jr.,** *In vivo* metabolism of [^{3}H] 7-dehydrocholesterol and [^{3}H] vitamin D_3 in marine fish, in Abstr. 4th Workshop Vitamin D, Berlin, February 18–22, 1979, 38.
91. **Gray, R. W., Omdahl, J. L., Ghazarian, J. G., and DeLuca, H. F.,** 25-Hydroxycholecalciferol-1-hydroxylase. Subcellular location and properties, *J. Biol. Chem.*, 247, 7528, 1972.
92. **Bikle, D. D. and Rasmussen, H.,** A comparison of the metabolism of 25-hydroxyvitamin D_3 by chick renal tubules, homogenates and mitochondria, *Biochim. Biophys. Acta*, 362, 439, 1974.
93. **Bikle, D. D., Murphy, E. W., and Rasmussen, H.,** The ionic control of 1,25-dihydroxyvitamin D_3 synthesis in isolated chick renal mitochondria, *J. Clin. Invest.*, 55, 299, 1975.
94. **Ghazarian, J. G., Schnoes, H. K., and DeLuca, H. F.,** Mechanism of 25-hydroxycholecalciferol 1α-hydroxylation. Incorporation of oxygen-18 into the 1α position of 25-hydroxycholecalciferol, *Biochemistry*, 12, 2555, 1973.
95. **Ghazarian, J. G., Jefcoate, C. R., Knutson, J. C., Orme-Johnson, W. H., and DeLuca, H. F.,** Mitochondrial Cytochrome P_{450}. A component of chick kidney 25-hydroxycholecalciferol-1α-hydroxylase, *J. Biol. Chem.*, 249, 3026, 1974.
96. **Pederson, J. I., Ghazarian, J. G., Orme-Johnson, N. R., and DeLuca, H. F.,** Isolation of chick renal mitochondrial ferredoxin active in the 25-hydroxyvitamin D_3-1α-hydroxylase system, *J. Biol. Chem.*, 251, 3933, 1976.
97. **Larkins, R. G., MacAuley, S. J., Rapoport, A., Martin, T. J., Tulloch, B. R., Byfield, P. G. H., Matthews, E. W., and MacIntyre, I.,** Effects of nucleotides, hormones, ions and 1,25-dihydroxycholecalciferol production on 1,25-dihydroxycholecalciferol production in isolated chick renal tubules, *Clin. Sci. Mol. Med.*, 46, 569, 1974.
98. **Larkins, R. G., MacAuley, S. J., and MacIntyre, I.,** Feedback control of vitamin D metabolism by a nuclear action of 1,25-dihydroxycholecalciferol on the kidney, *Nature (London)*, 252, 412, 1974.
99. **Henry, H. L.,** Metabolism of 25-hydroxy-vitamin D_3 by primary cultures of chick kidney cells, *Biochem. Biophys. Res. Commun.*, 74, 768, 1977.
100. **Omdahl, J. L. and Hunsaker, L. A.,** Direct modulation of 25-hydroxyvitamin D_3 hydroxylation in kidney tubules by 1,25-dihydroxyvitamin D_3, *Biochem. Biophys. Res. Commun.*, 81, 1073, 1978.
101. **Spanos, E., Barrett, D. I., Chong, K. T., and MacIntyre, I.,** Effect of oestrogen and 1,25-dihydroxycholecalciferol on 25-hydroxycholecalciferol metabolism in primary chick kidney cell cultures, *Biochem. J.*, 174, 231, 1978.
102. **Henry, H. L.,** Regulation of the hydroxylation of 25-hydroxyvitamin D_3 *in vivo* and in primary cultures of chick kidney cells, *J. Biol. Chem.*, 254, 2722, 1979.
103. **Shain, S. A.,** *In vitro* metabolism of 25-hydroxycholecalciferol by chick intestinal and renal cell preparations, *J. Biol. Chem.*, 247, 4393, 1972.
104. **Shain, S. A.,** The *in vitro* metabolism of 25-hydroxycholecalciferol to 1,25-dihydroxycholecalciferol by chick renal tubules, *J. Biol. Chem.*, 247, 4404, 1972.

105. **Bikle, D. D. and Rasmussen, H.,** The ionic control of 1,25-dihydroxyvitamin D_3 production in isolated chick renal tubules, *J. Clin. Invest.*, 55, 292, 1975.
106. **Rasmussen, H., Wong, M., Bikle, D., and Goodman, D. B. P.,** Hormonal control of the renal conversion of 25-hydroxycholecalciferol to 1,25-dihydroxycholecalciferol, *J. Clin. Invest.*, 51, 2502, 1972.
107. **Horiuchi, E., Suda, T., Sasaki, S., Ogata, E., Ezawa, I., Sano, Y., and Shimazawa, E.,** The regulatory role of calcium in 25-hydroxycholecalciferol metabolism in chick kidney *in vitro*, *Arch. Biochem. Biophys.*, 171, 540, 1975.
108. **Howard, G. A., Turner, R. T., Bottemiller, B. L., and Rader, J. I.,** Vitamin D metabolism in serum-free cultures of Japanese quail kidney cells, *J. Cell Biol.*, 79, 68a, 1978.
109. **Rosenthal, A. M., Jones, G., Fraser, D., and Kooh, S. W.,** 1,25-$(OH)_2$ vitamin D_3 and 24,25-$(OH)_2$ vitamin D_3 synthesis by the isolated perfused rat kidney, *Clin. Res.*, 26, A846, 1978.
110. **Knutson, J. C. and DeLuca, H. F.,** 25-Hydroxyvitamin-D_3-24-hydroxylase. Subcellular location and properties, *Biochemistry*, 13, 1543, 1974.
111. **Madhok, T. C., Schnoes, H. K., and DeLuca, H. F.,** Mechanism of 25-hydroxyvitamin D_3 24-hydroxylation: incorporation of oxygen-18 into the 24 position of 25-hydroxyvitamin D_3, *Biochemistry*, 16, 2142, 1977.
112. **Hill, L. F. and Stanbury, S. W.,** Vitamin D and the kidney, *Nephron*, 15, 369, 1975.
113. **Avioli, L. V., Birge, S., Lee, S. W., and Slatopolsky, E.,** The metabolic fate of vitamin D_3-^3H in chronic renal failure, *J. Clin. Invest.*, 47, 2239, 1968.
114. **Avioli, L. V., Birge, S. J., and Slatopolsky, E.,** The nature of vitamin D resistance of patients with chronic renal disease, *Arch. Intern. Med.*, 124, 451, 1969.
115. **Piel, C. F., Roof, B. S., and Avioli, L. V.,** Metabolism of tritiated 25-hydroxycholecalciferol in chronically uremic children before and after successful renal homotransplantation, *J. Clin. Endocrinol. Metab.*, 37, 944, 1973.
116. **Mawer, E. B., Backhouse, J., Holman, C. A., Lumb, G. A., and Stanbury, S. W.,** The distribution and storage of vitamin D and its metabolites in human tissues, *Clin. Sci.*, 43, 413, 1972.
117. **Mawer, E. B., Lumb, G. A., Schaefer, K., and Stanbury, S. W.,** The metabolism of isotopically labelled vitamin D_3 in man: the influence of the state of vitamin D nutrition, *Clin. Sci.*, 40, 39, 1971.
118. **Stanbury, S. W., Mawer, E. B., Lumb, G. A., Hill, L. F., Holman, C. A., Taylor, C. M., and Torkington, P.,** Vitamin D metabolism and renal bone disease, in *Clinical Aspects of Metabolic Bone Disease*, Frame, B., Parfitt, A. M. and Duncan, H., Eds., Elsevier, Amsterdam, 1973, 562.
119. **Holick, M. F., de Blanco, M. C., Clark, M. B., Henley, J. W., Neer, R. M., DeLuca, H. F., and Potts, J. T., Jr.,** The metabolism of [6-^{3}H] 1α, hydroxycholecalciferol to [6-^{3}H] 1α, 25-dihydroxycholecalciferol in a patient with renal insufficiency, *J. Clin. Endocrinol. Metab.*, 44, 595, 1977.
120. **Mawer, B. E., Backhouse, J. Taylor, C. M., Lumb, G. A., and Stanbury, S. W.,** Failure of formation of 1,25-dihydroxycholecalciferol in chronic renal insufficiency, *Lancet*, 1, 626, 1973.
121. **Lambert, P. W., Toft, D. O., Hodgson, S. F., Lindmark, E. A., Witrak, B. J., and Roos, B. A.,** An improved method for the measurement of 1,25-$(OH)_2D_3$ in human plasma, *Endocr. Res. Commun.*, 5, 293, 1978.
123. **Hartenbower, D. L., Coburn, J. W., Reddy, C. R., and Norman, A. W.,** Calciferol metabolism and intestinal calcium transport in the chick with reduced renal function, *J. Lab. Clin. Med.*, 83, 38, 1974.
124. **Van Stone, J. C., Frank, D. E., and Bradford, W. R.,** The effect of decreased renal function with and without reduction in renal mass on 1,25-dihydroxycholecalciferol production in rats, *J. Lab. Clin. Med.*, 89, 1168, 1977.
125. **Wong, R. G., Norman, A. W., Reddy, C. R., and Coburn, J. W.,** Biologic effects of 1,25-dihydroxycholecalciferol (a highly active vitamin D metabolite) in acutely uremic rats, *J. Clin. Invest.*, 51, 1287, 1972.
126. **Belsey, R., DeLuca, H. F., and Potts, J. T., Jr.,** Competitive binding assay for vitamin D and 25-OH vitamin D, *J. Clin. Endocrinol. Metab.*, 33, 554,1971.
127. **Haddad, J. G. and Chyu, K. J.,** Competitive protein-binding radioassay for 25-hydroxycholecalciferol, *J. Clin. Endocrinol. Metab.*, 33, 992, 1971.
128. **Taylor, C. M., Hughes, S. E., and de Silva, P.,** Competitive protein binding assay for 24,25-dihydroxycholecalciferol, *Biochem. Biophys. Res. Commun.*, 70, 1243, 1976.
129. **Norman, A. W., Henry, H., Bishop, J. E., and Coburn, J. W.,** Simultaneous measurement of 25(OH)D, 24,25$(OH)_2$D, and 1,25$(OH)_2$D in plasma samples by steroid competition assay, *Clin. Res.*, 26, A423, 1978.
130. **Whyte, M. P., Min, C., and Haddad, J. G., Jr.,** Dietary, substrate, and hormonal regulation of rat serum 24,25-dihydroxyvitamin D (24,25), *Clin. Res.*, 26, A430, 1978.

131. **Gray, T. K., Williams, M. E., and Dorr, A.,** Aging and the serum levels of 25-hydroxyvitamin D and 24,25-dihydroxyvitamin D in women, *Calcif. Tissue Int.*, 28, 174, 1979.
132. **Bishop, J. E., Roberts, P. A., Henry, H. L., Coburn, J. W., and Norman, A. W.,** Determination of concentration of 25(OH)D, 24,25$(OH)_2$D, and 1,25$(OH)_2$D in a 2.0 ml plasma sample, in Abstr. *4th Workshop Vitamin D,* Berlin, February 18–22, 1979, 55.
133. **Okano, K., Nakai, R., Goto, H., and Yoshikawa, M.,** Effects of age and diseases on human serum 25-hydroxycholecalciferol determined by competitive protein-binding assay, *Endocrinol. Jpn.*, 23, 265, 1976.
134. **Garcia-Pascual, B., Peytremann, A., Courvoisier, B., and Lawson, D. E. M.,** A simplified competitive protein-binding assay for 25-hydroxycholecalciferol, *Clin. Chim. Acta,* 68, 99, 1976.
135. **Rosen, J. F., Roginsky, M., Nathenson, G., and Finberg, L.,** 25-hydroxyvitamin D. Plasma levels in mothers and their premature infants with neonatal hypocalcemia, *Am. J. Dis. Child.,* 127, 220, 1974.
136. **Belsey, R. E., DeLuca, H. F., and Potts, J. T., Jr.,** A rapid assay for 25-OH-vitamin D_3 without preparative chromatography, *J. Clin. Endocrinol. Metab.*, 38, 1046, 1974.
137. **Imawari, M. and Goodman, D. S.,** Immunological and immunoassay studies of the binding protein for vitamin D and its metabolites in human serum, *J. Clin. Invest.,* 59, 432, 1977.
138. **Osborn, T. W. and Norman, A. W.,** Measurement of 25-hydroxycholecalciferol by a specific chick plasma competitive binding assay, *Fed. Proc. Fed. Am. Soc. Exp. Biol.*, 34, 893, 1975.
139. **Jones, G.,** Assay of vitamins D_2 and D_3, and 25-hydroxyvitamins D_2 and D_3, in human plasma by high-performance liquid chromatography, *Clin. Chem. Winston-Salem, N. C.*, 24, 287, 1978.
140. **Dokoh, S., Morita, R., Fukunaga, M., Yamamoto, I., Miyaji, A., and Torizuka, K.,** The measurement of various vitamin D derivatives in plasma using high-pressure liquid chromatography, in *Vitamin D: Basic Research and its Clinical Applieation,* Norman, A. W., Schaefer, K., Herrath, D.v., Grigoleit, H.-G., Coburn, J. W., DeLuca, H. F., Mawer, E. B., and Suda, T., Eds., De Gruyter, New York, 1979, 239.
141. **Haussler, M. R., Drezner, M. K., Pike, J. W., Chandler, J. S., and Hagan, L. A.,** Assay of 1,25-dihydroxyvitamin D and other active vitamin D metabolites in serum: application to animals and humans, in *Vitamin D:-Basic Research and its Clinical Application,* Norman, A. W., Schaefer, K., Herrath, D.v., Grigoleit, H.-G., Coburn, J. W., DeLuca, H. F., Mawer, E. B., and Suda, T., Eds., De Gruyter, New York, 1979, 189.
142. **Horst, R. L., Shepard, R. M., Jorgensen, N. A., and DeLuca, H. F.,** Assays for vitamin D and its metabolites, *in Vitamin D: Basic Research and its Clinical Application,* Norman, A. W., Schaefer, K., Herrath, D.v., Grigoleit, H.-G., Coburn, J. W., DeLuca, H. F., Mawer, E. B., and Suda, T., Eds., De Gruyter, New York, 1979, 213.
143. **Haussler, M. R., Hughes, M. R., McCain, T. A., Zerwekh, J. E., Brumbaugh, P. F., Jubiz, W., and Wasserman, R. H.,** 1,25-Dihydroxyvitamin D_3: mode of action in intestine and parathyroid glands, assay in humans and isolation of its glycoside from *Solanum malacoxylon, Calcif. Tiss. Res.*, Suppl. 22, 1, 1977.
144. **Hughes, M. R., Baylink, D. J., Jones, P. G., and Haussler, M. R.,** Radioligand receptor assay for 25-hydroxyvitamin D_2/D_3 and 1α,25-dihydroxyvitamin D_2/D_3, *J. Clin. Invest.,* 58, 61, 1976.
145. **Haussler, M. R., Baylink, D. J., Hughes, M. R., Brumbaugh, P. F., Wergedal, J. E., Shen, F. H., Nielsen, R. L., Counts, S. J., Bursac, K. M., and McCain, T. A.,** The assay of 1α-25-dihydroxy-vitamin D_3; physiologic and pathologic modulation of circulating hormone levels, *Clin. Endocrinol. Oxford,* 5 (Suppl.) 151s, 1976.
146. **Brumbaugh, P. F., Haussler, D. H., Bursac, K. M., and Haussler, M. R.,** Filter assay for 1α, 25-dihydroxyvitamin D_3. Utilization of the hormone's target tissue chromatin receptor, *Biochemistry,* 13, 4091, 1974.
147. **Pike, J. W., Spanos, E., Colston, K. W., MacIntyre, I., and Haussler, M. R.,** Influence of estrogen on renal vitamin D hydroxylases and serum 1α, 25-$(OH)_2D_3$ in chicks, *Am. J. Physiol.,* 235, E338, 1978.
148. **Pike, J. W., Parker, J. B., Haussler, M. R., Boass, A., and Toverud, S. U.,** Dynamic changes in circulating 1,25-dihydroxyvitamin D during reproduction in rats, *Science,* 204, 1427, 1979.
149. **Eisman, J. A., Hamstra, A. J., Kream, B. E., and DeLuca, H. F.** A sensitive, precise and convenient method for determination of 1,25-dihydroxyvitamin D in human plasma, *Arch. Biochem. Biophys.*, 176, 235, 1976.
150. **Wecksler, W. R. and Norman, A. W.,** An hydroxylapatite batch assay for the quantification of 1α, 25-dihydroxyvitamin D_3 -receptor complexes, *Anal. Biochem.,* 92, 314, 1979.
151. **Abel de la Cruz, L. A., Shieh, J.-C., Pollard, S. K., and Kenny, A. D.,** New radioreceptor assay for 1,25-dihydroxyvitamin D_3 using Japanese quail gut cytosolic receptor, *Fed. Proc. Fed. Am. Soc. Exp. Biol.,* 39, 559, 1980.

152. **Mellon, W. S. and DeLuca, H. F.,** Equilibrium and kinetic study of 1,25-dihydroxyvitamin D_3 binding to chicken intestinal cytosol employing high specific activity 1,25-dihydroxy-[^{3}H]-26,27-vitamin D_3, *Arch. Biochem. Biophys.*, 197, 90, 1979.

153. **Haussler, M. R., Drezner, M. K., Pike, J. W., and Hagan, L. A.,** 1,25-Dihydroxyvitamin D (1,25-(OH_2D) and parathyroid hormone (PTH) in calcium and phosphate homeostasis: biochemical, physiological and clinical aspects, *Acta Endocrinol. Copenhagen*, 91, 481, 1979.

154. **Wecksler, W.,** Kinetic and equilibrium binding properties of the 1,25-dihydroxyvitamin D_3-receptor from chick intestine, *Fed. Proc. Fed. Am. Soc. Exp. Biol.*, 37, 1789, 1978.

155. **Lawson, D. E. M. and Wilson, P. W.,** Intranuclear localization and receptor proteins for 1,25-dihydroxyvitamin D_3 in chick intestine, *Biochem. J.*, 144, 573, 1974.

156. **Brumbaugh, P. F. and Haussler, M. R.,** 1α, 25-dihydroxycholecalciferol receptors in intestine. II. Temperature-dependent transfer of the hormone to chromatin via a specific cytosol receptor, *J. Biol. Chem.*, 249, 1258, 1974.

157. **Peacock, M., Taylor, G. A., and Brown, W. B.,** Measurement of plasma 1,25$(OH)_2$ vitamin D by protein binding assay and radioimmunoassay, in *Vitamin D: Basic Research and its Clinical Application*, Norman, A. W., Schaefer, K., Herrath, D.v., Grigoleit, H.-G., Coburn, J. W., DeLuca, H. F., Mawer, E. B., and Suda, T., Eds., De Gruyter, New York, 1979, 179.

158. **Schaefer, P. C. and Goldsmith, R. S.,** Radioimmunoassay of vitamin D metabolites, in *Vitamin D: Basic Research and its Clinical Application*, Norman, A. W., Schaefer, K., Herrath, D.v., Grigoleit, H.-G., Coburn, J. W., DeLuca, H. F., Mawer, E. B., and Suda, T., Eds., De Gruyter, New York, 1979, 205.

159. **Schmidt-Gayk, H., Mayer, E., Schüer, R., Lichtwald, K., Bouillon, R., and Clemens, T. L.,** Studies on antisera against vitamin D metabolites, in *Vitamin D: Basic Research and its Clinical Application*, Norman, A. W., Schaefer, K., Herrath, D.v., Grigoleit, H.-G., Coburn, J. W., DeLuca, H. F., Mawer, E. B., and Suda, T., Eds., De Gruyter, New York, 1979, 233.

160. **Thomas, W. C., Jr., Morgan, H. G., Connor, T. B., Haddock, L., Bills, C. E., and Howard, T. E.,** Studies of antirachitic activity in sera from patients with disorders of calcium metabolism and preliminary observations on the mode of transport of vitamin D in human sera, *J. Clin. Invest.*, 38, 1078, 1959.

161. **DeCrousaz, P., Blanc, B., and Antener, I.,** Vitamin D activity in normal human serum and serum proteins, *Helv. Odontol. Acta*, 9, 151, 1965.

162. **Rikkers, H. and DeLuca, H. F.,** An *in vivo* study of the carrier proteins of ^{3}H-vitamins D_3 and D_4 in rat serum, *Am. J. Physiol.*, 213, 380, 1967.

163. **Peterson, P. A.,** Isolation and partial characterization of a human vitamin D-binding plasma protein, *J. Biol. Chem.*, 246, 7748, 1971.

164. **Daiger, S. P., Schanfield, M. S., and Cavalli-Sforza, L. L.,** Group-specific component (Gc) proteins bind vitamin D and 25-hydroxyvitamin D, *Proc. Natl. Acad. Sci. U.S.A.*, 72, 2076, 1975.

165. **Barragry, J. M., Corless, D., Auton, J., Carter, N. D., Long, R. G., Maxwell, J. D., and Switala, S.,** Plasma vitamin D-binding globulin in vitamin D deficiency, pregnancy and chronic liver disease, *Clin. Chim. Acta.*, 87, 359, 1978.

166. **Bouillon, R., Van Baelen, H., Rombauts, W., and de Moor, P.,** The isolation and characterization of the vitamin D-binding protein from rat serum, *J. Biol. Chem.*, 253, 4426, 1978.

167 **Trechsel, U., Bonjour, J.-P., and Fleisch, H.,** Regulation of 25-hydroxycholecalciferol-1-and-24-hydroxylases in cultured kidney cells, in *Vitamin D: Basic Research and its Clinical Application*, Norman, A. W., Schaefer, K., Herrath, D.v., Grigoleit, H.-G., Coburn, J. W., Deluca, H. F., Mawer, E. B. and Suda, T., Eds., De Gruyter, New York, 1979, 597.

168. **Edelstein, S., Lawson, D. E. M., and Kodicek, E.,** The transporting proteins of cholecalciferol and 25-hydroxycholecalciferol in serum of chicks and other species, *Biochem. J.*, 135, 417, 1973.

169. **Rosenstreich, S. J., Volwiler, W., and Rich, C.,** Metabolism and plasma protein transport of vitamin D_3 in the baboon, *Am. J. Clin. Nutr.*, 24, 897, 1971.

170. **Hay, A. W. M.,** The transport of 25-hydroxycholecalciferol in a New World monkey, *Biochem. J.*, 151, 193, 1975.

171. **Kida, K. and Goodman, D. S.,** Studies on the transport of vitamin D and of 25-hydroxyvitamin D in human plasma, *J. Lipid Res.*, 17, 485, 1976.

172. **Imawari, M., Kida, K., and Goodman, D. S.,** The transport of vitamin D and its 25-hydroxy metabolite in human plasma, *J. Clin. Invest.*, 58, 514, 1976.

173. **Bouillon, R., Van Baelen, H., and de Moor, P.,** 25-Hydroxyvitamin D and its binding protein in maternal and cord serum, *J. Clin. Endocrinol. Metab.*, 45, 679, 1977.

174. **Haddad, J. G., Hillman, L., and Rojanasathit, S.,** Human serum binding capacity and affinity for 25-hydroxygocalciferol and 25-hydroxycholecalciferol, *J. Clin. Endocrinol. Metab.*, 43, 86, 1976.

175. **Haddad, J. G., Jr. and Walgate, J.,** 25-Hydroxyvitamin D transport in human plasma, *J. Biol. Chem.,* 251, 4803, 1976.
176. **Rojanasathit, S. and Haddad, J. G.,** Ontogeny and effect of vitamin D deprivation on rat serum 25-hydroxyvitamin D binding protein, *Endocrinology,* 100, 642, 1977.
177. **Bouillon, R., van Baelen, H., Rombauts, W., and de Moor, P.,** The purification and characterization of the human-serum binding protein for the 25-hydroxycholecalciferol (Transcalciferin), *Eur. J. Biochem.,* 66, 285, 1976.
178. **Belsey, R., Clark, M. B., Bernat, M., Glowacki, J., Holick, M. F., DeLuca, H. F., and Potts, J. T.,** The physiologic significance of plasma transport of vitamin D and metabolites, *Am. J. Med.,* 57, 50, 1974.
179. **Hay, A. W. M. and Watson, G.,** Binding of 25-hydroxyvitamin D_2 to plasma protein in New World monkeys, *Nature (London)* 256, 150, 1975.
180. **Hay, A. W. M. and Watson, G.,** The plasma transport proteins of 25-hydroxycholecalciferol in fish, amphibians, reptiles and birds, *Comp. Biochem. Physiol. B,* 53, 167, 1976.
181. **Hay, A. W. M. and Watson, G.,** The plasma transport proteins of 25-hydroxycholecalciferol in mammals, *Comp. Biochem. Physiol. B,* 53, 163, 1976.
182. **Hay, A. W. M. and Watson, G.,** Binding properties of serum vitamin D transport proteins in vertebrates for 24R, 25-dihydroxycholecalciferol and 24S,25-dihydroxycholecalciferol *in vitro, Comp. Biochem. Physiol. B,* 58, 43, 1977.
183. **Tanaka, Y and DeLuca, H. F.,** The control of 25-hydroxyvitamin D metabolism by inorganic phosphorus, *Arch. Biochem. Biophys.,* 154, 566, 1973.
184. **Ribovich, M. L. and DeLuca, H. F.,** 1,25-dihydroxyvitamin D_3 metabolism, *Arch. Biochem. Biophys.,* 188, 164, 1978.
185. **Galante, L., Colston, K. W., Evans, I. M. A., Byfield, P. G. H., Matthews, E. W., and MacIntyre, I.,** The regulation of vitamin D metabolism, *Nature (London),* 244, 438, 1973.
186. **Omdahl, J. L. and DeLuca, H. F.,** Mediation of calcium adaptation by 1,25-dihydroxycholecalciferol, *J. Nutr.,* 107, 1975, 1977.
187. **Henry, H. L., Midgett, R. J., and Norman, A. W.,** Regulation of 25-hydroxyvitamin D_3-1-hydroxylase *in vivo, J. Biol. Chem.,* 249, 7584, 1974.
188. **Baksi, S. N. and Kenny, A. D.,** Vitamin D metabolism in Japanese quail: effects of lead exposure and dietary calcium, *Toxicol. Appl. Pharmacol.,* 51, 489, 1979.
189. **Haussler, M., Hughes, M., Baylink, D., Littledike, E. T., Cork, D., and Pitt, M.,** Influence of phosphate depletion on the biosynthesis and circulating level of 1α,25-dihydroxyvitamin D, in *Phosphate Metabolism,* Massry, S. G. and Ritz, E., Eds., Plenum Press, New York, 1977, 223.
190. **Hughes, M. R., Brumbaugh, P. F., Haussler, M. R., Wergedal, J. E., and Baylink, D. J.,** Regulation of serum 1α,25-dihydroxyvitamin D_3 by calcium and phosphate in the rat, *Science,* 190, 578, 1975.
191. **Swaminathan, R., Sommerville, B. A., and Care, A. D.,** Metabolism *in vitro* of 25-hydroxycholecalciferol in chicks fed on phosphorus-deficient diets, *Clin. Sci. Mol. Med.,* 54, 197, 1978.
192. **Montecuccoli, G., Bar, A., Risenfeld, G., and Hurwitz, S.,** The response of 25-hydroxycholecalciferol-1-hydroxylase activity, intestinal calcium absorption, and calcium-binding protein to phosphate deficiency in chicks, *Comp. Biochem. Physiol.,* 57, 331, 1977.
193. **Gray, R. W., Wilz, D. R., Caldas, A. E., and Lemann, J., Jr.,** The importance of phosphate in regulating plasma 1,25-$(OH)_2$-vitamin D levels in humans: studies in healthy subjects, in calcium-stone formers and in patients with primary hyperparathyroidism, *J. Clin. Endocrinol. Metab.,* 45, 299, 1977.
194. **Baxter, L. A. and DeLuca, H. F.,** Stimulation of 25-hydroxyvitamin D_3-1α-hydroxylase by phosphate depletion, *J. Biol. Chem.,* 251, 3158, 1976.
195. **Edelstein, S., Harell, A., Bar, A., and Hurwitz, S.,** The functional metabolism of vitamin D in chicks fed low-calcium and low-phosphorus diet, *Biochem. Biophys. Acta.,* 385, 438, 1975.
196. **Hughes, M. R., Baylink, D. J., Gonnerman, W. A., Toverud, S. U., Ramp, W. K., and Haussler, M. R.,** Influence of dietary vitamin D_3 on the circulating concentration of its active metabolites in the chick and rat, *Endocrinology,* 100, 799, 1977.
197. **Fraser, D. R. and Kodicek, E.,** Regulation of 25-hydroxycholecalciferol-1-hydroxylase activity in kidney by parathyroid hormone, *Nature (London), New Biol.,* 241, 163, 1973.
198. **Galante, L., Colston, K. W., MacAuley, S. J., and MacIntyre, I.,** Effect of calcitonin on vitamin D metabolism, *Nature (London),* 238, 271, 1972.
199. **Suda, T., Horiuchi, N., and Sasaki, S.,** Direct control by calcium of 25-hydroxycholecalciferol-1-hydroxylase activity in chick kidney mitochondria, *Biochem. Biophys. Res. Commun.,* 54, 512, 1973.
200. **Henry, H. L. and Norman, A. W.,** Studies on calciferol metabolism. Regulation of 25-hydroxyvitamin D_3-1-hydroxylase in isolated renal mitochondria, *Arch. Biochem. Biophys.,* 172, 582, 1976.

201. **Bikle, D. D. and Rasmussen, H.**, Ionic control of 1,25-dihydroxyvitamin D_3 production by isolated chick renal mitochondria, *Biochem. Biophys. Acta*, 538, 127, 1978.
202. **Kenny, A. D.**, Regulation of vitamin D metabolism in egg-laying birds, in *Calcium-Regulating Hormones*, Talmage, R. V., Owen, M., and Parson, J. A., Eds., Elsevier, Amsterdam, 1975, 408.
203. **Kenny, A. D., Lamb, J., David, N. R., and Losty, T. A.**, Regulation of vitamin D metabolism in egg-laying birds, *Fed. Proc. Fed. Am. Soc. Exp. Biol.*, 33, 679, 1974.
204. **Losty, T. A., Biellier, H. V., and Kenny, A. D.**, Regulation of vitamin D metabolism in egg-laying chickens, Prog. 56th Meeting Endocrine Soc. Atlanta, June 1974, A268.
205. **Kenny, A. D. and Baksi, S. N.**, Time of activation of renal 25-hydroxyvitamin D_3-1-hydroxylase in ovulating Japanese quail, *Fed. Proc. Fed. Am. Soc. Exp. Biol.*, 35, 662, 1976.
206. **Montecuccoli, G., Hurwitz, S., Cohen, A., and Bar, A.**, The role of 25-hydroxycholecalciferol-1-hydroxylase in the responses of calcium absorption to the reproductive activity in birds, *Comp. Biochem. Physiol. A*, 57, 335, 1977.
207. **Bar, A., Cohen, A., Edelstein, S., Shemesh, M., Montecuccoli, G., and Hurwitz, S.**, Involvement of cholecalciferol metabolism in birds in the adaptation of calcium absorption to the needs during reproduction, *Comp. Biochem. Physiol. B*, 59, 245, 1978.
208. **Sedrani, S. and Taylor, T. G.**, Metabolism of 25-hydroxycholecalciferol in Japanese quail in relation to reproduction, *J. Endocrinol.*, 72, 405, 1977.
209. **Abe, E., Tanabe, R., Suda, T., and Yoshiki, S.**, Circadian rhythm of 1α-25-dihydroxyvitamin D_3 production in egg-laying hens, *Biochem. Biophys. Res. Commun.*, 88, 500, 1979.
210. **Castillo, L., Tanaka, Y., Wineland, M. J., Jowsey, J. O., and DeLuca, H. F.**, Production of 1,25-dihydroxyvitamin D_3 and formation of medullary bone in the egg-laying hen, *Endocrinology*, 104, 1598, 1979.
211. **Spanos, E., Pike, J. W., Haussler, M. R., Colston, K. W., Evans, I. M. A., Goldner, A. M., McCain, T. A., and MacIntyre, I.**, Circulating 1α-25-dihydroxyvitamin D in the chicken: enhancement by injection of prolactin and during egg laying, *Life Sci.*, 19, 1751, 1976.
212. **Warren, D. C. and Scott, H. M.**, The time factor in egg formation, *Poult. Sci.*, 14, 195, 1935.
213. **Pike, J. W., Toverud, S., Boass, A., McCain, T., and Haussler, M. R.**, Circulating 1α,25-$(OH)_2D$ during physiological states of calcium stress, in *Vitamin D: Biochemical, Chemical and Clinical Aspects Related to Calcium Metabolism*, Norman, A. W., Schaefer, K., Coburn, J. W., DeLuca, H. F., Fraser, D., Grigoleit, H.-G. and Herrath, D. v., Eds., De Gruyter, New York, 1977, 187.
214. **Kumar, R., Cohen, W. R., Silva, P., and Epstein, F. H.**, Elevated 1,25-dihydroxyvitamin D plasma levels in normal human pregnancy and lactation, *J. Clin. Invest.*, 63, 342, 1979.
215. **Brown, D. J., Spanos, E., Raptis, P., and MacIntyre, I.**, Effect of pregnancy, acromegaly, primary hyperparathyroidism and prolactinoma on 1,25-dihydroxyvitamin D in man, in *Vitamin D: Basic Research and its Clinical Application*, Norman, A. W., Schaefer, K., Herrath, D. v., Grigoleit, H.-G., Coburn, J. W., DeLuca, H. F., Mawer, E. B., and Suda, T., Eds., De Gruyter, New York, 1979, 625.
216. **Lester, G. E., Gray, T. K., and Lorenc, R. S.**, Evidence for maternal and fetal differences in vitamin D metabolism, *Proc. Soc. Exp. Biol. Med.*, 159, 303, 1978.
217. **Boass, A., Toverud, S. U., McCain, T. A., Pike, J. W., and Haussler, M. R.**, Elevated serum levels of 1α,25-dihydroxycholecalciferol in lactating rats, *Nature (London)* 267, 630, 1977.
218. **Horiuchi, N., Suda, T., Sasaki, S., Takahashi, H., Shimazawa, E., and Ogata, E.**, Absence of regulatory effects of 1α,25-dihydroxyvitamin D_3 on 25-hydroxyvitamin D_3 metabolism in rats constantly infused with parathyroid hormone, *Biochem. Biophys. Res. Commun.*, 73, 869, 1976.
219. **Omdahl, J. L., Hunsaker, L. A., and Aschenbrenner, V. A.**, Control of kidney 25-hydroxyvitamin D_3 metabolism. Strontium and the involvement of parathyroid hormone, *Arch. Biochem. Biophys.*, 184, 172, 1977.
220. **Horiuchi, N., Suda, T., Takahashi, H. Shimazawa, E., and Ogata, E.**, *In vivo* evidence for the intermediary role of 3′,5′-cyclic AMP in parathyroid hormone-induced stimulation of 1α,25-dihydroxyvitamin D_3 synthesis in rats, *Endocrinology*, 101, 969, 1977.
221. **Omdahl, J. L.**, Interaction of the parathyroid and 1,25-dihydroxyvitamin D_3 in the control of renal 25-hydroxyvitamin D_3 metabolism, *J. Biol. Chem.*, 253, 8474, 1978.
222. **Rader, J. I., Baylink, D. J., Hughes, M. R., Safilian, E. F., and Haussler, M. R.**, Calcium and phosphorus deficiency in rats: effects on PTH and 1,25-dihydroxyvitamin D_3, *Am. J. Physiol.*, 236, E118, 1979.
223. **Hill, L. F. and Mawer, E. B.**, The interrelationships between vitamin D, parathyroid hormone and calcitonin, *Clin. Sci.*, 44, 4p, 1973.
224. **Lorenc, R., Tanaka, Y., DeLuca, H. F., and Jones, G.**, Lack of effect of calcitonin on the regulation of vitamin D metabolism in the rat, *Endocrinology*, 100, 468, 1977.

225. **Nagode, L. A. and Steinmeyer, C. L.,** Regulation of plasma levels of 1,25-dihydroxyvitamin D in growing dogs with thyroparathyroidectomy and varying amounts of parathyroid hormone, in *Vitamin D: Basic Research and its Clinical Application,* Norman, A. W., Schaefer, K., Herrath, D. v., Grigoleit, H.-G., Coburn, J. W., DeLuca, H. F., Mawer, E. B., and Suda, T., Eds., De Gruyter, New York, 1979, 567.
226. **Tanaka, Y., Lorenc, R. S., and DeLuca, H. F.,** The role of 1,25-dihydroxyvitamin D_3 and parathyroid hormone in the regulation of chick renal 25-hydroxyvitamin D_3-24-hydroxylase, *Arch. Biochem. Biophys.,* 171, 521, 1975.
227. **Kenny, A. D. and Dacke, C. G.,** The hypercalcemic response to parathyroid in Japanese quail, *J. Endocrinol.,* 62, 51, 1974.
228. **Dacke, C. G. and Kenny, A. D.,** Avian bioassay method for parathyroid hormone, *Endocrinology,* 92, 463, 1973.
229. **Booth, B. E., Tsai, H. C., and Morris, R. C., Jr.,** Parathyroidectomy reduces 25-hydroxyvitamin D_3-1α-hydroxylase activity in the hypocalcemic vitamin D-deficient chick, *J. Clin. Invest.,* 60, 1314, 1977.
230. **Larkins, R. G., Colston, K. W., Galante, L. S., MacAuley, S. J., Evans, I. M. A., and MacIntyre, I.,** Regulation of vitamin-D metabolism without parathyroid hormone, *Lancet,* 2, 289, 1973.
231. **Pento, J. T., Waite, L. C., Tracy, P. J., and Kenny, A. D.,** Adaptation to calcium deprivation in the rat: effects of parathyroidectomy, *Am. J. Physiol.,* 232, E336, 1977.
232. **Turner, R. T., Howard, G. A., Rader, J. I., Bottemiller, B. L., and Baylink, D. J.,** *In vitro* regulation of 25-hydroxyvitamin D_3 metabolism by avian kidney cells in serum-free medium, in *Vitamin D: Basic Research and its Clinical Application,* Norman, A. W., Schaefer, K., Herrath, D. v., Grigoleit, H.-G., Coburn, J. W., DeLuca, H. F., Mawer, E. B., and Suda, T., Eds. De Gruyter, New York, 1979, 617.
233. **Baksi, S. N. and Kenny, A. D.,** Influence of sex on renal 25-hydroxyvitamin D_3 metabolism in Japanse quail, in Prog. 58th Meeting Endocrine Soc. San Francisco, 1976, 262.
234. **Tanaka, Y., Castillo, L., Wineland, M. J., and DeLuca, H. F.,** Synergistic effect of progesterone, testosterone and estradiol in the stimulation of chick renal 25-hydroxyvitamin D_3-1α-hydroxylase, *Endocrinology,* 103, 2035, 1978.
235. **Sommerville, B. A., Swaminathan, R., and Scanes, C. G.,** The effects of dietary calcium and of oestrogen on the metabolism of 25-hydroxycholecalciferol in vitamin D-replete chicks, *Calcif. Tissue Res.,* Suppl. 22, 51, 1977.
236. **Kenny, A. D. and Baksi, S. N.,** Estradiol-induced stimulation of vitamin D metabolism in antiandrogen-treated Japanese quail, Prog. 60th Meeting Endocrine Soc. Miami, 1978, 321.
237. **Kenny, A. D.,** Plasma estradiol levels in Japanese quail: relationship to vitamin D metabolism, *Calcif. Tissue Int.,* 28, 175, 1979.
238. **Spanos, E., Colston, K. W., and MacIntyre, I.,** Effect of glucocorticoids on vitamin D metabolism, *FEBS Lett.,* 75, 73, 1977.
239. **Baksi, S. N. and Kenny, A. D.,** Estradiol stimulation of 1,25-dihydroxyvitamin D_3 production in normal rats, *Pharmacologist,* 19, 186, 1977.
240. **Gallagher, J. C., Riggs, B. L., Hamstra, A., and DeLuca, H. F.,** Effect of estrogen therapy on calcium absorption and vitamin D metabolism in postmenopausal osteoporosis, *Clin. Res.,* 26, 32A, 1978.
241. **Nicholson, R. A., Akhtar, M., and Taylor, T. G.,** Metabolism of cholecalciferol in the liver of Japanese quail (Coturnix coturnix japonica) with particular reference to the effects of estrogen, *Biochem. J.,* 182, 745, 1979.
242. **Kenny, A. D. and Baksi, S. N.,** Stimulation of renal-vitamin D endocrine system by physiological doses of estradiol in Japanese quail, *Fed. Proc. Fed. Am. Soc. Exp. Biol.,* 37, 926, 1978.
243. **Spanos, E., Colston, K. W., Evans, I. M. S., Galante, L. S., MacAuley, S. J., and MacIntyre, I.,** Effect of prolactin on vitamin D metabolism, *Mol. Cell. Endocrinol.,* 5, 163, 1976.
244. **MacIntyre, I., Brown, D. J., and Spanos, E.,** Prolactin, growth hormone and vitamin D metabolism, in *Vitamin D: Basic Research and its Clinical Application,* Norman, A. W., Schaefer, K., Herrath, D. v., Grigoleit, H.-G., Coburn, J. W., DeLuca, H. F., Mawer, E. B., and Suda, T., Eds., De Gruyter, New York, 1979, 523.
245. **Spencer, E. M., Tobiassen, O., Ling, P., and Braunstein, E.,** Growth hormone and prolactin action on vitamin D metabolism in the rat, in *Vitamin D: Basic Research and its Clinical Application,* Norman, A. W., Schaefer, K., Herrath, D. v., Griogleit, H.-G., Coburn, J. W., DeLuca, H. F., Mawer, E. B., and Suda, T., Eds., De Gruyter, New York, 1979, 475.
246. **Kenny, A. D. and Dacke, C. G.,** Parathyroid hormone and calcium metabolism, in *World Review of Nutrition and Dietetics,* Vol. 20, Bourne, G. H., Ed., S. Karger, Basel, 1975, 231.
247. **Pang, P. K. T., Schreibman, M. P., and Griffith, R. W.,** Pituitary regulation of serum calcium levels in the killifish, *Fundulus heteroclitus,* L., *Gen. Comp. Endocrinol.,* 21, 536, 1973.

248. **Spencer, E. M. and Tobiassen, O.**, Growth hormone's stimulation of intestinal calcium absorption is mediated by vitamin D, *Clin. Res.*, 25, 162A, 1977.

249. **James, M. F., Spanos, E., Robinson, E. J., Makeen, A. M., Snowball, S. Colston, K. W., Hillyard, C., and MacIntyre, I.**, Effect of anterior pituitary and related peptide hormones on calcium absorption and the metabolism of vitamin D, *J. Endocrinol.*, 79, 38P, 1979.

250. **Spanos, E., Barrett, D., MacIntyre, I., Pike, J. W., Safilian, E. F., and Haussler, M. R.**, Effect of growth hormone on vitamin D metabolism, *Nature (London)*, 273, 246, 1978.

251. **Gertner, J. M., Horst, R. L., Genel, M., and Rasmussen, H.**, The effect of human growth hormone replacement on parathyroid function and vitamin D metabolism, in *Vitamin D: Basic Research and its Clinical Application*, Norman, A. W., Schaefer, K., Herrath, D. v., Grigoleit, H.-G., Coburn, J. W., DeLuca, H. F., Mawer, E. B., and Suda, T., Eds., De Gruyter, New York, 1979, 265.

252. **Kumar, R., Merimee, T. J., Silva, P., and Epstein, F. H.**, The effect of chronic excess or deficiency of growth hormone on plasma 1,25-dihydroxyvitamin D levels in man, in *Vitamin D: Basic Research and its Clinical Application*, Norman, A. W., Schaefer, K., Herrath, D. v., Grigoleit, H.-G., Coburn, J. W., DeLuca, H. F., Mawer, E. B., and Suda, T., Eds., De Gruyter, New York, 1979, 1005.

253. **Lund, B., Sørensen, O. H., and Lund, B.**, Clinical application of the $1,25(OH)_2D$ assay, in *Vitamin D: Basic Research and its Clinical Application*, Norman, A. W., Schaefer, K., Herrath, D. v., Grigoleit, H.-G., Coburn, J. W., DeLuca, H. F., Mawer, E. B., and Suda, T., Eds., De Gruyter, New York, 1979, 991.

254. **Herrath, D. v., Opitz, A., Koch, H.-U., Knoop, H., and Schaefer, K.**, Effect of cortisone on vitamin D metabolism in rat plasma, *Klin. Wochenschr.*, 49, 48, 1971.

255. **Schaefer, K., Herrath, D. v., Koch, H.-U., and Opitz, A.**, Effect of cortisone on vitamin D metabolism, *Isr. J. Med. Sci.*, 7, 533, 1971.

256. **Lukert, B. P. and Adams, J. S.**, Vitamin D metabolism in man. Effect of corticosteroids, *Arch. Intern. Med.*, 136, 1241, 1976.

257. **Favus, M. J., Kimberg, D. V., Millar, G. N., and Gershon, E.**, Effects of cortisone administration on the metabolism and localization of 25-hydroxycholecalciferol in the rat, *J. Clin. Invest.*, 52, 1328, 1973.

258. **Lukert, B. P., Stanbury, S. W., and Mawer, E. B.**, Vitamin D and intestinal transport of calcium: effects of prednisolone, *Endocrinology*, 93, 718, 1973.

259. **Chesney, R. W., Mazess, R. B., Hamstra, A. J., and DeLuca, H. F.**, Reduction of serum-1,25-dihydroxyvitamin-D_3 in children receiving glucocorticoids, *Lancet*, 2, 1123, 1978.

260. **Sorrel, M. and Rosen, J. F.**, Interactions of lead, calcium, vitamin D and nutrition in lead-burdened children, *Arch. Environ. Health*, 32, 160, 1977.

261. **Hill, L. F., Lumb, G. A., Mawer, E. B., and Stanbury, S. W.**, Indirect inhibition of the biosynthesis of 1,25-dihydroxycholecalciferol in rats treated with a diphosphonate, *Clin. Sci.*, 44, 335, 1973.

262. **Baxter, L. A., DeLuca, H. F., Bonjour, J.-P., and Fleisch, H. A.**, Inhibition of vitamin D metabolism by ethane-1-hydroxy-1, 1-diphosphonate, *Arch. Biochem. Biophys.*, 164, 655, 1974.

263. **Guilland, D., Trechsel, U., Bonjour, J.-P., and Fleisch, H.**, Stimulation of calcium absorption and apparent increased intestinal 1,25-dihydroxycholecalciferol in rats treated with low doses of ethane-1-hydroxy-1, 1-diphosphonate, *Clin. Sci. Mol. Med.*, 48, 157, 1975.

264. **Omdahl, J. L. and DeLuca, H. F.**, Rachitogenic activity of dietary strontium, *J. Biol. Chem.*, 247, 5520, 1972.

265. **Omdahl, J. L. and DeLuca, H. F.**, Strontium induced rickets: metabolic basis, *Science*, 174, 949, 1971.

266. **Berger, E. Y.**, Intestinal absorption and excretion, in *Mineral Metabolism: An Advanced Treatise*, Vol. 1, Comar, C. L. and Bronner, F., Eds., Academic Press, New York, 1960, 249.

267. **Berger, E. Y.**, Techniques for studying ion transfer across the alimentary tract, in *The Transfer of Calcium and Strontium Across Biological Membranes*, Wasserman, R. H., Ed., Academic Press, New York, 1963, 57.

268. **Levin, R. J.**, Techniques, terminology and parameters in intestinal absorption, *Br. Med. Bull.*, 23, 209, 1967.

269. **Wilson, T. H. and Wiseman, G.**, The use of sacs of everted small intestine for the study of the transference of substances from the mucosal to the serosal surface, *J. Physiol. (London)*, 123, 116, 1954.

270. **Duthie, H. L.**, Methods for studies of intestinal absorption in man, *Br. Med. Bull.*, 23, 213, 1967.

271. **Henry, K. M. and Kon, S. K.**, The relationship between calcium retention and body stores of calcium in the rat: effect of age and of vitamin D, *Br. J. Nutr.*, 7, 147, 1953.

272. **Benson, J. D., Emery, R. S., and Thomas, J. W.**, Effects of previous calcium intakes on adaptation to low and high calcium diets in rats, *J. Nutr.*, 97, 53, 1969.

273. **Hurwitz, S. and Griminger, P.,** Observations on the calcium balance of laying hens, *J. Agric. Sci. Camb.*, 54, 373, 1960.
274. **Gershoff, S. N., Legg, M. A., and Hegsted, D. M.,** Adaptation to different calcium intakes in dogs, *J. Nutr.*, 64, 303, 1958.
275. **Bauer, W., Albright, F., and Aub, J. C.,** Studies of calcium and phosphorus metabolism. II. The calcium excretion of normal individuals in a low calcium diet, also data on a case of pregnancy, *J. Clin. Invest.*, 7, 75, 1929.
276. **Comar, C. L., Monroe, R. A., Visek, W. J., and Hansard, S. L.,** Comparison of two isotope methods for determination of endogenous fecal calcium, *J. Nutr.*, 50, 459, 1953.
277. **Visek, W. J., Monroe, R. A., Swanson, E. W., and Comar, C. L.,** Calcium metabolism in dairy cows as studied with Ca^{45}, *J. Dairy Sci.*, 36, 373, 1953.
278. **Hansard, S. L. and Crowder, H. M.,** The physiological behavior of calcium in the rat, *J. Nutr.*, 62, 325, 1957.
279. **Hansard, S. L. and Plumlee, M. P.** Effects of dietary calcium and phosphorus levels upon the physiological behavior of calcium and phosphorus in the rat, *J. Nutr.*, 54, 17, 1954.
280. **Shah, B. G. and Draper, H. H.,** Depression of calcium absorption in parathyroidectomized rats, *Am. J. Physiol.*, 211, 963, 1966.
281. **Sammon, P. J., Stacey, R. E., and Bronner, F.,** Role of parathyroid hormone in calcium homeostasis and metabolism, *Am. J. Physiol.*, 218, 479, 1970.
282. **Bronner, F. and Harris, R. S.,** Absorption and metabolism of calcium in human beings, studied with $calcium^{45}$, *Ann. N. Y. Acad. Sci.*, 64, 314, 1956.
283. **Bronner, F.,** Calcium absorption, *Am. J. Clin. Nutr.*, 22, 376, 1969.
284. **Bronner, F. and Aubert, J.-P.,** Bone metabolism and regulation of the blood calcium level in rats, *Am. J. Physiol.*, 209, 887, 1965.
285. **Bronner, F.,** Dynamics and function of calcium, in *Mineral Metabolism: An Advanced Treatise*, Vol. 2, (Part A) Comar, C. L. and Bronner, F., Eds., Academic Press, New York, 1964, 341.
286. **Cramer, C. F.,** Participation of parathyroid glands in control of calcium absorption in dogs, *Endocrinology*, 72, 192, 1963.
287. **Cramer, C. F.,** *In vivo* intestinal transport of calcium and water from solutions recycled through healed gut loops in dogs, *J. Nutr.*, 84, 118, 1964.
288. **Cramer, C. F.,** Sites of calcium absorption and the calcium concentration of gut contents in the dog, *Can. J. Physiol. Pharmacol.*, 43, 75, 1965.
289. **Cramer, C. F.,** Effect of Ca/P ratio and pH on calcium and phosphorus absorption from dog gut loops *in vivo*, *Can. J. Physiol. Pharmacol.*, 46, 171, 1968.
290. **Cramer, C. F. and Dueck, J.,** *In vivo* transport of calcium from healed Thiry-vella fistulas in dogs, *Am. J. Physiol.*, 202, 161, 1962.
291. **Cramer, C. F. and Hagg, T. A.,** The effect of flow rate and osmolarity of lumen contents on calcium and water absorption from Thiry-Vella fistulas in dogs, *Can. J. Biochem. Physiol.*, 41, 127, 1963.
292. **Cramer, C. F., Parkes, C. O., and Copp, D. H.,** The effect of chicken and hog calcitonin on some parameters of Ca, P, and Mg metabolism in dogs, *Can. J. Physiol. Pharmacol.*, 47, 181, 1969.
293. **Care, A. D. and van't Klooster, A. T.,** *In vivo* transport of magnesium and other cations across the wall of the gastrointestinal tract of sheep, *J. Physiol. (London)*, 177, 174, 1965.
294. **Phillipson, A. T. and Storry, J. E.,** The absorption of calcium and magnesium from the rumen and small intestine of the sheep, *J. Physiol. (London)*, 181, 130, 1965.
295. **Scott, D.,** Factors influencing the secretion and absorption of calcium and magnesium in the small intestine of the sheep, *Q. J. Exp. Physiol.*, 50, 312, 1965.
296. **Hydéh, S.,** A turbidimetric method for the determination of higher polyethylene glycols in biological materials, *Ann. Agric. Coll. Sweden*, 22, 139, 1955.
297. **Dumont, P. A., Curran, P. F., and Solomon, A. K.,** Calcium and strontium in rat small intestine, their fluxes and their effect on Na flux, *J. Gen. Physiol.*, 43, 1119, 1960.
298. **Krawitt, E. L.,** Effect of thyrocalcitonin on duodenal calcium transport, *Proc. Soc. Exp. Biol. Med.*, 125, 1084, 1967.
299. **Krawitt, E. L. and Schedl, H. P.,** *In vivo* calcium transport by rat small intestine, *Am. J. Physiol.*, 214, 232, 1968.
300. **Wasserman, R. H., Kallfelz, F. A., and Comar, C. L.,** Active transport of calcium by rat duodenum *in vivo*, *Science*, 133, 883, 1961.
301. **Holdsworth, E. S.,** Vitamin D_3 and calcium absorption in the chick, *Biochem. J.*, 96, 475, 1965.
302. **Waldron-Edward, D., Paul, T. M., and Skoryna, S. C.,** Effects of the counter ion and pH on intestinal absorption of calcium and strontium, *Proc. Soc. Exp. Biol. Med.*, 123, 532, 1966.
303. **Wasserman, R. H.,** Studies on vitamin D_3 and the intestinal absorption of calcium and other ions in the rachitic chick, *J. Nutr.*, 77, 69, 1962.

304. **Wasserman, R. H. and Comar, C. L.,** The parathyroids and the intestinal absorption of calcium, strontium and phosphate ions in the rat, *Endocrinology*, 69, 1074, 1961.
305. **Wasserman, R. H., Taylor, A. N., and Kallfelz, F. A.,** Vitamin D and transfer of plasma calcium to intestinal lumen in chicks and rats, *Am. J. Physiol.*, 211, 419, 1966.
306. **Winter, M., Morava, E., and Simon, G.,** Effect of cortisone on the intestinal absorption of calcium in rats, *Med. Exp.*, 19, 52, 1969.
307. **Winter, M., Morava, E., Simon, G., and Sós, J.,** The role of the parathyroid glands in the absorption of calcium from the small intestine, *J. Endocrinol.*, 47, 65, 1970.
308. **Corradino, R. A. and Wasserman, R. H.,** Strontium inhibition of vitamin D_3-induced calcium-binding protein (CaBP) and calcium absorption in chick intestine, *Proc. Soc. Exp. Biol. Med.*, 133, 960, 1970.
309. **Coates, M. E., Harrison, G. F., and Holdsworth, E. S.,** The effect of a rachitogenic factor on calcium metabolism in chicks, *Br. J. Nutr.*, 15, 149, 1961.
310. **Coates, M. E. and Holdsworth, E. S.,** Vitamin D_3 and absorption of calcium in the chick, *Br. J. Nutr.*, 15, 131, 1961.
311. **Ebel, J. G., Taylor, A. N., and Wasserman, R. H.,** Vitamin D-induced calcium-binding protein of intestinal mucosa. Relation to vitamin D dose level and lag period, *Am. J. Clin. Nutr.*, 22, 431, 1969.
312. **Feher, J. J. and Wasserman, R. H.,** Calcium absorption and intestinal calcium-binding protein: quantitative relationship, *Am. J. Physiol.*, 236, E556, 1979.
313. **Gershoff, S. N. and Hegsted, D. M.,** Effect of vitamin D and Ca: P ratios on chick gastrointestinal tract, *Am. J. Physiol.*, 187, 203, 1956.
314. **Harmeyer, J. and DeLuca, H. F.,** Calcium-binding protein and calcium absorption after vitamin D administration, *Arch. Biochem. Biophys.*, 133, 247, 1969.
315. **Hurwitz, S., Harrison, H. C., and Harrison, H. E.,** Effect of vitamin D_3 on the in vitro transport of calcium by the chick intestine, *J. Nutr.*, 91, 319, 1967.
316. **Neville, E. and Holdsworth, E. S.,** A "second messenger" for vitamin D, *FEBS Lett.*, 2, 313, 1969.
317. **Sallis, J. D. and Holdsworth, E. S.,** Influence of vitamin D on calcium absorption in the chick, *Am. J. Physiol.*, 203, 497, 1962.
318. **Wasserman, R. H., Corradino, R. A., and Taylor, A. N.,** Binding proteins from animals with possible transport function, *J. Gen. Physiol.*, 54, 114s, 1969.
319. **Wasserman, R. H. and Kallfelz, F. A.,** Vitamin D_3 and unidirectional calcium fluxes across the rachitic chick duodenum, *Am. J. Physiol.*, 203, 221, 1962.
320. **Webling, D. D'A. and Holdsworth, E. S.,** The effect of bile, bile acids and detergents on calcium absorption in the chick, *Biochem. J.*, 97, 408, 1965.
321. **Kallfelz, F. A. and Wasserman, R. H.,** Correlation between ^{47}Ca absorption and intestinal calcium-binding activity in the golden hamster, *Proc. Soc. Exp. Biol. Med.*, 139, 77, 1972.
322. **Schedl, H. P., Osbaldiston, G. W., and Mills, I. H.,** Absorption, secretion and precipitation of calcium in the small intestine of the dog, *Am. J. Physiol.*, 214, 814, 1968.
323. **Schachter, D. and Rosen, S. M.,** Active transport of Ca^{45} by the small intestine and its dependence on vitamin D, *Am. J. Physiol.*, 196, 357, 1959.
324. **Rasmussen, H.,** The influence of parathyroid function upon the transport of calcium in isolated sacs of rat small intestine, *Endocrinology*, 65, 517, 1959.
325. **Oswald, N. and Binswanger, U.,** Proximal and distal intestinal calcium transport in vitro as influenced by low calcium diet, uremia, parathyroidectomy and 1,25-dihydroxycholecalciferol treatment in rats, *Res. Exp. Med.*, 175, 19, 1979.
326. **Avioli, L. V., Scott, S., Lee, S. W., and DeLuca, H. F.,** Intestinal calcium absorption: nature of defect in chronic renal disease, *Science*, 166, 1154, 1969.
327. **Avioli, L. V., Lee, S. W., Birge, S. J., Slatopolsky, E., and DeLuca, H. F.,** The nature of the defect in intestinal calcium absorption in chronic renal disease, *J. Clin. Invest.*, 48, 4a, 1969.
328. **Blunt, J. W., Tanaka, Y., and DeLuca, H. F.,** The biological activity of 25-hydroxycholecalciferol, a metabolite of vitamin D_3, *Proc. Natl. Acad. Sci. U.S.A.*, 61, 1503, 1968.
329. **Dowdle, E. B., Schachter, D., and Schenker, H.,** Requirement for vitamin D for the active transport of calcium by the intestine, *Am. J. Physiol.*, 198, 269, 1960.
330. **Finkelstein, J. D. and Schachter, D.,** Active transport of calcium by intestine: effects of hypophysectomy and growth hormone, *Am. J. Physiol.*, 203, 873, 1962.
331. **Gruson, M., Cerland, M., Miravet, L., Paul, J., and Hioco, D.,** Action de la calcitonine de porc sur le transfert *in vitro* du Ca^{45} au niveau du duodénum de rat normal et thyroparathyroïdectomisé, *C. R. Acad. Sci.*, 270, 1014, 1970.
332. **Harrison, H. C. and Harrison, H. E.,** Calcium transport by rat colon *in vitro*, *Am. J. Physiol.* 217, 121, 1969.

333. **Kessner, D. M. and Epstein, F. H.,** Effect of magnesium deficiency on gastrointestinal transfer of calcium, *Proc. Soc. Exp. Biol. Med.,* 122, 721, 1966.
334. **Kimberg, D. V., Schachter, D., and Schenker, H.,** Active transport of calcium by intestine: effects of dietary calcium, *Am. J. Physiol.,* 200, 1256, 1961.
335. **Lifshitz, F., Harrison, H. C., and Harrison, H. E.,** Intestinal transport of calcium and phosphate in experimental magnesium deficiency, *Proc. Soc. Exp. Biol. Med.,* 125, 19, 1962.
336. **Lifshitz, F., Harrison, H. C., and Harrison, H. E.,** Response to vitamin D of magnesium deficient rats, *Proc. Soc. Exp. Biol. Med.,* 125, 472, 1967.
337. **Lifshitz, F., Harrison, H. C., and Harrison, H. E.,** Influence of parathyroid function upon the *in vitro* transport of calcium and phosphate by the rat intestine, *Endocrinology,* 84, 912, 1969.
338. **Martin, D. L. and DeLuca, H. F.,** Influence of sodium on calcium transport by the rat small intestine, *Am. J. Physiol.,* 216, 1351, 1969.
339. **Noble, H. M. and Matty, A. J.,** The effect of thyroxine on the movement of calcium and inorganic phosphate through the small intestine of the rat, *J. Endocrinol.,* 37, 111, 1967.
340. **Armbrecht, H. J. and Wasserman, R. H.,** Enhancement of Ca^{++} uptake by lactose in the rat small intestine, *J. Nutr.,* 106, 1265, 1976.
341. **Schachter, D., Dowdle, E. B., and Schenker, H.,** Active transport of calcium by the small intestine of the rat, *Am. J. Physiol.,* 198, 263, 1960.
342. **Schachter, D., Kowarski, S., Finkelstein, J. D., and Ma, R. I. W.,** Tissue concentration differences during active transport of calcium by intestine, *Am. J. Physiol.,* 211, 1131, 1966.
343. **Schachter, D., Kowarski, S., and Reid, P.,** Active transport of calcium by intestine: studies with a calcium activity electrode, in *A Symposium on Calcium and Cellular Function,* Cuthbert, A. W., Ed., St. Martin's Press, New York, 1970, 108.
344. **Urban, E. and Schedl, H. P.,** Comparison of *in vivo* and *in vitro* effects of vitamin D on calcium transport in the rat, *Am. J. Physiol.,* 217, 126, 1969.
345. **Urban, E. and Schedl, H. P.,** Effect of vitamin D on tissue calcium of rat and duodenum, *Scand. J. Gastroenterol.,* 5, 33, 1970.
346. **Wasserman, R. H.,** Metabolic basis of calcium and strontium discrimination: studies with surviving intestinal segments, *Proc. Soc. Exp. Biol. Med.,* 104, 92, 1960.
347. **Wasserman, R. H. and Taylor, A. N.,** The non-essentiality of sodium ions for intestinal calcium transport, *Proc. Soc. Exp. Biol. Med.,* 114, 479, 1963.
348. **Williams, G. A., Bowser, E. N., Henderson, W. J., and Uzgiries, V.,** Effects of vitamin D and cortisone on intestinal absorption of calcium in the rat, *Proc. Soc. Exp. Biol. Med.,* 106, 664, 1961.
349. **Williams, G. A., Bowser, E. N., Henderson, W. J., and Uzgiries, V.,** Calcium absorption in the rat in relation to excessive vitamin D and cortisone, *Proc. Soc. Exp. Biol. Med.,* 110, 889, 1962.
350. **Morehead, R. M. and Kessner, D. M.,** Effects of Mg deficiency and parathyroidectomy on gastrointestinal Ca transport in the rat, *Am. J. Physiol.,* 217, 1608, 1969.
351. **Parsons, D. S. and Paterson, C. R.,** Fluid and solute transport across rat colonic mucosa, *Q. J. Exp. Physiol.,* 50, 220, 1965.
352. **Schachter, D.,** Vitamin D and the active transport of calcium by the small intestine, in *The Transfer of Calcium and Strontium Across Biological Membranes,* Wasserman, R. H., Ed., Academic Press, New York, 1963, 197.
353. **Wasserman, R. H. and Taylor, A. N.,** Some aspects of the intestinal absorption of calcium with special reference to vitamin D, in *Mineral Metabolism: An Advanced Treatise,* Vol. 3, Comar, C. L. and Bronner, F., Eds., Academic Press, New York, 1969, 321.
354. **Crane, R. K. and Wilson, T. H.,** *In vitro* method for the study of the rate of intestinal absorption of sugars, *J. Appl. Physiol.,* 12, 145, 1958.
355. **Batt, E. R. and Schachter, D.,** Developmental pattern of some intestinal transport mechanisms in newborn rats and mice, *Am. J. Physiol.,* 216, 1064, 1969.
356. **Martin, D. L. and DeLuca, H. F.,** Calcium transport and the role of vitamin D, *Arch. Biochem. Biophys.,* 134, 139, 1969.
357. **Ziporin, Z. Z., Isaac, G. J., Liddle, C. G., and Waring, P. P.,** Effect of actinomycin D on vitamin D-mediated uptake of ^{45}Ca by intestinal slices, *Calcif. Tissue Res.,* 13, 187, 1973.
358. **Schachter, D., Dowdle, E. B., and Schenker, H.,** Accumulation of Ca^{45} by slices of the small intestine, *Am. J. Physiol.,* 198, 275, 1960.
359. **Rasmussen, H., Waldorf, A., Dziewiatkowski, D. D., and DeLuca, H. F.,** Calcium exchange in isolated intestinal villi, *Biochem. Biophys. Acta,* 75, 250, 1963.
360. **Ussing, H. H. and Zerahn, K.,** Active transport of sodium as the source of electric current in the short-circuited isolated frog skin, *Acta Physiol. Scand.,* 23, 110, 1951.
361. **Helbock, H. J., Forte, J. G., and Saltman, P.,** The mechanism of calcium transport by rat intestine, *Biochim. Biophys. Acta,* 126, 81, 1966.

362. **Walling, M. W. and Rothman, S. S.,** Phosphate-independent, carrier-mediated active transport of calcium by rat intestine, *Am. J. Physiol.*, 217, 1144, 1969.
363. **Corradino, R. A.,** Cadmium inhibition of vitamin D-mediated responses in organ-cultured embryonic chick duodenum, *Toxicol. Appl. Pharmacol.*, 48, 257, 1979.
364. **Corradino, R. A.,** 1,25-dihydroxycholecalciferol: inhibition of action of organ-cultured intestine by actimomycin D and *α*-amanitin, *Nature (London)* 243, 41, 1973.
365. **Corradino, R. A.,** Diphenylhydantoin: direct inhibition of the vitamin D_3-mediated calcium absorptive mechanism in organ-cultured duodenum, *Biochem. Pharmacol.*, 25, 863, 1976.
366. **Corradino, R. A.,** Embryonic chick intestine in organ culture: hydrocortisone and vitamin D-mediated processes, *Arch. Biochem. Biophys.*, 192, 302, 1979.
367. **Corradino, R. A.,** Embryonic chick intestine in organ culture: response to vitamin D_3 and its metabolites, *Science*, 179, 402, 1973.
368. **Corradino, R. A.,** Embryonic chick intestine in organ culture: interaction of adenylate cyclase system and vitamin D_3-mediated calcium absorption mechanism, *Endocrinology*, 94, 1607, 1974.
369. **Corradino, R. A. and Wasserman, R. H.,** Vitamin D_3: induction of calcium-binding protein in embryonic chick intestine in vitro, *Science*, 172, 731, 1971.
370. **Corradino, R. A., Fullmer, C. S., and Wasserman, R. H.,** Embryonic chick intestine in organ culture: stimulation of calcium transport by exogenous vitamin D-induced calcium-binding protein, *Arch. Biochem. Biophys.*, 174, 738, 1976.
371. **Malm, O. J.,** *Calcium Requirements and Adaptation in Adult Men*, Oslo University Press, 1958.
372. **Blau, M., Spencer, H., Swernov, H., and Laszlo, D.,** Utilization and intestinal excretion of calcium in man, *Science*, 120, 1029, 1954.
373. **Bronner, F.,** Dynamics and function of calcium, in *Mineral Metabolism: An Advanced Treatise*, Vol. 2, Comar, C. L. and Bronner, F., Eds., Academic Press, New York, 1964, 341.
374. **Avioli, L. V., McDonald, J. E., Singer, R. A., and Henneman, P. H.,** A new oral isotopic test of calcium absorption, *J. Clin. Invest.*, 44, 128, 1965.
375. **Caniggia, A., Gennari, C., Bianchi, V., and Guideri, R.,** Intestinal absorption of ^{45}Ca in senile osteoporosis, *Acta Med. Scand.*, 173, 613, 1963.
376. **Curtis, F. K., Fellows, H., and Rich, C.,** Estimation of human calcium absorption by external radioisotope counting, *J. Lab. Clin. Med.*, 69, 1036, 1967.
377. **Jaworski, Z. F., Brown, E. M., Fedoruk, S., and Seitz, H.,** A method for the study of calcium absorption by the human gut using a standard dose of calcium labeled with calcium^{47}, *N. Engl. J. Med.*, 269, 1103, 1963.
378. **Rose, G. A., Reed, G. W., and Smith, A. H.,** Isotpoic method for measurement of calcium absorption from the gastrointestinal tract, *Br. Med. J.*, 1, 690, 1965.
379. **Samachson, J.,** Plasma values after oral ^{45}calcium and ^{85}strontium as an index of absorption, *Clin. Sci.*, 25, 17, 1963.
380. **Spencer, H., Menczel, J., Lewin, I., and Samachson, J.,** Absorption of calcium in osteoporosis, *Am. J. Med.*, 37, 223, 1964.
381. **Spencer, H., Lewin, I., Fowler, J., and Samachson, J.,** Effect of sodium fluoride on calcium absorption and balances in man, *Am. J. Clin. Nutr.*, 22, 381, 1969.
382. **Birge, S. J., Peck, W. A., Berman, M., and Whedon, G. D.,** Study of calcium absorption in man: a kinetic analysis and physiologic model, *J. Clin. Invest.*, 48, 1705, 1969.
383. **Szymendera, J., Heaney, R. P., and Saville, P. D.,** Intestinal calcium absorption: concurrent use of oral and intravenous tracers and calculations by the inverse convolution method, *J. Lab. Clin. Med.*, 79, 570, 1972.
384. **Wensel, R. H., Rich, C., Brown, A. C., and Volwiler, W.,** Absorption of calcium measured by intubation and perfusion of the intact human small intestine, *J. Clin. Invest.*, 48, 1768, 1969.
385. **Wilson, T. H.,** *Intestinal Absorption*, W. B., Saunders, Philadelphia, 1962.
386. **Koefoed-Johnsen, V. and Ussing, H. H.,** Ion transport, in *Mineral Metabolism*, Vol. 1, Comar, C. L. and Bronner, F. Eds., Academic Press, New York, 1960, 169.
387. **Ussing, H. H.,** The distinction by means of tracers between active transport and diffusion. The transfer of iodide across the isolated frog skin, *Acta Physiol. Scand.*, 19, 43, 1949.
388. **Adams, T. H., Wong, R. G., and Norman, A. W.,** Vitamin D mediated calcium transport, *Fed. Proc. Fed. Am. Soc. Exp. Biol.*, 28, 759, 1969.
389. **Aubert, J.-P., Bronner, F., and Richelle, L. J.,** Quantitation of calcium metabolism theory, *J. Clin. Invest.*, 42, 885, 1963.
390. **Michalska, L., Wróbel, J., and Niemiro, R.,** Phosphate and vitamin D sensitive movement of calcium in rat distal ileum, *Acta Biochim. Pol.*, 19, 333, 1972.
391. **Winter, M., Morava, E., Simon, G., and Gyure, A.,** The effect of vitamin D_3 and 25-hydroxycholecalciferol on intestinal transport of calcium *in vivo* and *in vitro*, *Experientia*, 28, 659, 1972.

392. **Hurwitz, S., Bar, A., and Cohen, I.,** Regulation of calcium absorption by fowl intestine, *Am. J. Physiol.*, 225, 150, 1973.
393. **Hurwitz, S. and Bar, A.,** Absorption of calcium and phosphorus along the gastrointestinal tract of the laying fowl as influenced by dietary calcium and egg shell formation, *J. Nutr.*, 86, 433, 1965.
394. **Hurwitz, S. and Bar, A.,** Rate of passage of calcium-45 and yttrium-91 along the intestine, and calcium absorption in the laying fowl, *J. Nutr.*, 89, 311, 1966.
395. **Bar, A., Eisner, U., Montecuccoli, G., and Hurwitz, S.,** Regulation of intestinal absorption in the laying quail: independence of kidney vitamin D hydroxylation, *J. Nutr.*, 106, 1336, 1976.
396. **DeLuca, H. F.,** Recent advances in the metabolism and function of vitamin D, *Fed. Proc. Fed. Am. Soc. Exp. Biol.*, 28, 1678, 1969.
397. **DeLuca, H. F.,** Mechanism of action of 25-hydroxycholecalciferol: the active form of vitamin D, *Calif. Tissue Res.*, 4, 283, 1969.
398. **Martin, D. L., Melancon, M. J., and DeLuca, H. F.,** Vitamin D-stimulated, calcium-dependent adenosine triphosphatase from brush borders of rat small intestine, *Biochem. Biophys. Res. Commun.*, 35, 819, 1969.
399. **Melancon, M. J.,** Vitamin D-induced, calcium-dependent adenosine triphosphatase in chick intestinal brush borders, *Fed. Proc. Fed. Am. Soc. Exp. Biol.*, 29, 268, 1970.
400. **Melancon, M. J. and DeLuca, H. F.,** Vitamin D stimulation of calcium-dependent adenosine triphosphatase in chick intestinal brush borders, *Biochemistry*, 9, 1658, 1970.
401. **Taylor, A. N. and Wasserman, R. H.,** Vitamin D stimulation of calcium-binding protein and brush border enzyme activities, *Fed. Proc. Fed. Am. Soc. Exp. Biol.*, 29, 368, 1970.
402. **Harrison, H. E. and Harrison, H. C.,** Sodium, potassium, and intestinal transport of glucose, L-tyrosine, phosphate, and calcium, *Am. J. Physiol.*, 205, 107, 1963.
403. **Wasserman, R. H., and Taylor A. N.,** Metabolic roles of fat soluble vitamins D, E, and K, *Annu. Rev. Biochem.*, 41, 179, 1972.
404. **Moriuchi, S. and DeLuca, H. F.,** The effect of vitamin D_3 metabolites on membrane proteins of chick duodenal brush borders, *Arch. Biochem. Biophys.*, 174, 367, 1976.
405. **Wilson, P. W. and Lawson, D. E. M.,** Incorporation of [^{3}H] leucine into an actin-like protein in response to 1,25-dihydroxycholecalciferol in chick intestinal brush borders, *Biochem. J.*, 173, 627, 1978.
406. **Goodman, D. B. P., Haussler, M. R., and Rasmussen, H.,** Vitamin D_3 induced alteration of microvillar membrane lipid composition, *Biochem. Biophys. Res. Commun.*, 46, 80, 1972.
407. **Wasserman, R. H. and Taylor, A. N.,** Vitamin D_3-induced calcium-binding protein in chick intestinal mucosa, *Science*, 152, 791, 1966.
408. **Taylor, A. N. and Wasserman, R. H.,** Vitamin D_3-induced calcium-binding protein: partial purification, electrophoretic visualization, and tissue distribution, *Arch. Biochem. Biophys.*, 119, 536, 1967.
409. **Wasserman, R. H., Corradino, R. A., and Taylor, A. N.,** Vitamin D-dependent calcium-binding protein: purification and some properties, *J. Biol. Chem.*, 243, 3978, 1968.
410. **Taylor, A. N. and Wasserman, R. H.,** Vitamin D-induced calcium-binding protein: comparative aspects in kidney and intestine, *Am. J. Physiol.*, 223, 110, 1972.
411. **Wasserman, R. H., Corradino, R. A., Fullmer, C. S., and Taylor, A. N.,** Some aspects of vitamin D action; calcium absorption and the vitamin D-dependent calcium-binding protein, *Vitam. Horm. (N.Y.)*, 32, 299, 1974.
412. **Bar, A., Hurwitz, S., and Edelstein, S.,** Response of renal calcium-binding protein independence of kidney vitamin D hydroxylation, *Biochim. Biophys. Acta*, 411, 106, 1975.
413. **Taylor, A. N.,** Chick brain calcium-binding protein: comparison with intestinal vitamin D-induced calcium-binding protein, *Arch. Biochem. Biophys.*, 161, 100, 1974.
414. **Taylor, A. N.,** Chick brain calcium-binding protein: response to cholecalciferol and some developmental aspects, *J. Nutr.*, 107, 480, 1977.
415. **Milhaud, G., Moukhtar, M. S., Cherian, G., and Pirault, A. M.,** Effet de l'administration du thyrocalcitonine sur les principaux paramétres du metabolisme de calcium du rat normal et du rat thyroparathyroïdectomisé, *C. R. Acad. Sci. Paris*, 262, 511, 1966.
416. **Bruns, M. E. H., Fausto, A., and Avioli, L. V.,** Placental calcium binding protein in rats: apparent identity with vitamin D-dependent calcium binding protein from rat intestine, *J. Biol. Chem.*, 253, 3186, 1978.
417. **Corradino, R. A., Wasserman, R. H., Pubols, M. H., and Chang, S. I.,** Vitamin D_3 induction of a calcium-binding protein in the uterus of the laying hen, *Arch. Biochem. Biophys.*, 125, 378, 1968.
418. **Taylor, A. N. and Wasserman, R. H.,** A vitamin D_3-dependent factor influencing calcium binding by homogenates of chick intestinal mucosa, *Nature (London)*, 205, 248, 1965.

419. **Pointillart, A., Thomasset, M., and Garel, J. M.,** Effects of vitamin D deficiency on calcium-binding proteins (CaBP) and on plasma calcitonin (CT) and parathyroid hormone (PTH) levels in growing pigs, in *Vitamin D: Basic Research and its Clinical Application,* Norman, A. W., Schaefer, K., Herrath, D. v., Grigoleit, H.-G., Coburn, J. W., DeLuca, H. F., Mawer, E. B., and Suda, T., Eds., De Gruyter, New York, 1979, 275.
420. **Morrissey, R. L. and Wasserman, R. H.,** Calcium absorption and calcium-binding protein in chicks on differing calcium and phosphorus intakes, *Am. J. Physiol.,* 220, 1509, 1971.
421. **Bar, A., Hurwitz, S., and Cohen, I.,** Relationship between duodenal calcium-binding protein, parathyroid activity and various parameters of mineral metabolism in the rachitic and vitamin D-treated chick, *Comp. Biochem. Physiol.,* 43A, 519, 1972.
422. **Bar, A. and Hurwitz, S.** Relationship of duodenal calcium-binding protein to calcium absorption in the laying fowl, *Comp. Biochem. Physiol. B,* 41, 735, 1972.
423. **Fullmer, C. S. and Wasserman, R. H.,** Isolation and partial charactization of intestinal calcium-binding proteins from the cow, pig, horse, guinea pig, and chick, *Biochim, Biophys. Acta,* 393, 134, 1975.
424. **Spencer, R., Charman, M., Wilson, P. W., and Lawson, D. E. M.,** The relationship between vitamin D-stimulated calcium transport and intestinal calcium-binding protein in the chicken, *Biochem. J.,* 170, 93, 1978.
425. **Parkes, C. O. and Reynolds, J. J.,** The effect of parathyroid hormone and vitamin D_3 metabolism on CaBP synthesis by embryonic duodenum, in vitro, *Horm. Metab. Res.,* 10, 75, 1978.
426. **Feher, J. J. and Wasserman, R. H.,** Evidence for a membrane-bound fraction of chick intestinal calcium-binding protein, *Biochim. Biophys. Acta,* 540, 134, 1978.
427. **Hamilton, J. W. and Holdsworth, E. S.,** The role of calcium binding protein in the mechanism of action of cholecalciferol (vitamin D_3), *Aust. J. Exp. Biol. Med. Sci.,* 53, 469, 1975.
428. **Friedlander, E. J., Henry, H. L., and Norman, A. W.,** Studies on the mode of action of calciferol. Effects of dietary calcium and phosphorus on the relationship between the 25-hydroxyvitamin D_3-1α-hydroxylase and production of chick intestinal calcium-binding protein, *J. Biol. Chem.,* 252, 8677, 1977.
429. **Wasserman, R. H. and Combs, G. F., Jr.,** Relation of vitamin D-dependent intestinal calcium-binding protein to calcium absorption during the ovulatory cycle in Japanese quail, *Proc. Soc. Exp. Biol. Med.,* 159, 286, 1978.
430. **Drescher, D. and DeLuca, H. F.,** Vitamin D stimulated calcium binding protein from rat intestinal mucosa. Purification and some properties, *Biochemistry,* 10, 3877, 1971.
431. **Oku, T., Moriucki, S., and Hosoya, N.,** Vitamin D_3 binding protein in rat intestinal mucosa, *J. Vitaminol.,* 17, 81, 1971.
432. **Bronner, F. and Freund, T.,** Intestinal CaBP: a new quantitative index of vitamin D deficiency in the rat, *Am. J. Physiol.,* 229, 689, 1975.
433. **Moriuchi, S., Yamanouchi, T., and Hosoya, N.,** Demonstration of two different vitamin D-dependent calcium-binding proteins in rat intestinal mucosa, *J. Nutr. Sci. Vitaminol.,* 21, 251, 1975.
434. **Peshin, J., Ornoy, A., and Menczel, J.,** Transplacental effects of thyrocalcitonin on intestinal calcium-binding protein, alkaline phosphatase activity and ossification of long bones in rat fetuses, *Isr. J. Med. Sci.,* 12, 248, 1976.
435. **Ooizumi, K., Moriuchi, S., and Hosoya, N.,** Vitamin D dependent calcium binding protein in rat intestinal mucosa, *J. Vitaminol.,* 16, 228, 1970.
436. **Marche, P., Pradelles, P., Gros, C., and Thomasset, M.,** Radioimmunoassay for a vitamin D-dependent calcium-binding protein in rat duodenal mucosa, *Biochem. Biophys. Res. Commun.,* 76, 1020, 1977.
437. **Bruns, M. E. H., Fliesher, E. B., and Avioli, L. V.,** Control of vitamin D-dependent calcium-binding protein in rat intestine by growth and fasting, *J. Biol. Chem.,* 252, 4145, 1977.
438. **Thomasset, M., Redel, J., Marche, P., and Cuisinier-Gleizes, P.,** Duodenal calcium-binding protein (CaBP) and bone calcium mobilization in response to 24R,25 and 24S,25-dihydroxycholecalciferol in intact and nephrectomized rats, *J. Steroid Biochem.,* 9, 159, 1978.
439. **Eisman, J. A. and DeLuca, H. F.,** Intestinal 1,25-dihydroxyvitamin D_3 binding protein: specificity of binding, *Steroids,* 30, 245, 1977.
440. **Chapman, M. W., Taylor, A. N., Wasserman, R. H., and Pond, W. G.,** Detection and distribution of intestinal calcium-binding protein in the young adult male guinea pig, *Proc. Soc. Exp. Biol. Med.,* 154, 546, 1977.
441. **Hitchman, A. J. W., Kerr, M. K., and Harrison, J. E.,** The purification of pig vitamin D-induced intestinal calcium binding protein, *Arch. Biochem. Biophys.,* 155, 221, 1973.
442. **Fox, J., Pickard, D. W., Care, A. D., and Murray, T. M.,** Effect of low phosphorus diets on intestinal calcium absorption and the concentration of calcium-binding protein in intact and parathyroidectomized pigs, *J. Endocrinol.,* 78, 379, 1978.

443. **Fullmer, C. S. and Wasserman, R. H.,** Bovine intestinal calcium-binding proteins. Purification and some properties, *Biochim. Biophys. Acta,* 317, 172, 1973.
444. **Huang, W. Y., Cohn, D. M., and Hamilton, J. W.,** Calcium-binding protein of bovine intestine. The complete amino acid sequence, *J. Biol. Chem.,* 250, 7647, 1975.
445. **Fullmer, C. S., Wasserman, R. H., Hamilton, J. W., Huang, W. Y., and Cohn, D. V.,** The effect of calcium on the tryptic digestion of bovine intestinal calcium-binding protein, *Biochem. Biophys. Acta,* 412, 256, 1975.
446. **Oldham, S. B., Smith, R., Hartenbower, D. L., and Henry, H.,** Effects of 1α,25-dihydroxyvitamin D_3 (1α,25$(OH)_2D_3$) on serum calcium (SCa), immunoreactive parathyroid hormone (IPTH) and intestinal and parathyroid calcium binding proteins (ICaBPS PCaBP) in the dog, *Fed. Proc. Fed. Am. Soc. Exp. Biol.,* 35, 302, 1976.
447. **Taylor, A. N., Wasserman, R. H., and Jowsey, J.,** A vitamin D-dependent calcium-binding protein in canine intestinal mucosa, *Fed. Proc. Fed. Am. Soc. Exp. Biol.,* 27, 675, 1968.
448. **Wasserman, R. H. and Taylor, A. N.,** Evidence for a vitamin D_3-induced calcium-binding protein in new world primates, *Proc. Soc. Exp. Biol. Med.,* 136, 25, 1971.
449. **Alpers, D. H., Lee, S. W., and Avioli, L. V.,** Partial isolation of human duodenal calcium-binding proteins, *Clin. Res.,* 18, 605, 1970.
450. **Helmke, K., Federlin, K., Piazolo, P., Ströder, J., Jeschke, R., and Franz, H. E.,** Localization of calcium-binding protein in intestinal tissue by immunofluorescence in normal, vitamin-D-deficient and uraemic subjects, *Gut,* 15, 875, 1974.
451. **Taylor, A. N. and Wasserman, R. H.,** Immunofluorescent localization of vitamin D-dependent calcium-binding protein, *J. Histochem. Cytochem.,* 18, 107, 1970.
452. **Lippiello, L. and Wasserman, R. H.,** Fluorescent antibody localization of the vitamin D-dependent calcium-binding protein in the oviduct of a laying hen, *J. Histochem. Cytochem.,* 23, 111, 1975.
453. **Morrissey, R. L., Empson, R. N., Jr., Zolock, D. T., Bikle, D. D., and Bucci, T. J.,** Intestinal response to 1α,25-dihydroxycholecalciferol. II. A timed study of the intracellular localization of calcium binding protein, *Biochim. Biophys. Acta,* 538, 34, 1978.
454. **Morrissey, R. L., Zolock, D. T., Bucci, T. J., and Bikle, D. D.,** Immunoperoxidase localization of vitamin D dependent calcium binding protein, *J. Histochem. Cytochem.,* 26, 628, 1978.
455. **Arnold, B. M., Kavacs, K., and Murray, T. M.,** Cellular localization of intestinal calcium-binding protein in pig duodenum, *Digestion,* 14, 77, 1976.
456. **Marche, P., Le Guern, C., and Cassier, P.,** Cytoplasmic localization of the calcium binding protein in rat duodenal absorptive cells, in *Vitamin D. Basic Research and its Clinical Application,* Norman, A. W., Schaefer, K., Herrath, D. v., Grigoleit, H.-G., Coburn, J. W., DeLuca, H. F., Mawer, E. B., and Suda, T., Eds., De Gruyter, New York, 1979, 643.
458. **Morrissey, R. L., Bucci, T. J., Empson, R. N., Jr., and Lufkin, E. B.,** Calcium-binding protein: its cellular localization in jejunum, kidney and pancreas, *Proc. Soc. Exp. Biol. Med.,* 149, 56, 1975.
459. **Piazolo, P. Hotz, J., Helmke, K., Franz, H. E., and Schleyer, M.,** Calcium-binding protein in the duodenal mucosa of uremic patients and normal subjects, *Kidney Int.,* 8, 110, 1975.
460. **Dorrington, K. J., Hui, A., Hofmann, T., Hitchman, A. J. W., and Harrison, J. E.,** Porcine intestinal calcium-binding protein. Molecular properties and the effect of binding calcium ions, *J. Biol. Chem.,* 249, 199, 1974.
461. **Wasserman, R. H. and Taylor, A. N.,** Vitamin D-dependent calcium-binding protein: response to some physiological and nutritional variables, *J. Biol. Chem.,* 243, 3987, 1968.
462. **Bar, A. and Wasserman, R. H.,** Duodenal calcium binding protein in the chick: a new bioassay for vitamin D, *J. Nutr.,* 104, 1202, 1974.
463. **Spencer, R., Charman, M., Emtage, J., S. and Lawson, D. E. M.,** Production and properties of vitamin-D-induced mRNA for chick calcium-binding protein, *Eur. J. Biochem.* 71, 399, 1976.
464. **Morrissey, R. L. and Wasserman, R. H.,** Adaptation, calcium binding protein (CaBP) and the intestinal absorption of calcium, *Fed. Proc. Fed. Am. Soc. Exp. Biol.,* 29, 847, 1970.
465. **Taylor, A. N. and Wasserman, R. H.,** Correlation between the vitamin D-induced calcium-binding protein and intestinal absorption of calcium, *Fed. Proc. Fed. Am. Soc. Exp. Biol.,* 28, 1834, 1969.
466. **Bar, A. and Wasserman, R. H.,** Control of calcium absorption and intestinal calcium-binding protein synthesis, *Biochem. Biophys. Res. Commun.,* 54, 191, 1973.
467. **Corradino, R. A., Ebel, J. G., Craig, P. H., Taylor, A. N., and Wasserman, R. H.,** Calcium absorption and the vitamin D_3-dependent calcium-binding protein. I. Inhibition by dietary strontium, *Calcif. Tissue Res.,* 7, 81, 1971.
468. **Corradino, R. A., Ebel, J. G., Craig, P. H., Taylor, A. N., and Wasserman, R. H.,** Calcium absorption and the vitamin D_3-dependent calcium-binding protein. II. Recovery from dietary strontium inhibition, *Calcif. Tissue Res.,* 7, 93, 1971.

469. **Wasserman, R. H.**, Calcium absorption and calcium-binding protein synthesis: *solanum malacoxylon* reverses strontium inhibition, *Science*, 183, 1092, 1974.

470. **Kimberg, D. V., Baerg, R. D., Gershon, E., and Graudusius, R. T.**, Effect of cortisone treatment on the active transport of calcium by the small intestine, *J. Clin. Invest.*, 50, 1309, 1971.

471. **Edelstein, S., Noff, D., Matitiahu, A., Spair, R., and Harrel, A.**, The functional metabolism of vitamin D in rats treated with cortisol, *FEBS Lett.*, 82, 115, 1977.

472. **Krawitt, E. L.**, The role of intestinal transport proteins in cortisol-mediated suppression of Ca^2+ absorption, *Biochim. Biophys. Acta*, 274, 170, 1972.

474. **Corradino, R. A. and Wasserman, R. H.**, Actinomycin D inhibition of vitamin D_3-induced calcium-binding protein (CaBP) formation in chick duodenal mucosa, *Arch. Biochem. Biophys.*, 126, 957, 1968.

475. **Spencer, R., Charman, M., and Lawson, D. E. M.**, Stimulation of intestinal calcium-binding-protein mRNA synthesis in the nucleus of vitamin D-deficient chicks by 1,25-dihydroxycholecalciferol, *Biochem. J.*, 175, 1089, 1978.

476. **Spencer, R., Charman, M., Wilson, P., and Lawson, E.**, Vitamin D-stimulated intestinal calcium-absorption may not involve calcium-binding protein directly, *Nature*, 263, 161, 1976.

477. **Emtage, J. S., Lawson, D. E. M., and Kodicek, E.**, The response of the small intestine to vitamin D. Correlation between calcium-binding-protein production and increased calcium absorption, *Biochem. J.*, 144, 339, 1974.

478. **Sernka, T. J. and Borle, A. B.**, Calcium in the intestinal contents of rats on different calcium diets, *Proc. Soc. Exp. Biol. Med.*, 131, 1420, 1969.

469. **Cramer, C. F. and Copp, D. H.**, Progress and rate of absorption of radiostrontium through intestinal tracts of rats, *Proc. Soc. Exp. Biol. Med.*, 102, 514, 1959.

480. **Lengemann, F. W.**, Over-all aspects of calcium and strontium absorption, in *The Transfer of Calcium and Strontium Across Biological Membranes*, Wasserman, R. H., Ed., Academic Press, New York, 1963, 85.

481. **Marcus, C. S. and Lengemann, F. W.**, Use of radioyttrium to study food movement in the small intestine of the rat, *J. Nutr.*, 76, 179, 1962.

482. **Marcus, C. S. and Lengemann, F. W.**, Absorption of Ca^{45} and Sr^{85} from solid and liquid food at various levels of the alimentary tract of the rat, *J. Nutr.*, 77, 155, 1962.

483. **Schachter, D., Kimberg, D. V., and Schenke, H.**, Active transport of calcium by intestine: action and bio-assay of vitamin D, *Am. J. Physiol.*, 200, 1263, 1961.

484. **Avioli, L. V.**, Absorption and metabolism of vitamin D_3 in man, *Am. J. Clin. Nutr.*, 22, 437, 1969.

485. **Wasserman, R. H.**, Vitamin D and the absorption of calcium and strontium *in vivo*, in *The Transfer of Calcium and Strontium Across Biological Membranes*, Wasserman, R. H., Ed., Academic Press, New York, 1963, 211.

486. **Wasserman, R. H.**, Calcium transport by the intestine: a model and comment on vitamin D action, *Calcif. Tissue Res.*, 2, 301, 1968.

487. **Henry, K. M. and Kon, S. K.**, The effect of age and of the supply of phosphorus on the assimilation of calcium by the rat, *Biochem. J.*, 41, 169, 1947.

488. **Lemaire, R.**, Modifications du métabolisme calcique avec l'âge, *C. R. Soc. Biol.*, 161, 726, 1967.

489. **Draper, H. H.**, The relationship of age and the intestinal absorption of calcium, in *The Transfer of Calcium and Strontium Across Biological Membranes*, Wasserman, R. H., Ed., Academic Press, New York, 1963, 97.

490. **Hironaka, R., Draper, H. H., and Kastelic, J.**, Physiological aspects of aging. III. The influence of aging on calcium metabolism in rats, *J. Nutr.*, 71, 356, 1960.

491. **Hansard, S. L., Comar, C. L., and Davis, G. K.**, Effects of age upon the physiological behavior of calcium in cattle, *Am. J. Physiol.*, 177, 383, 1954.

492. **Gallagher, J. C., Riggs, B. L., and DeLuca, H. F.**, Effect of age on calcium absorption and serum $1,25(OH)_2D$, *Clin. Res.*, 26, 680A, 1978.

493. **Simkiss, K.**, *Calcium in Reproductive Physiology: A Comparative Study of Vertebrates*, Chapman & Hall, London, 1967.

494. **Fournier, P and Susbielle, H.**, Les échanges de calcium chez le rat au cours de la gestation, de la lactation et du sevrage. I. Influence d'un régime riche en calcium, *J. Physiol. (Paris)*, 44, 123, 1952.

495. **Fournier, P. and Susbeille, H.**, Les échanges de calcium chez le rat au cours de la gestation, de la lactation et du sevrage. II. Influence d'un régime pauvre en calcium, *J. Physiol. (Paris)*, 44, 575, 1952.

496. **Plumlee, M. P.**, Placental Transfer of Calcium in Cattle and Rats using Radioactive $Calcium^{45}$, Ph.D. thesis, Purdue University, Ind., 1953.

497. **Comar, C. L.**, Radiocalcium studies in pregnancy, *Ann. N.Y. Acad. Sci.*, 64, 281, 1956.

498. **Ramberg, C. F., Phang, J. M., and Kronfield, D. S.,** A compartmental model of calcium metabolism in cows, in *Parturient Hypocalcemia,* Anderson, J. J. B., Ed., Academic Press, New York, 1970, 119.
499. **Coons, C. M., and Blunt, K.,** The retention of nitrogen, calcium, phosphorus, and magnesium by pregnant women, *J. Biol. Chem.,* 86, 1, 1930.
500. **Macy, I. G., Hunscher, H. A., Nims, B., and McCosh, S. S.,** Metabolism of women during the reproductive cycle. I. Calcium and phosphorus utilization in pregnancy, *J. Biol. Chem.,* 86, 17, 1930.
501. **Kleiber, M. and Luick, J. R.,** Calcium and phosphorus transfer in intact dairy cows, *Ann. N.Y. Acad. Sci.,* 64, 299, 1956.
502. **Mayer, G. P., Ramberg, C. F., and Kronfeld, D. S.,** Calcium homeostasis in the cow, *Clin. Orthop.,* 62, 79, 1969.
503. **Conaway, H. H., Leddicotte, G. W., and Kenny, A. D.,** Neutron activation analysis of rat bone: simultaneous determination of calcium, chlorine, magnesium and sodium, *Anal. Biochem.,* 39, 218, 1971.
504. **Bar, A., Cohen, A., Edelstein, S., Shemesh, M., Montetcuccoli, G., and Hurwitz, S.,** Involvement of cholecalciferol metabolism in birds in the adaptation of calcium absorption to the needs during reproduction, *Comp. Biochem. Physiol.,* 59B, 245, 1978.
505. **Mueller, W. J., Schraer, R., and Schraer, H.,** Calcium metabolism and skeletal dynamics of laying pullets, *J. Nutr.,* 84, 20, 1964.
506. **Hurwitz, S. and Bar, A.,** Intestinal calcium absorption in the laying fowl and its importance in calcium homeostasis, *Am. J. Clin. Nutr.,* 22, 391, 1969.
507. **Kenny, A. D.,** Parathyroid glands and calcium metabolism, in *World Review of Nutrition and Dietetics,* Vol. 2, Bourne, G. H., Ed., Pitman Medical Publishing, London, 1960, 159.
508. **Nicolaysen, R.,** The absorption of calcium as a function of the body saturation with calcium, *Acta Physiol. Scand.,* 5, 200, 1943.
509. **Nicolaysen, R.,** Studies in calcium metabolism in rats. III. The adaptation to low Ca intakes of old rats, *Acta Physiol. Scand.,* 36, 114, 1956.
510. **Rottensten, K. V.,** The effect of body stores on the efficiency of calcium utilization, *Biochem. J.,* 32, 1285, 1938.
511. **Hurwitz, S. and Bar, A.,** Calcium depletion and repletion in laying hens. I. Effect on calcium in various bone segments in egg shells and in blood plasma, and on calcium balance, *Poult. Sci.,* 45, 345, 1966.
512. **Ribovich, M. L. and DeLuca, H. F.,** Effect of dietary calcium and phosphorus on intestinal calcium absorption and vitamin D metabolism, *Arch. Biochem. Biophys.,* 188, 145, 1978.
513. **Bonjour, J.-P., Fleisch, H., and Trechsel, U.,** Calcium absorption in diphosphonate-treated rats: effect of parathyroid function, dietary calcium and phosphorus, *J. Physiol. (London),* 264, 125, 1977.
514. **Swaminathan, R., Sommerville, B. A., and Care, A. D.,** The effect of dietary calcium on the activity of 25-hydroxycholecalciferol-1-hydroxylase and Ca absorption in vitamin D-replete chicks, *Br. J. Nutr.,* 38, 47, 1977.
515. **Walling, M. W. and Rothman, S. S.,** Apparent increase in carrier affinity for intestinal calcium transport following dietary calcium restriction, *J. Biol. Chem.,* 245, 5007, 1970.
516. **Favus, M. J., Walling, M. W., and Kimberg, D. V.,** Effects of dietary calcium restriction and chronic thyroparathyroidectomy on the metabolism of [^{3}H]25-hydroxyvitamin D_3 and the active transport of calcium by rat intestine, *J. Clin. Invest.,* 53, 1139, 1974.
517. **Fox, R., Swaminathan, R., Murray, T. M., and Care, A. D.,** Role of the parathyroid glands in the enhancement of intestinal calcium absorption in response to a low calcium diet, *J. Endocrinol.,* 74, 345, 1977.
518. **Kemm, J. R.,** The effect of parathyroidectomy and large doses of cholecalciferol on the ability of rats to adapt to changes in dietary intake of calcium, *J. Physiol. (London),* 256, 103, 1976.
519. **Greep, R. O.,** The physiology and chemistry of the parathyroid hormone, in *The Hormones: Physiology, Chemistry and Applications,* Vol. 1, Pincus, G. and Thimann, K. V., Eds., Academic Press, New York, 1948, 255.
520. **Pento, J. T.,** A Study of Calcium Transport in the Small Intestine of the Rat, Ph.D. thesis, University of Missouri, 1970.
521. **Pento, J. T. and Kenny, A. D.,** Mechanism of adaptation to calcium deprivation in the rat, Prog. 52nd Meeting Endocrine Soc. St. Louis, 121, 1970.
522. **Casewell, M. W. and Fennell, R. H.,** Supernumerary parathyroid structures in the neck and thymus of parathyroidectomized rats and their relationship to recovery from hypocalcaemia, *Br. J. Exp. Pathol.,* 51, 197, 1970.

523. **Van Dyke, J. H.**, Aberrant parathyroid tissue and the thymus: postnatal development of accessory parathyroid glands in the rat, *Anat. Rec.*, 134, 185, 1959.
524. **Kenny, A. D.**, Survival and serum calcium levels of rats after parathyroidectomy, *Endocrinology*, 70, 715, 1962.
525. **Taylor, T. G., Morris, T. R., and Hertelendy, F.**, The effect of pituitary hormones on ovulation in calcium deficient pullets, *Vet. Rec.*, 74, 123, 1962.
526. **Olson, E. B., Jr., DeLuca, H. F., and Potts, J. T., Jr.**, Calcitonin inhibition of vitamin D-induced intestinal calcium absorption, *Endocrinology*, 90, 151, 1972.
527. **Malm, O. J.**, *Calcium Requirement and Adaptation in Adult Men*, Oslo University Press, 1958.
528. **Nicolaysen, R., Eeg-Larsen, N., and Malm, O. J.**, Physiology of calcium metabolism, *Physiol. Rev.*, 33, 424, 1953.
529. **Walker, A. R. P., Fox, F. W., and Irving, J. T.**, Studies in human mineral metabolism. I. The effect of bread rich in phytate phosphorus on the metabolism of certain mineral salts with special reference to calcium, *Biochem. J.*, 42, 452, 1948.
530. **Bronner, F. Richelle, L. J., Saville, P. D., Nicholas, J. A., and Cobb, J. R.**, Quantitation of calcium metabolism in postmenopausal osteoporosis and in scoliosis, *J. Clin. Invest.*, 42, 898, 1963.
531. **Heaney, R. P. and Skillman, T. G.**, Secretion and excretion of calcium by the human gastrointestinal tract, *J. Lab. Clin. Med.*, 64, 29, 1964.
532. **Irving, J. T.**, *Calcium Metabolism*, Methuen, London, 1957.
533. **Malm, O. J.**, On phosphates and phosphoric acid as dietary factors in the calcium balance of man, *Scand. J. Clin. Lab. Invest.*, 5, 75, 1953.
534. **Davis, G. K.**, Interactions of calcium with other nutrients in intestinal absorption, in *The Transfer of Calcium and Strontium Across Biological Membranes*, Wasserman, R. H., Ed., Academic Press, New York, 1963, 129.
535. **Spencer, H., Menczel, J., Lewin, I., and Samachson, J.**, Effect of high phosphorus intake on calcium and phosphorus metabolism in man, *J. Nutr.*, 86, 125, 1965.
536. **Clark, I.**, Metabolic interrelations of calcium, magnesium and phosphate, *Am. J. Physiol.*, 217, 871, 1969.
537. **Wasserman, R. H.**, Lactose-stimulated intestinal absorption of calcium: a theory, *Nature (London)*, 201, 997, 1964.
538. **Ribovich, M. L. and DeLuca, H. F.**, The influence of dietary calcium and phosphorus on intestinal calcium transport in rats given vitamin D metabolites, *Arch. Biochem. Biophys.*, 170, 529, 1975.
539. **Clark, I. and Rivera-Cordero, F.**, Effects of endogenous parathyroid hormone on calcium, magnesium and phosphate metabolism in rats, II. Alterations in dietary phosphate, *Endocrinology*, 96, 360, 1974.
540. **Alcock, N. and MacIntyre, I.**, Inter-relation of calcium and magnesium absorption, *Clin. Sci.*, 22, 185, 1962.
541. **Alcock, N. and MacIntyre, I.**, Some effects of magnesium repletion on calcium metabolism in the rat, *Clin. Sci.*, 26, 219, 1964.
542. **Clark, I.**, Relation of magnesium ions to calcium and phosphate absorption, *Nature (London)*, 207, 982, 1965.
543. **Clark, I.**, Effects of magnesium ions on calcium and phosphorus metabolism, *Am. J. Physiol.*, 214, 348, 1968.
544. **Clark, I.**, Effects of magnesium on calcium and phosphate metabolism in parathyroidectomized rats, *Endocrinology*, 85, 1103, 1969.
545. **Ebel, J. G. and Comar, C. L.**, Effect of dietary magnesium on strontium-calcium discrimination and incorporation into bone of rats, *J. Nutr.*, 96, 403, 1968.
546. **Forbes, R. M.**, Mineral utilization in the rat. I. Effects of varying dietary ratios of calcium, magnesium and phosphorus, *J. Nutr.*, 80, 321, 1963.
547. **Heaton, F. W. and Parson, F. W.**, The metabolic effect of high magnesium intakes, *Clin. Sci.*, 21, 273, 1961.
548. **Miller, E. R., Ullrey, D. E., Zutaut, C. L., Hoefer, J. A., and Luecke, R. W.**, Mineral balance studies with the baby pig: effects of dietary vitamin D_2 level upon calcium, phosphorus and magnesium balance, *J. Nutr.*, 85, 255, 1965.
549. **Hsu-Fang, C., Wasserman, R. H., and Schwartz, R.**, Effect of magnesium deficiency on intestinal calcium transport in rats, *Proc. Soc. Exp. Biol. Med.*, 159, 171, 1978.
550. **Hsu-Fang, C., Schwartz, R., Krook, L., and Wasserman, R. H.**, Intestinal calcium absorption and bone morphology in magnesium deficient chicks, *Cornell Vet.*, 69, 88, 1979.
551. **Hendrix, J. Z., Alcock, N. W., and Archibald, R. M.**, Competition between calcium, strontium, and magnesium for absorption in the isolated rat intestine, *Clin. Chem.*, 9, 734, 1963.

552. **Fourman, P., Royer, P., Levell, M. J., and Morgan, D. B.,** *Calcium Metabolism and the Bone,* 2nd ed., Blackwell Scientific, Oxford, 1968.
553. **Henneman, P. H., Dempsey, E. F., Carroll, E. L., and Albright, F.,** The cause of hypercalcuria in sarcoid and its treatment with cortisone and sodium phytate, *J. Clin. Invest.,* 35, 1229, 1956.
554. **Harris, R. F.,** Phytic acid and its importance in human nutrition, *Nutr. Rev.,* 13, 257, 1955.
555. **Bronner, F., Harris, R. S., Meletskos, C. J., and Benda, C. E.,** Studies in calcium metabolism. Effect of food phytates on calcium^{45} uptake in children on low-calcium breakfasts, *J. Nutr.,* 54, 523, 1954.
556. **Chang, Y. O. and Hegsted, D. M.,** Lactose and calcium transport in gut sacs, *J. Nutr.,* 82, 297, 1964.
557. **Lengemann, F. W.,** The site of action of lactose in the enhancement of calcium utilization, *J. Nutr.,* 69, 23, 1959.
558. **Lengemann, F. W., Wasserman, R. H., and Comar, C. L.,** Studies on the enhancement of radiocalcium and radiostrontium absorption by lactose in the rat, *J. Nutr.,* 68, 443, 1959.
559. **Wasserman, R. H. and Comar, C. L.,** Carbohydrates and gastrointestinal absorption of radiostrontium and radiocalcium in the rat, *Proc. Soc. Exp. Biol. Med.,* 101, 314, 1959.
560. **Wasserman, R. H. and Lengemann, F. W.,** Further observations on lactose stimulation of the gastrointestinal absorption of calcium and stontium in the rat, *J. Nutr.,* 70, 377, 1960.
561. **Greenwald, E., Samachson, J., and Spencer, H.,** Effect of lactose on calcium metabolism in man, *J. Nutr.,* 79, 531, 1963.
562. **Pansu, D., Chapuy, M. C., and Bernard, J.,** L'Absorption de calcium en présence de lactose chez des sujets ostéoporotiques intolérants ou non au lactose, *C. R. Acad. Sci. Paris,* 268, 1310, 1969.
563. **Raven, A. M., Lengemann, F. W., and Wasserman, R. H.,** Studies of the effect of lysine on the absorption of radiocalcium and radiostrontium by the rat, *J. Nutr.,* 72, 29, 1960.
564. **Wasserman, R. H., Comar, C. L., and Nold, M. M.,** The influence of amino acids and other organic compounds on the gastrointestinal absorption of calcium^{45} and strontium^{89} in the rat, *J. Nutr.,* 59, 371, 1956.
565. **Wasserman, R. H., Comar, C. L., Schooley, J. C., and Lengemann, F. W.,** Interrelated effects of L-lysine and other dietary factors on the gastrointestinal absorption of calcium 45 in the rat and chick, *J. Nutr.,* 62, 367, 1957.
566. **Spencer, H. and Samachson, J.,** Effect of lysine on calcium metabolism in man, *J. Nutr.,* 81, 301, 1963.
567. **Spencer, H., Kramer, L., Osis, D., and Morris, C.,** Effect of a high protein (meat) intake on calcium metabolism in man, *Am. J. Clin. Nutr.,* 31, 2167, 1978.
568. **Schachter, D., Finkelstein, J. D., and Kowarski, S.,** Metabolism of vitamin D. I. Preparation of radioactive vitamin D and its intestinal absorption in the rat, *J. Clin. Invest.,* 43, 787, 1964.
569. **Lengemann, F. W. and Dobbins, J. W.,** The role of bile in calcium absorption, *J. Nutr.,* 66, 45, 1958.
570. **Webling, D. D'A., and Holdsworth, E. S.,** Bile salts and calcium absorption, *Biochem. J.,* 100, 652, 1966.
571. **Vaughan, O. W. and Filer, L. J.,** The enhancing action of certain carbohydrates on the intestinal absorption of calcium in the rat, *J. Nutr.,* 71, 10, 1960.
572. **Briscoe, A. M. and Ragan, C.,** Enhancement of calcium absorption in man by a bile acid sequestrant, *Am. J. Clin. Nutr.,* 13, 277, 1963.
573. **Thompson, W. G. and Thompson, G. R.,** Effect of cholestyramine on the absorption of vitamin D_3 and calcium, *Gut,* 10, 717, 1969.
574. **DeLuca, H. F.,** Mechanism of action and metabolic fate of vitamin D, *Vitam. Horm. (N.Y.),* 25, 315, 1967.
575. **DeLuca, H. F.,** *Vitamin D. Metabolism and Function,* Springer-Verlag, New York, 1979.
576. **Nicolaysen, R. and Eeg-Larsen, H.,** The biochemistry and physiology of vitamin D, *Vitam. Horm. (N.Y.),* 11, 29, 1953.
577. **Carlsson, A.,** The effect of vitamin D on the absorption of inorganic phosphate, *Acta Physiol. Scand.,* 31, 301, 1954.
578. **Conrad, H. R. and Hansard, S. L.,** Effects of massive doses of vitamin D on physiological behavior of calcium in cattle, *J. Appl. Physiol.,* 10, 98, 1957.
579. **Underwood, E., Fisch, S., and Hodge, H. C.,** Metabolism of calcium in normal, rachitic and vitamin D-treated rats as evidenced.by radiocalcium Ca^{45} studies, *Am. J. Physiol.,* 166, 387, 1951.
580. **Hamilton, J. W. and Holdsworth, E. S.,** Calcium transport by the chick small intestine. The role of vitamin D_3, the mitochondria and binding protein, *Calcif. Tissue Res.,* 4, 284, 1969.
581. **Younoszai, M. K., Urban, E., and Schedl, H. P.,** Vitamin D and intestinal calcium fluxes in vivo in the rat, *Am. J. Physiol.,* 225, 287, 1973.

582. **Harrison, H. E. and Harrison, H. C.**, Studies with radiocalcium: the intestinal absorption of calcium, *J. Biol. Chem.*, 188, 83, 1951.
583. **Harrison, H. E. and Harrison, H. C.**, Transfer of Ca^{45} across intestinal wall *in vitro* in relation to action of vitamin D and cortisol, *Am. J. Physiol.*, 199, 265, 1960.
584. **Harrison, H. E. and Harrison, H. C.**, Vitamin D and permeability of intestinal muscosa to calcium, *Am. J. Physiol.*, 208, 370, 1965.
585. **Harrison, H. E. and Harrison, H. C.**, Actinomycin D inhibition of intestinal transport of calcium and of vitamin D action, *Proc. Soc. Exp. Biol. Med.*, 121, 312, 1966.
586. **Czarnowska-Misztal, E., Zull, J. E., and DeLuca, H. F.**, Response to vitamin D in adrenalectomized animals, *Nature (London)*, 210, 96, 1966.
587. **Harrison, H. C. and Harrison, H. E.**, Dibutyryl cyclic AMP, vitamin D and intestinal permeability to calcium, *Endocrinology*, 86, 756, 1970.
588. **Kessner, D. M. and Epstein, F. H.**, Effect of renal insufficiency on gastrointestinal transport of calcium, *Am. J. Physiol.*, 209, 141, 1965.
589. **Morii, H., Lund, J., Neville, P. F., and DeLuca, H. F.**, Biological activity of a vitamin D metabolite, *Arch, Biochem. Biophys.*, 120, 508, 1967.
590. **Zull, J. E., Czarnowska-Misztal, E., and DeLuca, H. F.**, Actinomycin D inhibition of vitamin D action, *Science*, 149, 182, 1965.
591. **Zull, J. E., Czarnowska-Misztal, E., and DeLuca, H. F.**, On the relationship between vitamin D action and actinomycin-sensitive processes, *Proc. Natl., Acad. Sci. U.S.A.*, 55, 177, 1966.
592. **Petith, M. M., Wilson, H. D., and Schedl, H. P.**, Vitamin D dependence of in vivo calcium transport and mucosal calcium binding protein in rat large intestine, *Gastroenterology*, 76, 99, 1979.
593. **Adams, T. H., Wong, R. G., and Norman, A. W.**, Studies on the mechanism of action of calciferol, II. Effects of the polyene antibiotic, filipin, on vitamin D-mediated calcium transport, *J. Biol. Chem.*, 245, 4432, 1970.
594. **Adams, T. H. and Norman, A. W.**, Studies on the mechanism of action of calciferol. I. Basic parameters of vitamin D-mediated calcium transport, *J. Biol. Chem.*, 245, 4421, 1970.
595. **DeLuca, H. F.**, 25-Hydroxycholecalciferol, the probable metabolically active form of vitamin D, *Am. J. Clin. Nutr.*, 22, 412, 1969.
596. **Harrison, H. E. and Harrison, H. C.**, Theories of vitamin D action, in *The Transfer of Calcium and Strontium Across Biological Membranes*, Wasserman, R. H., Ed., Academic Press, New York, 1963, 229.
597. **Sallis, J. D. and Holdsworth, E. S.**, Calcium metabolism in relation to vitamin D_3 and adrenal function in the chick, *Am. J. Physiol.*, 203, 506, 1962.
598. **O'Donnell, J. M. and Smith, M. W.**, Influence of cholecalciferol (vitamin D_3) on the initial kinetics of the uptake of calcium by rat small-intestinal mucosa, *Biochem. J.*, 134, 667, 1973.
599. **Moriuchi, S., Watanabe, T., and Hosoya, N.**, Distribution of orally administered ^{45}Ca in rat intestinal tissues and vitamin D_3 effect, *J. Vitaminol.*, 16, 58, 1970.
600. **Schachter, D. and Kowarski, S.**, Radioactive vitamin D: preparation, metabolism, and mechanism of action, *Bull, N.Y. Acad. Med.*, 41, 241, 1965.
601. **Bosmann, H. B. and Chen, P. S.**, Actinomycin D inhibition of vitamin D- and dihydrotachysterol-induced responses in the chick, *J. Nutr.*, 90, 405, 1966.
602. **Norman, A. W.**, Actinomycin D and the response to vitamin D, *Science*, 149, 184, 1965.
603. **Norman, A. W.**, Actinomycin D effect on lag in vitamin D-mediated calcium absorption in the chick, *Am. J. Physiol.*, 211, 829, 1966.
604. **Norman, A. W., Haussler, M. R., Adams, T. H., Myrtle, J. F., Roberts, P., and Hibberd, K. A.**, Basic studies on the mechanism of action of vitamin D, *Am. J. Clin. Nutr.*, 22, 396, 1969.
605. **Lawson, D. E. M., Wilson, P. W., Barker, D. C., and Kodicek, E.**, Isolation of chick intestinal nuclei. Effect of vitamin D_3 on nuclear metabolism, *Biochem. J.*, 115, 263, 1969.
606. **Norman, A. W.**, Vitamin D-mediated synthesis of rapidly labelled RNA from intestinal mucosa, *Biochem. Biophys. Res. Commun.*, 23, 335, 1966.
607. **Stohs, S. J., Zull, J. E., and DeLuca, H. F.**, Vitamin D stimulation of [^3H] orotic acid incorporation into ribonucleic acid of rat intestinal mucosa, *Biochemistry*, 6, 1304, 1967.
608. **Haussler, M. R. and Norman, A. W.**, The subcellular distribution of physiological doses of vitamin D_3, *Arch. Biochem. Biophys.*, 118, 145, 1967.
609. **Stohs, S. J. and DeLuca, H. F.**, Subcellular location of vitamin D and its metabolites in intestinal mucosa after a 10-IU dose, *Biochemistry*, 6, 3338, 1967.
610. **Brumbaugh, P. F. and Haussler, M. R.**, Nuclear and cytoplasmic receptors for 1,25-dihydroxy-cholecalciferol in intestinal mucosa, *Biochem. Biophys, Res. Commun.*, 51, 74, 1973.

611. **Brumbaugh, P. F. and Haussler, M. R.,** 1α,25-Dihydroxycholecalciferol receptors in intestine. I. Association of 1α,25-dihydroxycholecalciferol with intestinal mucosa chromatin, *J. Biol. Chem.*, 249, 1251, 1974.
612. **Kream, B. E., Yamada, S., Schnoes, H. K., and DeLuca, H. F.,** Specific cytosol binding protein for 1,25-dihydroxyvitamin D_3 in rat intestine, *J. Biol. Chem.*, 252, 4501, 1977.
613. **Kream, B. E., Jose, M. J. L., and DeLuca, H. F.,** The chick intestine cytosol binding protein for 1,25-dihydroxyvitamin D_3: a study of analog binding, *Arch. Biochem. Biophys.*, 179, 462, 1977.
614. **MacGregor, R. R., Hamilton, J. W., and Cohn, D. V.,** The induction of calcium-binding protein biosynthesis in intestine by vitamin D_3, *Fed. Proc. Fed. Am. Soc. Exp. Biol.*, 29, 368, 1970.
615. **Kallfelz, F. A., Taylor, A. N., and Wasserman, R. H.,** Vitamin D-induced calcium-binding factor in rat intestinal mucosa, *Proc. Soc. Exp. Biol. Med.*, 125, 54, 1967.
616. **Skou, J. C.,** Enzymatic basis for active transport of Na^+ and K^+ across cell membranes, *Physiol. Rev.*, 45, 596, 1965.
617. **DeWolff, F. A.,** Stimulation of vitamin D-dependent Ca-ATPase and of intestinal calcium absorption by diphenylhydantoin, *Eur. J. Pharmacol.*, 33, 71, 1975.
618. **Kowarski, S. and Schachter, D.,** Vitamin D and adenosine triphosphatase dependent on divalent cations in rat intestinal mucosa, *J. Clin. Invest.*, 52, 2765, 1973.
619. **Bonjour, J.-P., Russell, R. G. G., Morgan, D. B., and Fleisch, H. A.,** Intestinal calcium absorption, Ca-binding protein, and Ca-ATPase in diphosphonate-treated rats, *Am. J. Physiol.*, 224, 1011, 1972.
620. **Nagode, L. A., Haussler, M. R., Boyce, D. W., Pechet, M., and Rasmussen, H.,** Vitamin D induced phosphatases in bone and intestine: inhibitions by theophylline and diphosphonates, *Fed. Proc. Fed. Am. Soc. Exp. Biol.*, 29, 368, 1970.
621. **Delling, G., Hehrmann, R., and Montz, R.,** Effect of dibutyryl cyclic AMP (DBcAMP) and parathyroid hormone (PTH) on intestinal calcium absorption (in vivo studies with ^{47}Ca), *Horm. Metab. Res.*, 4, 59, 1972.
622. **Corradino, R. A.,** Involvement of cyclic AMP in the vitamin D mediated intestinal calcium absorptive mechanism, in *Calcium-regulating Hormones*, Talmage, R. V., Owen, M., and Parsons, J. A., Eds., American Elsevier, New York, 1975, 346.
623. **Miravet, L., Redel, J., Carre, M., Quellé, M. L., and Bordier, P.,** The biological activity of synthetic 25,26-dihydroxycholecalciferol and 24,25-dihydroxycholecalciferol in vitamin D-deficient rats, *Calcif. Tissue Res.*, 21, 145, 1976.
624. **Boyle, I. T., Ohmdahl, J. L., Gray, R. W. and DeLuca, H. F.,** The biological activity and metabolism of 24,25-dihydroxyvitamin D_3, *J. Biol. Chem.*, 248, 4174, 1973.
625. **Walling, M. W., Hartenbower, D. L., Coburn, J. W., and Norman, A. W.,** Effects of 1α,25-,24R,25-, and 1α,24R,25-hydroxylated metabolites of vitamin D_3 on calcium and phosphate absorption by duodenum from intact and nephrectomized rats, *Arch. Biochem. Biophys.*, 182, 251, 1977.
626. **Henry, H. L., Norman, A. W., Taylor, A. N., Hartenbower, D. L., and Coburn, J. W.,** Biological activity of 24,25-dihydroxycholecalciferol in chicks and rats, *J. Nutr.*, 106, 724, 1976.
627. **Szymendera, J. and Galus, K.,** Effect of 24,25-dihydroxycholecalciferol on calcium absorption in proximal small intestine in uraemia, *Br. Med. J.*, 2, 1465, 1978.
628. **Pang, P. K. T., Tenner, T. E., Jr., Yee, J. A., Yang, M., and Janssen, H. F.,** Hypotensive action of parathyroid hormone preparations on rats and dogs, *Proc. Natl. Acad. Sci. U.S.A.*, 77, 675, 1980.
629. **Pang, P. K. T., Yang, M., Oguro, C., Phillips, J. G., and Yee, J. A.,** Hypotensive actions of parathyroid hormone preparations in vertebrates, *Gen. Comp. Endocrinol.*, 41, 135, 1980.
630. **Charbon, G. A.,** A rapid and selective vasodilator effect of parathyroid hormone, *Eur. J. Pharmacol.*, 3, 275, 1968.
631. **Charbon, G. A.,** Vasodilator action of parathyroid hormone used as bioassay, *Arch. Int. Pharmacodyn. Ther.*, 178, 296, 1969.
632. **Charbon, G. A.,** Quick acting, short-lived effects of parathyroid hormone on arterial hepatic blood flow, *Digestion*, 6, 267, 1972.
633. **Charbon, G. A. and Pieper, E. E. M.,** Effect of calcitonin on parathyroid hormone-induced vasodilation, *Endocrinology*, 91, 828, 1972.
634. **Charbon, G. A. and Hulstaert, P. F.,** Augmentation of arterial hepatic and renal flow by extracted and synthetic parathyroid hormone, *Endocrinology*, 95, 621, 1974.
635. **Aubert, J.-P., Cherian, A. G., Moukhtar, M. S., and Milhaud, G.,** Etude du métabolisme du calcium chez le rat àl'aide de calcium 45. V. La thyroparathyroïdectomie et l'effet de la thyroxine et de la parathormone, *Biochem. Pharmacol.*, 13, 31, 1964.
636. **Milhaud, G. and Moukhtar, M. S.,** Thyrocalcitonin: effects on calcium kinetics in the rat, *Proc. Soc. Exp. Biol. Med.*, 123, 207, 1966.

637. **Clark, I. and Rivera-Cordero, F.**, Effect of parathyroid function on absorption and excret. calcium, magnesium and phosphate by rats, *Endocrinology*, 88, 302, 1971.
638. **Cramer, C. F., Suiker, A. P., and Copp, D. H.**, Parathyroid influence on calcium and phosphorus absorption by the gut, in *The Parathyroids*, Greep, R. O. and Talmage, R. V., Eds., Charles C Thomas, Springfield, Ill., 1961, 158.
639. **Talmage, R. V. and Elliott, J. R.**, Influence of parathyroids on intestinal absorption of radiocalcium and radiostrontium, *Fed. Proc. Fed. Am. Soc. Exp. Biol.*, 17, 160, 1958.
640. **Kodicek, E., Cruickshank, E. M., DeLuca, H. F., and Raisz, L. G.**, Effects of vitamin D and parathyroidectomy on the absorption of Ca^{45} from *in vivo* loops of small intestine, in *Bone and Tooth*, Blackwood, H. J. J., Ed., MacMillan, New York, 1964, 363.
641. **Larsson, S.-E. and Ahlgren, O.**, The role of the parathyroids for the adaptation to a low calcium intake, *Acta Pathol. Microbiol. Scand. A*, 83, 603, 1975.
642. **Nelson, T. E., Tavernor, W. D., Jones, E. W., and Tillman, A. D.**, Influence of age and calcium-free diet on thyroparathyroidectomized sheep, *J. Nutr.*, 97, 359, 1969.
643. **Payne, J. M. and Sansom, B. F.**, Calcium metabolism in normal and thyro-parathyroidectomized goats, *J. Physiol. (London)*, 184, 433, 1966.
644. **Bone, H. G., III, Zerwekh, J. E., Haussler, M. R., and Pak, C. Y. C.**, Effect of parathyroidectomy on serum 1α,25-dihydroxyvitamin D and intestinal calcium absorption in primary hyperparathyroidism, *J. Clin. Endocrinol. Metab.*, 48, 877, 1979.
645. **Robinson, C. J., Matthews, E. W., and MacIntyre, I.**, The effect of parathyroid hormone and thyrocalcitonin on the intestinal absorption of calcium and magnesium, in *Les Tissus Calcifiés, Ve Symposium Européen, Bordeaux, France*, Milhaud, G., Owen, M., and Blackwood, H. J. J., Eds., Société d'Edition d'Enseignement Supérieur, Paris, 1968, 279.
646. **Parsons, J. A., Zanelli, J. M., Gray, D., Rafferty, B., and Stevenson, R. W.**, Double isotope estimates of intestinal calcium absorption in rats: enhancement by parathyroid hormone and 1,25-dihydroxycholecalciferol, *Calcif. Tissue Res.*, Suppl. 22, 127, 1976.
647. **Birge, S. J., Switzer, S. C. and Leonard, D. R.**, Influence of sodium and parathyroid hormone on calcium release from intestinal mucosal cells, *J. Clin. Invest.*, 54, 702, 1974.
648. **Wills, M. R., Wortsman, J., Pak, C. Y. C., and Bartter, F. C.**, The role of parathyroid hormone in the gastrointestinal absorption of calcium, *Clin. Sci.*, 39, 89, 1970.
649. **Toverud, S. U.**, Parathyroid effect on intestinal absorption of calcium and on secretion of calcium with the digestive juices in vitamin D-deficient rats, Acta Physiol. Scand., 62 (Suppl. 234) 1, 1964.
650. **Garabedian, M., Tanaka, Y., Holick, M. F., and DeLuca, H. F.**, Response of intestinal calcium transport and bone calcium mobilization to 1,25-dihydroxyvitamin D_3 in thyroparathyroidectomized rats, *Endocrinology*, 94, 1022, 1974.
651. **Corradino, R. A.**, Parathyroid hormone and calcitonin; no direct effect of vitamin D_3-mediated, intestinal calcium absorptive mechanism, *Horm. Metab. Res.*, 8, 485, 1976.
652. **Hirsch, P. F., Voelkel, E. F. and Munson, P. L.**, Thyrocalcitonin: hypocalcemic hypophosphatemic principle of the thyroid gland, *Science*, 146, 412, 1964.
653. **Munson, P. L., Hirsch, P. F., Tashjian, A. H., and Aliapoulios, M. A.**, Calcitonin and thyrocalcitonin: evaluation of hypocalcemic factors, in *Methods in Drug Evaluation*, Mantegazza, P. and Piccinini, F., Eds., North-Holland, Amsterdam, 1966, 467.
654. **Kenny, A. D. and Heiskell, C. A.**, Effect of crude thyrocalcitonin on calcium and phosphorus metabolism in rats, *Proc. Soc. Exp. Biol. Med.*, 120, 269, 1965.
655. **Wase, A. W., Peterson, A., Rickes, E., and Solewski, J.**, Some effects of thyrocalcitonin on the calcium metabolism of the rat, *Endocrinology*, 79, 687, 1966.
656. **Loreau, N., Blain, F., and Ardaillou, R.**, Effets de la calcitonine sur les transferts de phosphates, calcium et sodium à tranvers le jéjunum du rat, *J. Physiol. (Paris)*, 63, 249A, 1971.
657. **Cramer, C. F.**, Effect of salmon calcitonin on *in vivo* calcium absorption in rats, *Calcif. Tissue Res.*, 13, 169, 1973.
658. **Walling, M. W., Brasitus, T. A., and Kimberg, D. V.**, Effects of calcitonin and substance P on the transport of Ca, Na, and Cl across rat ileum in vitro, *Gastroenterology*, 73, 89, 1977.
659. **Kraintz, L. and Cramer, C. F.**, Lack of effect of thyrocalcitonin on calcium absorption from gut loops in the dog, Prog. 48th Meeting Endocrine Soc. Chicago, 1966, 70.
660. **Kisloff, B. and Moore, E. W.**, Effects of intravenous calcitonin on water, electrolyte, and calcium movement across *in vivo* rabbit jejunum and ileum, *Gastroenterology*, 72, 462, 1977.
661. **Swaminathan, R., Ker, J., and Care, A. D.**, Calcitonin and intestinal calcium absorption, *Endocrinology*, 61, 83, 1974.
662. **Care, A. D.**, The effects of pancreozymin and secretion on calcitonin release, *Fed. Proc. Fed. Am. Soc. Exp. Biol.*, 29, 253, 1970.

663. **Kimberg, D. V.,** Effects of vitamin D and steroid hormones on the active transport of calcium by the intestine, *N. Engl. J. Med.*, 280, 1396, 1969.

664. **Favus, M. J., Walling, M. W., and Kimberg, D. V.,** Effects of 1,25-dihydroxycholecalciferol on intestinal calcium transport in cortisone-treated rats, *J. Clin. Invest.*, 52, 1680, 1973.

665. **Younoszai, M. K. and Ghishan, F. K.,** *In vivo* intestinal calcium absorption in infant rats: influence of methylprednisolone and vitamin D, *Proc. Soc. Exp. Biol. Med.*, 158, 174, 1978.

666. **Fox, J., Care, A. D., and Marshall, D. H.,** Reversal of betamethasone-induced inhibition of intestinal calcium absorption by 1α-hydroxycholecalciferol, *J. Endocrinol.*, 78, 187, 1978.

667. **Klein, R. G., Arnaud, S. B., Gallagher, J. C., DeLuca, H. F., and Riggs, B. L.,** Intestinal calcium absorption in exogenous hypercortisonism. Role of 25-hydroxyvitamin D and corticosteroid dose, *J. Clin. Invest.*, 60, 253, 1977.

668. **Avioli, L. V., Birge, S. J., and Lee, S. W.,** Effects of prednisone on vitamin D metabolism in man, *J. Clin. Endocrinol. Metab.*, 28, 1341, 1968.

669. **Miravet, L., Carre, M., Fisher-Ferraro, C., and Mautalen, C.,** Action of *Solanum malacoxylon* on intestinal calcium transport in vitamin D-deficient-prednisolone treated rats, *J. Clin. Endocrinol. Metab.*, 45, 1230, 1977.

670. **Clark, I. and Smith, M. R.,** Effects of parathyroidectomy and hydrocortisone on the intestinal absorption of calcium and phosphates, *Endocrinology*, 74, 421, 1964.

671. **Friedland, J. A., Williams, G. A., Bowser, E. N., Henderson, W. J., and Hoffeins, E.,** Effect of hyperthyroidism on intestinal absorption of calcium in the rat, *Proc. Soc. Exp. Biol. Med.*, 120, 20, 1965.

672. **Jones, J. E., Desper, P. C., Shane, S. R., and Flink, E. B.,** Magnesium metabolism in hyperthyroidism and hypothyroidism, *J. Clin. Invest.*, 45, 891, 1966.

673. **Gallagher, J. C., Riggs, B. L., Hamstra, A., and DeLuca, H. F.,** Effect of estrogen therapy on calcium absorption and vitamin D metabolism in postmenopausal osteoporosis, *Clin. Res.*, 26, 415A, 1978.

674. **Fujita, T.,** Effect of tetragastrin on calcium absorption from rat duodenal loop *in vivo*, *Endocrinol. Jpn.*, 20, 407, 1973.

675. **Swaminathan, R., Winter, M., and Care, A. D.,** The lack of effect of pentagastrin on intestinal calcium absorption in the rat, *Horm. Metab. Res.*, 7, 273, 1975.

676. **Fleisch, H., Russell, R. G. G., and Francis, M. D.,** Diphosphonates inhibit hydroxyapatite dissolution in vitro and bone resorption in tissue culture and in vivo, *Science*, 165, 1262, 1969.

677. **Fleisch, H., Russell, R. G. G., Bisaz, S., Mühlbauer, R. C., and Williams, D. A.,** The inhibitory effect of phosphonates on the formation of calcium phosphate crystals in vitro and on aortic and kidney calcification in vivo, *Eur. J. Clin. Invest.*, 1, 12, 1970.

678. **Francis, M. D.,** The inhibition of calcium hydroxyapatite crystal growth by polyphosphonates and polyphosphates, *Calcif. Tissue Res.*, 3, 151, 1969.

679. **Francis, M. D., Russell, R. G. G., and Fleisch, H.,** Diphosphonates inhibit formation of calcium phosphate crystals in vitro and pathological calcification in vivo, *Science*, 165, 1264, 1969.

680. **Russell, R. G. G., Mühlbauer, R. C., Bisaz, S., Williams, D. A., and Fleisch, H.,** The influence of pyrophosphate, condensed phosphates, phosphonates and other phosphate compounds on the dissolution of hydroxyapatite in vitro and on bone resorption induced by parathyroid hormone in tissue culture and in thyroparathyroidectomized rats, *Calcif. Tissue Res.*, 6, 183, 1970.

681. **Gasser, A. B., Morgan, D. B., Fleisch, H. A., and Richelle, L. J.,** The influence of two diphosphonates on calcium metabolism in the rat, *Clin Sci.*, 43, 31, 1972.

682. **Bonjour, J.-P., DeLuca, H. F., Fleisch, H., Trechsel, U., Matejowec, L. A., and Omdahl, J. L.,** Reversal of the EHDP inhibition of calcium absorption by 1,25-dihydroxycholecalciferol, *Eur. J. Clin. Invest.*, 3, 44, 1973.

683. **Trechsel, U., Schenk, R., Bonjour, J.-P., Russell, R. G. G., and Fleisch, H.,** Relation between bone mineralization, Ca absorption and plasma Ca in phosphonate-treated rats, *Am. J. Physiol.*, 232, E298, 1977.

684. **Krawitt, E. L., Sampson, H. W., Kunin, A. S., and Matthews, J. L.,** Effect of ethane-1-hydroxy-1, 1-diphosphonate (EHDP) administration on duodenal calcium transport, *Calcif. Tissue Res.*, 15, 21, 1974.

685. **Peterson, P., Gray, P., and Tolman, K. G.,** Calcium balance in drug-induced osteomalacia: response to vitamin D, *Clin. Pharmacol. Ther.*, 19, 63, 1976.

686. **Harrison, H. C. and Harrison, H. E.,** Inhibition of vitamin D-stimulated active transport of calcium of rat intestine by diphenylhydantoin-phenobarbital treatment, *Proc. Soc. Exp. Biol. Med.*, 153, 220, 1976.

687. **Caspary, W. F.,** Inhibition of intestinal calcium transport by diphenylhydantoin in rat duodenum, *N. Engl. J. Med.*, 274, 146, 1972.

688. **Koch, H. U., Kraft, D., von Herrath, D., and Schaefer, K.**, Influence of diphenylhydantoin and phenobarbital on intestinal calcium transport in the rat, *Epilepsia*, 13, 829, 1972.
689. **Hahn, T. J., Hendin, B. A., Scharp, C. R., and Haddad, J. G., Jr.**, Effect of chronic anticonvulsant therapy on serum 25-hydroxycalciferol levels in adults, *N. Engl. J. Med.*, 287, 900, 1972.
690. **Worker, N. A. and Carillo, B. J.**, "Enteque seco", calcification and wasting in grazing animals in the Argentine, *Nature (London)*, 215, 72, 1967.
691. **O'Donnell, J. M. and Smith, M. W.**, Vitamin D-like action of *Solanum malacoxylon* on calcium transport by rat intestine, *Nature (London)*, 244, 357, 1973.
692. **Wasserman, R. H., Henion, J. D., Haussler, M. R., and McCain, T. A.**, Calcinogenic factor in *Solanum malocoxylon:* evidence that it is 1,25-dihydroxyvitamin D_3-glycoside, *Science*, 194, 853, 1976.
693. **Wasserman, R. H., Corradino, R. A., Krook, L., Hughes, M. R., and Haussler, M. R.**, Studies on the 1α,25-dihydroxycholecalciferol-like activity in a calcinogenic plant, *Cestrum diurnum*, in the chick, *J. Nutr.*, 106, 457, 1976.
694. **Wasserman, R. H., Corradino, R. A., and Krook, L. P.**, *Lestrum diurnum:* a domestic plant with 1,25-dihydroxycholecalciferol-like activity, *Biochem. Biophys. Res. Commun.*, 62, 85, 1975.
695. **Wasserman, R. H.**, Active vitamin D-like substances in *Solanum malacoxylon* and other calcinogenic plants, *Nutr. Rev.*, 33, 1, 1975.
696. **Walling, M. W. and Kimberg, D. V.**, Effects of 1α,25-dihydroxyvitamin D_3 and *Solanum glaucophyllum* on intestinal calcium and phosphate transport and on plasma Ca, Mg, and P levels in the rat, *Endocrinology*, 97, 1567, 1975.
697. **Heggeness, F. W.**, Effect of antibiotics on the gastrointestinal absorption of calcium and magnesium in the rat, *J. Nutr.*, 68, 573, 1959.
698. **Migicovsky, B. B., Nielson, A. M., Gluck, M., and Burgess, R.**, Pencillin and calcium absorption, *Arch. Biochem. Biophys.*, 34, 479, 1951.
699. **Reddy, B. S., Pleasants, J. R., and Wostmann, B. S.**, Calcium phosphorus and magnesium metabolism in germfree rats, *Fed. Proc. Fed. Am. Soc. Exp. Biol.*, 27, 311, 1968.
700. **Abel de la Cruz, L. A., Pollard, S. K., and Kenny, A. D.**, Plasma 1,25-dihydroxyvitamin D levels determined by new radioreceptor assay using egg-laying Japanese quail gut cytosolic receptor, in *Abstr. 7th Int. Conf. Calcium Regulating Hormones*, September 1980, in press.
701. **Kaetzel, D. M., Jr. and Soares, J. H., Jr.**, Effect of age on plasma 1,25-dihydroxyvitamin D_3 in laying hens and quail, *Fed. Proc. Fed. Am. Soc. Exp. Biol.*, 39, 661, 1980.
702. **Lund, B. and Sørensen, O. H.**, Measurement of 25-hydroxyvitamin D and its relation to sunshine, age and vitamin D intake in the Danish population, *Scand. J. Clin. Lab. Invest.*, 39, 23, 1979.
703. **Riggs, B. L., Gallagher, J. C., DeLuca, H. F., Edis, A. J., Lambert, P. W., and Arnaud, C. D.**, A syndrome of osteoporosis, increased serum immunoreactive parathyroid hormone, and inappropriately low serum 1,25-dihydroxyvitamin D, *Mayo Clin. Proc.*, 53, 701, 1978.
704. **Haussler, M. R., Hughes, M. R., Pike, J. W., and McCain, T. A.**, Radioligand receptor assay for 1,25-dihydroxyvitamin D: biochemical, physiologic and clinical applications, in *Vitamin D: Biochemical, Chemical and Clinical Aspects Related to Calcium Metabolism*, Norman, A. W., Schaefer, K., Coburn, J. W., DeLuca, H. F., Fraser, D., Grigoleit, H. G. and Herrath, D. v., Eds., De Gruyter, New York, 1977, 473.
705. **Preece, A., O'Riordan, J. L. H., Lawson, D. E. M. and Kodicek, E.**, A competitive protein-binding assay for 25-hydroxycholecalciferol and 25-hydroxyergocalciferol in serum, *Clin. Chim. Acta*, 54, 235, 1974.
706. **Hahn, T. J. and Halstead, L. R.**, Anticonvulsant drug-induced osteomalacia: alterations in mineral metabolism and response to vitamin D_3 administration, *Calcif Tissue Int.*, 27, 13, 1979.
707. **Scriver, C. R., Reade, T. M., DeLuca, H. F., and Hamstra, A. J.**, Serum 1,25-dihydroxyvitamin D levels in normal subjects and in patients with heriditary rickets on bone disease, *N. Engl. J. Med.*, 299, 976, 1978.
708. **Björkhem, I., Holmberg, I., Kristiansen, T., and Pedersen, J. I.**, Assay of 1,25-dihydroxy vitamin D_3 by isotope dilution — mass fragmentography, *Clin. Chem.*, 25, 584, 1979.
709. **Horst, R. L., Jorgensen, N. A., and DeLuca, H. F.**, Plasma 1,25-dihydroxyvitamin D and parathyroid hormone levels in paretic dairy cows, *Am. J. Physiol.*, 235, E634, 1978.
710. **Barlet, J.-P., Argemi, B., Davicco, M.-J., and Lefaivre, J.**, Plasma concentrations of 25-hydroxy vitamin D in pregnant and lactating ewes and foetal and newborn lambs, *J. Endocrinol.*, 79, 149, 1978.
711. **Whyte, M., Haussler, M., Lee, S. W., and Avioli, L. V.**, Circulating vitamin D metabolites in the male and female trout, *Clin. Res.*, 27, A704, 1979.
712. **Turner, R. T.**, personal communication.
713. **Pollard, S. K. and Kenny, A. D.**, unpublished observations
714. **Kenny, A. D.**, unpublished observations.

Index

INDEX

A

B

C

D

E

F

G

H

I

R

S

T

U

V